EU Rule of Law Promotion

Do EU institutions have an influence on the implementation of the rule of law in potential candidate countries and, if so, of what kind? During the compliance monitoring process related to the effective rule of law and democracy the EU Commission tests and criticizes the effectiveness of the judiciary and strengthens the rule of law in preparation for accession. In the Western Balkans this was a process fraught with difficulties.

Despite the fact that academic scholarship and democratic politics agree on rule of law as a legitimizing principle for the exercise of state authority, there is no uniform European standard for institution-building or monitoring activities by the EU in this area. With focus on the reform of the judiciary in five case study countries of Bosnia and Herzegovina, Kosovo, Macedonia, Montenegro, and Serbia, this empirical research investigates the EU's transformative power with regard to the effectiveness of rule of law and judicial sector reform in its infancy. It analyzes the depth and limitations of EU rule of law promotion in the Western Balkans and presents policy recommendations intended to address the shortcomings in judiciary reform.

This book aims to fill the gap in the existing academic scholarship of EU politics, law and Western Balkans literature.

Marko Kmezić is a Lecturer and Senior Researcher at the Centre for Southeast European Studies, University of Graz, Austria.

Southeast European Studies

Series Editor: Florian Bieber

The Balkans are a region of Europe widely associated over the past decades with violence and war. Beyond this violence, the region has experienced rapid change in recent times though, including democratization, economic and social transformation. New scholarship is emerging which seeks to move away from the focus on violence alone to an understanding of the region in a broader context drawing on new empirical research.

The Southeast European Studies Series seeks to provide a forum for this new scholarship. Publishing cutting-edge, original research and contributing to a more profound understanding of Southeastern Europe while focusing on contemporary perspectives the series aims to explain the past and seeks to examine how it shapes the present. Focusing on original empirical research and innovative theoretical perspectives on the region the series includes original monographs and edited collections. It is interdisciplinary in scope, publishing high-level research in political science, history, anthropology, sociology, law and economics and accessible to readers interested in Southeast Europe and beyond.

Titles in the series:

Croatia and the European Union: Changes and Development
Edited by Pero Maldini and Davor Paukovic

Citizenship in Bosnia and Herzegovina, Macedonia and Montenegro: Effects of Statehood and Identity Challenges
Jelena Džankic

Austerity and the Third Sector in Greece: Civil Society at the European Frontline
Edited by Jennifer Clarke and Asteris Huliaras

State-Building and Democratization in Bosnia and Herzegovina
Edited by Soeren Keil and Valery Perry

EU Rule of Law Promotion

Judiciary Reform in the Western Balkans

Marko Kmezić

Routledge
Taylor & Francis Group
LONDON AND NEW YORK

First published 2017
by Routledge

2 Park Square, Milton Park, Abingdon, Oxfordshire OX14 4RN
711 Third Avenue, New York, NY 10017

Routledge is an imprint of the Taylor & Francis Group, an informa business

First issued in paperback 2018

This book is published with the support of the University of Graz.

British Library Cataloguing in Publication Data
A catalogue record for this book is available from the British Library

Library of Congress Cataloging in Publication Data
Names: Kmezic, Marko, author.
Title: EU rule of law promotion : judiciary reform in the Western Balkans / Marko Kmezic.
Other titles: European Union rule of law promotion
Description: New York, NY : Routledge, 2017. | Includes bibliographical references and index.
Identifiers: LCCN 2016005914 | ISBN 9781472485557 (hardback) | ISBN 9781315580722 (ebook)
Subjects: LCSH: Rule of law–European Union countries. | Rule of law–Balkan peninsula. | Law reform–Balkan peninsula. | Balkan Peninsula–Foreign relations–European Union countries. | European Union countries–Foreign relations–Balkan peninsula.
Classification: LCC KJC4426 .K84 2017 | DDC 347.496–dc23
LC record available at http://lccn.loc.gov/2016005914

ISBN: 978-1-4724-8555-7 (hbk)
ISBN: 978-1-138-36142-3 (pbk)

Typeset in Times New Roman
by Integra Software Services Pvt. Ltd.

"Never forget that if you leave your law to judges and your religion to bishops, you will presently find yourself without either law or religion." Bernard Shaw

Contents

List of figures and tables

Figures

Tables

Preface and acknowledgements

In Serbia, when you park your car in a spot not intended for parking, you can expect your four wheeled pet to be towed. In a more favorable scenario (for your library research on the other side of the town, not necessarily your wallet) you would find a ticket on your windshield that was due in a week. What happens, however, when upon further inspection you determine that according to the horizontal traffic signalization you had actually parked properly, while the vertical signalization (read "no parking" sign) is now a bare metal pole and the sign has been removed. For sure, the rule of law state embodied in its judicial institutions is there to warrant your right to park in the space provided for it and to correct obvious failure of the officer on duty.

The place of this true story is New Belgrade, Serbia, near the farmers' market in blok 45, the time is late fall 2010, and the main actor is the author of this book, raddled with thoughts about the topic of his doctoral dissertation. Upon the first half minute of blank staring at the piece of paper stuck on my windshield, on the edge of coming to terms with the fact that the start of my research project will cost me 5,000 Serbian dinars, I realized the oversight of the above mentioned police officer. The fact that, not that long ago, I had passed my exam in procedural law at Belgrade University enabled me to foresee two strategies so as to avoid payment (of the undeserved ticket). The first was simply not pay the ticket and forget about the whole case after the first corner. After all, in the rule of law abiding state of Serbia, there was a very small probability that I would get to a court hearing before the lapse of ticked expiry (two years for cases with a "relatively small monetary sum"), regardless of the small print at the bottom of the ticket warning otherwise. The second was to go willingly to the court and prove my innocence. The first strategy seemed quite appealing. However, at that time I had been living and working in Graz, Austria, and my grandparents lived at the address I was residing fictitiously during the late 1990s in order to evade potential army conscription in Belgrade at that time. Immediately I realized I should spare my honest old folks from an unnecessary visit from the uniformed police officer. So, straight to the courthouse.

I prepared by collecting photographs of the place of the alleged parking violation, which included a photo of the "unlawfully" parked vehicle, a photo of the pole without the traffic sign, as well as a photo of barely visible remnants of a parking spot drawn on the concrete. Just in case, I browsed through textbooks from law school so as to not embarrass myself in front of the judge after I had established my profession as an assistant at the law faculty.

During my next visit to Belgrade I went to the courthouse in Vračar. I had to explore the building to find the judges' chambers handling my case, which turned out to be an airless and shabby attic room. I was ready to make a long speech denigrating the whole process, including the police officer who had written the ticket. However, instead of the judge I was greeted by the administrative assistant who was astounded by my intent to willingly show in front of the court. She told me that the judge was on a business trip to Kosovska Mitrovica and the he would not be in court at least for a month. I would not be in Belgrade for even longer and thus hoped that in the meantime police officers would not be visiting my grandparents.

The next time, I was committed to finishing the whole ordeal as I really did not want to waste any more time in the courthouse attic. This time there was no administrative assistant, but the judge. He looked at me speechless, eyes wide open, in obvious disbelief while I was explaining the reason of my visit. He apologized for the assistant's absence due to which he could not tell how long it would take to find my case. He opened one of the drawers, and, I think, pretended to be looking for my case. He shook his head doubtfully. As I was not interrupting, he decided that two minutes were enough and admitted that he could not find my case as it probably may not have even be there. Actually, he told me, even if the case appeared, why would I inconvenience myself with another visit? Even if the court found me guilty for the non-existent violation and if I filed a complaint, the case would surely get outdated, so I would not be damaged by anything. I decided there was no reason for arguing with the bewildered judge and left the courthouse.

This true story established several facts key to my intention to explore the reform of the rule of law system in the Western Balkans. Namely, the law apparatus in the region is not efficient, non-accountable, works under extremely poor conditions and it is not computerized. Will it change during the ongoing negotiations with the EU?

During later stages of writing the book, the case described in this story became outdated/expired, without any closure by the court. In the meantime, a whole set of new rules on judiciary has been accepted, while the work of courts became regularly monitored by the European Commission. The subject of this book is thus the establishment of a relationship between these two processes, namely, the influence of Europeanization on the rule of law in Southeast Europe.

In turning to extend the customary thanks, I would first like to mention the continued support in my research by the Swiss Agency for Development and Cooperation for which I am greatly indebted. I am particularly grateful for the support of Jasmina Opardija-Šušnjar and Niclas Hayoz from the Interfaculty Institute for Central and Eastern Europe at the University of Fribourg, who have generously supported my research for close to two years through the

Regional Research Promotion Program. In addition, I am thankful to the various officials, scholars, and friends both within and outside the Western Balkans region with whom I have discussed this research: Frank Schimmelfennig, Antoaneta Dimitrova, Adam Fagan, Adnan Kadribašić, Adaleta Bibezić, Vladimir Misev, Gresa Caka, Sanja Kmezić, Pierre Mirel and Erwan Fuere. This work could not have been completed without a constant source of academic inspiration coming from my colleagues at the Centre for Southeast European Studies at the University of Graz: Florian Bieber, Kerem Öktem, Dario Brentin, Karabekir Akkoyunlu, Edith Marko-Stöckl, Emma Lantschner, Armina Galijaš, Hrvoje Paić, Güler Alkan, Lura Pollozhani, Beate Hainschek and Tanja Bilaver. They are of course in no way responsible for my account and my conclusions. Most of all, I would like to thank Florian Bieber for his exceptionally helpful comments on chapters of this book, and Joseph Marko for his invaluable guidance and support during the research and initial drafting process of this study. Their thought-provoking and questioning observations and constructive suggestions were critical to improving the structure, substance and essence of this book.

Finally, my utmost gratitude goes to my family for their unwavering support, encouragement and love. I would like to thank my parents, my sister Jelena, my wife Sanja, and my son Nikola.

Marko Kmezić
Graz, Austria

List of abbreviations

ABA/Ceeli	American Bar Association/Central and East-European Legal Initiative
AIRE	Advice on Individual Rights in Europe
BD	Brčko District
BiH	Bosnia and Herzegovina
CARDS	Community Assistance for Reconstruction Development and Stabilisation
CCEJ	Consultative Council of European Judges
CF	Constitutional Framework
CMS	Case Management System
DJA	Department of Judicial Administration
DOJ	Department of Justice
DPS	Democratic Party of Socialists of Montenegro
EAR	European Agency for Reconstruction
EC	European Commission
ECHR	European Court of Human Rights
EIPA	European Institute for Public Administration
EJN	European Judicial Network
EJTN	European Judicial Training Network
ENCJ	European Network of Councils for Judiciary
ENP	European Neighbourhood Policy
EPAP	European Partnership Action Plan
EPD	Enhanced Permanent Dialogue
ESPD	European Security and Defence Policy
EU	European Union
EULEX	European Union Rule of Law Mission in Kosovo
EUSR	European Union Special Representative
FBiH	Federation of BiH
FRY	Federal Republic of Yugoslavia
GDP	Gross Domestic Product
HJPC	High Judicial and Prosecutorial Council
HLAD	High-Level Accession Dialogue
IA	Interim Agreement on trade and trade-related matters
ICJ	International Court of Justice

ICO	International Civilian Office
ICR	International Civilian Representative
ICTY	International Criminal Tribunal for Former Yugoslavia
IPA	Instrument for Pre-Accession
ISG	International Steering Group
JHA	Justice and Home Affairs
JIS	Judicial Information System
JPTC	Judicial and Prosecutorial Training Centre
JRCB	Joint Rule of Law Coordination Board
JSRS	Justice Sector Reform Strategy
KJC	Kosovo Judicial Council
KJI	Kosovo Judicial Institute
KJPC	Kosovo Judicial and Prosecutorial Council
KPC	Kosovo Prosecutorial Council
MOJ	Ministry of Justice
MPS	Ministry of Public Services
NATO	North Atlantic Treaty Organization
NGO	Non-governmental organization
NPI	National Programme for the Integration
ODC	Office of Disciplinary Council
ODP	Office of the Disciplinary Prosecutor
OHR	Office of the High Representative
OSCE	Organization for Security and Co-operation in Europe
PARiM	Public Administration Reform in Montenegro
RCC	Regional Cooperation Council
RS	Republika Srpska
SAA	Stabilisation and Association Agreement
SAP	Stabilisation Association Process
SAPD	Stabilisation Association Process Dialogue
SEE	Southeastern Europe
SFRY	Socialist Federal Republic of Yugoslavia
SNS	Serbian Progressive Party
SPRK	Special Prosecution Office of the Republic of Kosovo
SPS	Socialist Party of Serbia
SRSG	Special Representative of the Secretary General
STM	Stabilisation and Association Process Tracking Mechanism
TAIEX	Technical Assistance and Information Exchange
TL	Treaty of Lisbon
UNDP	United Nations Development Programme
UNMIK	United Nations Mission in Kosovo
UNSCR	United Nations Security Council Resolution
WB	Western Balkans
WBCs	Western Balkan countries

Part I

1 Introduction

Southeastern Europe in transition

The countries of Southeastern Europe (SEE) lag behind other European states in the process of consolidation of economy and democracy and accession to the European Union. While three countries joined the European Union (EU), Romania and Bulgaria in 2007 as laggards of the 2004 enlargement and Croatia in 2013, the remainder of the region remains excluded with no foreseeable accession date in sight. Furthermore, state dissolution and the legacy of violent conflict shaped the transformation in the former Yugoslavia, which included the need for a long period of reconstruction of the state and economy, and reconciliation between peoples. In addition to the dual political and economic transformation from communist rule and a planned economy to democracy and market liberalism, most countries of SEE, in particular the successor states of former Yugoslavia, are weak states with dysfunctional institutions, notwithstanding the considerable diversity among these states.[1] These multiple challenges are crucial to explaining the delay in the EU integration process in the Western Balkan countries (WBC).[2] The EU sought to account for these particularities with the Stabilisation and Association Process (SAP).

However, in spite of the fact that the SAP was launched already 15 years ago, the WBC are still far away from the full EU membership. After losing the momentum of change gained after the democratic revolution in Serbia and the second democratic revolution in Croatia in 2000, the current situation can best be described as the "consolidation of unconsolidated democracies."[3] The latest edition of the *Nations in Transit* report presents a record of backsliding and stagnation in all key governance indicators across all the countries of the region.[4] While liberal democratic Western Balkan governments seem to identify with the EU, they often remain overshadowed by the high number of domestic formal and informal "gate keeper" elites that continue to control the state in an effort to preserve their private economic interests and their grip on political power.[5] The reconciliation after the violent conflicts of the 1990s is still not fully achieved, while a climate of revenge, fear and hatred still drives decisions of the political elites and, more importantly, the attitudes of common people. Bilateral relationships, particularly between Serbia and

Kosovo and Macedonia and Greece, remain overburdened by historical legacies, and threaten to export tension to the level of regional cooperation as well. While the dynamics of the EU integration seem to announce a new phase in regional relations, relapse into the doctrine of the ethnically pure state and ethnic extremism is all but impossible.

Moreover, Bosnia-Herzegovina and Kosovo—notwithstanding the latter's declaration of independence in 2008—remain internationally administered territories.[6] Macedonia managed to avoid a full-scale war and to reduce inter-ethnic tensions with the mostly successful implementation of the Ohrid Framework Agreement of 2001, but the political system is not fully consolidated,[7] while the countries' Euro-Atlantic integration is consistently vetoed by Greece due to the mutual name issue dispute. After the dissolution of the common state with Montenegro in 2006 and Kosovo's declaration of independence in 2008, Serbia is currently in the hands of "reformed" Milošević allies who have turned pro-European. At the same time its political elites are searching for a way to escape the dilemmas over state- and nationhood issues. Having gained independence in 2006, Montenegro has nearly completed the state-building processes. However, the country's newly achieved independence did not result in a swift resolution of key challenges, such as weak governance and widely perceived corruption.[8] Albania did not take part in the violent ex-Yugoslav wars and therefore had an easier path towards democratic consolidation than the countries analyzed above, but it has nonetheless undergone a very slow democratic and economic transition hampered by the internal political polarization of the ruling elites, the dominant influence of informal centers of power, and high levels of corruption throughout all branches of government.[9]

Romania and Bulgaria did not have to cope with violent state dissolution like that seen by the former Socialist Federal Republic of Yugoslavia (SFRY) and, consequently, did not have to undergo a phase of reconstruction and reconciliation and experienced fewer challenges to democratic consolidation processes. Instead, these two countries were finally successful in their legal and institutional reform efforts and joined the European Union with the accession in 2007, which completed the EU's fifth enlargement. However, despite the far-reaching reforms enacted in preparation for EU membership, Bulgaria and Romania still had some way to go in the adaptation of their legal systems to guarantee an effective system of rule of law.[10] To ensure that these reform efforts continue beyond accession, the Commission has established a package of transitional measures within the Cooperation and Verification Mechanism to ensure the smooth integration of Bulgaria and Romania.[11] Hence, both countries are still subject to a specific post-accession monitoring system. Finally, Croatia managed to consolidate its democracy after the second democratic "revolution" in 2000, but was delayed multiple times in the accession process, first by insufficient cooperation with the International Criminal Tribunal for the former Yugoslavia (ICTY), and later due to an unresolved border dispute with Slovenia.[12] In July 2013, Croatia became the 28th member state of the EU as the second country from the former Yugoslavia to enter the EU, and the first country after Greece to join the Union in a single country enlargement. Croatia managed to avoid the post-accession monitoring instruments concerning the improvement of rule of law imposed by the EU on Bulgaria and Romania. Bearing in mind the experience from the 2007 enlargement, the EU took a more austere negotiating position with Croatia in closing Chapters 23 and 24 pertaining to "Judiciary and Fundamental Rights," and "Justice, Freedom and Security," respectively. While one could argue that Croatia escaped the post-accession monitoring because it was forced to do a better job than Bulgaria and Romania in implementation of an effective rule of law system, the fact is that the EU officials became aware of the "limited effects"[13] of the Cooperation and Verification Mechanism, and therefore decided to rely more on "soft pressure" to ensure the effective implementation of rule of law in Croatia.

This shows that not only EU candidate countries, but even the EU member states[14] did not manage to resolve all the problems with regard to a functioning system of rule of law, which places the rule of law implementation in SEE high on the agenda of future legal and political science research interest. What is particularly sticking, and what also presents the driving impetus for the research behind this book, is the fact that despite constantly growing EU efforts in promoting democracy and rule of law in SEE,[15] the dynamics of international impact, and particularly the causal impact of international instruments on domestic outcomes, remains a highly under-theorized and under-researched area. More precisely, this study treats the experience of the EU's transformative engagement in the candidate countries taking part in the SAP within the field of reform of the judiciary.

Framing the challenge

Strengthening of the rule of law and the accession to the EU have been fraught with difficulties in Southeastern Europe for over 20 years. In line with previous scholarship on "Europeanization,"[16] this book treats this phenomenon as a *politically* driven process, i.e. as a way in which EU institutions, rules and policy-making processes impact the legal systems, institutional mechanisms and creation of collective cultural identity in non-EU member states. Hence, the research question of this book remains the same: Whether and what kind of influence the EU institutions have on the implementation of the rule of law in the Southeastern Europe.

Although there is no uniform EU standard regarding the rule of law, it can be observed that rule of law as a constitutional principle and institutional mechanisms in legal textbooks' descriptions are different from practical requirements with regard to the conceptualization and operationalization of benchmarks for monitoring processes in the Stabilisation and Association Process. Namely, during the monitoring process of the (potential) candidate countries' compliance with the Copenhagen conditionality criteria related to the effective rule of law and democracy principle, the EU Commission tests and criticizes various issues included in the Justice and Home Affairs (JHA) policies of the EU, stretching from asylum and border control to the fight against corruption and organized crime.

This book deliberately chooses not to deal with the effect of EU policies in this sector covered by Chapter 24, but focuses on the normative and empirical analysis of the effective functioning of the judiciary in five case study countries. The central focus of this study, then, is the reform of the judiciary in those five case study countries: Bosnia and Herzegovina, Kosovo, Macedonia, Montenegro, and Serbia.

More specifically, this study scrutinizes the institutional reform carried out in the judicial sector by means of content analysis of legal rules and administrative regulations adopted for this purpose, as well as their implementation. Furthermore, this book tests whether the EU Commission uses a double standard or whether a coherent framework of analysis is created and used in the monitoring process.

As previously has been observed with regard to the EU monitoring activities in the Eastern enlargement process,[17] the performance of the judicial system remains difficult to measure mostly due to the lack of coherent European standards. For this reason this study borrows a comprehensive set of judicial independence, accountability, efficiency and effectiveness "benchmarks" already elaborated on behalf of EuropeAid by Joseph Marko et al.[18] Namely political, economic and ethnic challenges to judicial *independence* stemming from the establishment of such new institutions as High Judicial Councils whose members are appointed by parliaments and/or the executive, the low level of salaries paid in the judiciary, or proportional ethnic representation (where applicable) even in the judiciary, which raises challenges for the notion of "fair trial" that have not been empirically studied so far. Secondly, independence must be balanced with *accountability* against the danger of a "gouvernement des juges."[19] Thirdly, independence and accountability are of no effect if judges and prosecutors are not *efficient* and *effective*. Hence, capacity-building in the judicial sector and the effectiveness of its institutional mechanisms are functions that have to be studied both from a normative and an empirical perspective.

The investigation of the state of the judiciary is based on an analysis of the institutional reforms thus far performed in the five case study countries. Particular focus is given to newly established institutions such as the High Judicial and Prosecutorial Council with the goal to assess whether they provide political independence to the judiciary. This task has been executed through an empirical study based on 52 semi-structured interviews with representatives of the judiciary, government employees and relevant domestic and international experts (legal scholars, NGO representatives, journalists, EU representatives), as well as a review of media reporting.[20] With regard to accountability, this study has empirically tested whether the judicial institutions are effective in this matter, again with a special focus on the newly established institutions and their role in maintaining accountability in working habits. The analysis of the training of judges organized by the Organization for Security and Co-operation in Europe (OSCE) and expert non-governmental organizations (NGOs) (such as the Belgrade and Sarajevo Human Rights Centers) in terms of capacity building helped to determine the efficiency of the judicial institutions in the SEE. Special focus is given to the effectiveness of the newly established Judicial Academies throughout the region, which are partially founded and financed by the EU Commission. Finally, the effectiveness of the judiciary is assessed through an analysis of the legal and institutional reforms of, for instance, civil procedure in order to shorten the length of civil law suits, as well as through an assessment of the work of the newly established "special" courts (labor courts, administrative courts etc.) and chambers (war crimes chamber, organized crime chamber etc.).

Based on such a comprehensive comparative study of the judicial sector reform in the selected countries, this study will identify the possible "misfit"[21] between the criteria established in the EU monitoring process, and the laws adopted by the parliaments of EU (potential) candidate countries on the one hand, and the effectiveness of the judiciaries, on the other. From this basic analytical framework, a subset of more concrete research questions follows:

1 What EU requirements are developed in the monitoring process?
2 Which organizational-institutional reforms have been made?
3 Which elites (e.g. political, economic, ethnic, etc.) resisted these reforms?
4 Who (e.g. critical civil society actors, opposition political parties, etc.) has supported these reforms?
5 What have been the effects and how did they change over the last decade with regard to judiciary independence, accountability, efficiency, and effectiveness benchmarks?
6 Finally, does the current EU approach to the rule of law reform in candidate countries work beyond the critical phase of norm adoption.

This book looks into the institutional changes in the judiciary of SEE countries from 2000 until the present. The year 2000 in SEE was marked by the collapse of Slobodan Milošević's authoritarian regime in Serbia and Montenegro, and the "second" democratic revolution through general elections in Croatia. These events provided the path for the democratic consolidation and economic reform of the region based on a commitment of all relevant political actors to EU integration. Furthermore, at the same time the EU launched its new Western Balkans policy based on the SAP, which offered the countries of the region the "perspective" of eventual EU membership. By taking the whole 15 years into account, the research elaborated in this study will hopefully be able to critically answer the question of whether and how this process can be more effective in the future.

Book structure

The book is organized in three major parts. Besides the introduction, Part I provides an overview of the existing literature on Europeanization with specific focus on its effect on the rule of law. Part II attempts to provide accurate and up-to-date normative and empirical analysis of the state of judiciary reforms in Bosnia and Herzegovina, Kosovo, Macedonia, Montenegro, and Serbia. Finally, Part III offers answers to the question of the success of the Europeanization by rule of law implementation in SEE in the form of a comprehensive conclusion chapter, as well as policy recommendations intended to address the shortcomings in judiciary reform in SEE observed during the research that led to this book, as well as ideas for how the EU could enhance its influence in the rule of law promotion during the accession phase.

Part II begins with a commentary on the role of the legacies and cultural predispositions on the reform of the judiciary in five case study countries. It continues with an analysis of the current state of play in European integrations process in the SEE. Finally, the largest part of this section of the book is dedicated to the empirical and normative analysis of the reform of the judiciary in Bosnia and Herzegovina, Kosovo, Macedonia, Montenegro, and Serbia. This is timely, given the apparent problematic surrounding the implementation of the effective rule of law in the region addressed by the European Commission (EC) in the process of European integration. Furthermore, as will be shown, rule of law norm socialization in SEE remains understudied and undertheorized. The rich and diverse insights in Part II may in due course contribute to the understanding and conceptualization of this phenomenon in the Western Balkans region.

In Part III of the book we shall conclude the scope, depth and limitations of EU rule of law promotion in the Western Balkans. This study finds that the accession process generates unique, broad-based and long-term support for the establishment of the rule of law in the (potential) candidate states. However, at the same time it goes on to show a number of shortcomings and wrong assumptions in EU's rule of law export strategy to the candidate states. Hence, this book offers specific recommendations in order to foster the process.

The innovative character and broader impact of the book

First, the traditional top-down approach in Europeanization studies has in many cases underestimated the constructivist institutionalist approach. In this regard, already in 2006, Sedelmeier called for more conceptualization efforts, to which this book provides an answer.[22] The proposed re-conceptualization of the "spiral theory," the selection of countries for comparison and the elaboration of a comprehensive framework of analysis trying to overcome the theoretical dichotomies will thus provide new innovative ground.

Secondly, while there are a number of single case studies, no comprehensive and comparative empirical studies exist so far to test pre-accession monitoring of and compliance with the rule of law implementation in the Western Balkans (WB), and/or to analyze the different roles that various gate-keeper elites play. In addition, the reform of the rule-of-law sector has generally been neglected and has not been the object of comprehensive scientific research to date.

From the perspective of applied research, the book thus intends not just to advance scholarship on this topic, but also to have an impact on the policy strategy for the accession processes in the Western Balkans beyond the "wait-and-see"[23] approach pursued by EU institutions today.

Thirdly, the entire book, based on a neo-institutional approach, will strengthen interdisciplinary research in the study of the EU. By drawing on research methodology from political science and law, this book is intended to help to overcome the gap between scholars of EU law and comparative constitutional law on the one hand, and political science on the other.

Finally, this study on how to strengthen rule of law in transition societies and weak or failed states could potentially have a broader implication for EU foreign policy not only in the sphere of democratization, but also for sustainable economic development. In this regard, this book may be of interest also for other international institutions, such as the World Bank or the United Nations Development Programme's economic research and strategies' development in the fight against poverty.

Notes

1 See S. Keil. and Z. Arkan. (eds.). 2015. *The EU and Member State Building: European Foreign Policy in the Western Balkans* (Routledge: New York).

2 At this point the author would like to introduce several terminological clarifications, chiefly for the use of the term Western Balkans. Namely, most international scholars, and in recent years even domestic authors, have chosen to follow the lead of the European Union, which since 1999 has considered the geographical region of Southeastern Europe to be composed of two parts. The first subgroup is composed of four EU members—Greece, Slovenia, Bulgaria and Romania. The other subgroup consists of the four initial successor states to the former Yugoslavia, plus newly independent Montenegro and Kosovo, together with Albania. These states are dubbed the Western Balkans simply due to their geographical location to the west of Bulgaria and Romania. Some authors contest the term Western Balkans for several reasons. First, it is often used as a pejorative synonym for violence and ethnic hatred; second, the difference between the Western Balkans and the rest of the Southeast Europe is not so pronounced beyond the European Union enlargement context; and finally, to bring in more confusion, EU member states, Slovenia and Croatia, are located on the western frontier of the Western Balkans. Acknowledging the aforementioned arguments, the author proposes the use of the term Western Balkans contextually, and only for the purpose of this research, since it includes all the countries under scrutiny. This, however, is not the only open terminological issue. The official EU documents use the term Former Yugoslav Republic of Macedonia. The author will employ the term Macedonia, unless citing an official EU document. Similarly, Kosova is the preferred usage by local authorities, but this research will use the term Kosovo, which is more frequently used in English-language sources.

3 This term is first used to describe the state of democracy in the Western Balkans in F. Bieber. 2012. "The Western Balkans are Dead – Long Live the Balkans! Democratization and the Limits of the EU," in V. Džihić and D. Hamilton (eds.). *Unfinished Business: The Western Balkans and the International Community* (Washington D.C.: Brookings Institution Press): 3–10; and later in C. Gordon, M. Kmezić and J. Opardija (eds.). 2013. *Stagnation and Drift in the Western Balkans: The Challenges of Political, Economic and Social Change* (Bern: Peter Lang AG).

4 *Nations in Transit*. 2015. Freedom House. Available at https://freedomhouse.org/sites/default/files/FH_NIT2015_06.06.15_FINAL.pdf.
5 See in M. Kmezić. 2014. "Overcoming the Crisis of Enlargement," *Contemporary Southeastern Europe*, 1(1).
6 See for example in J. Marko. 2008. "The New Kosovo Constitution in a Regional Comparative Perspective," *Review of Central and East European Law* 33: 437–450; M. Weller. 2009. *Contested Statehood: Kosovo's Struggle for Independence* (Oxford: Oxford University Press); F. Bieber. 2010. "Bosnia and Herzegovina since 1990," in S. P. Ramet (ed.), *Central and Southeast European Politics since 1989* (Cambridge: Cambridge University Press): 311–328; and O. Tansey. 2010. *Regime-Building: Democratization and International Administration* (Oxford: Oxford University Press).
7 Balkans in Europe Policy Advisory Group. 2015. *Unraveling the Political Crisis in Macedonia: Toward Resolution or Calm Before the Storm?* Available at http://www.suedosteuropa.uni-graz.at/biepag/node/158.
8 Transparency International. 2014. "Montenegro: Overview of Political Corruption." Available at http://www.transparency.org/files/content/corruptionqas/Montenegro_Overview_of_Political_Corruption_2014.pdf.
9 T. Cierco. 2014. "Albania's Difficult Path towards Democracy," *Canadian-American Slavic Studies*, 48(4): 468–491.
10 A. L. Dimitrova. 2010. "The New Member States of the EU in the Aftermath of Enlargement: Do new European Rules Remain Empty Shells?," *Journal of European Public Policy* 17(1): 137–148.
11 For more details on Cooperation and Verification Mechanism see A. L. Dimitrova. 2015. "The Effectiveness and Limitations of Political Integration in Central and Eastern European Member States: Lessons from Bulgaria and Romania," *MAXCAP Working Papers* No. 10.
12 D. Winland. 2008. "Ten Years Later: The Changing Nature of Transnational Ties in Post-independence Croatia," in D. Kostovicova and V. Bojičić-Dželilović, *Transnationalism in the Balkans* (New York: Routledge): 79–93.
13 K. Ott. 28 June 2013. *Croatia and the EU: The Catch-Up Issue* (CEPS Commentary).
14 See U. Sedelmeier. 2014. "Anchoring Democracy from Above? The European Union and Democratic Backsliding in Hungary and Romania after Accession." *Journal of Common Market Studies*, 52(1): 105–121.
15 See for instance see T. Carothers (ed.). 2006. *Promoting the Rule of Law Abroad* (Washington D.C.: Carnegie Endowment for International Peace); A. Magen and L. Morlino. 2008. *International Actors, Democratization and the Rule of Law* (New York: Routledge); L. J. Cohen and J. R. Lampe (eds.). 2011. *Embracing Democracy in the Western Balkans: From Post-conflict Struggles toward European Integration* (Washington, D.C.: Woodrow Wilson Center Press).
16 See in particular U. Sedelmeier. 2006 "Europeanization in New Member and Candidate States," *Living Reviews in European Governance* 1(3); and U. Sedelmeier. 2011. "Europeanization in New Member and Candidate States," *Living Reviews in European Governance* 6(1).
17 A. Mungiu-Pippidi. 2008. "The EU as a Transformation Agent. Lessons Learned from Governance Reforms in East Central Europe," *Hertie School of Governance – Working Papers* 33.
18 J. Marko, F. Palermo, and J. Woelk. July 2004. "Re-enforcement of the Rule of Law. Division of Competences and Interrelations between Courts, Prosecutors, the Police, Executive and the Legislative Powers in the Western Balkans Countries." Strategic Studies in CARDS 2003. Final Report.
19 W. Sadurski, A. Czarnota and M. Krygier (eds.). 2006. *Spreading Democracy and the Rule of Law: The Impact of EU Enlargement on the Rule of Law, Democracy and Constitutionalism in Post-Communist Legal Orders* (Netherlands: Springer).

20 In order to secure respondents anonymity, throughout the book names of the interviewed persons will not be disclosed. Instead, respondents' demographic details, professional affiliation as well as the date of the conducted interview will be revealed.

21 G. Falkner. 2003. "Comparing Europeanisation Effects: From Metaphor to Operationalisation," *European Integration Online Papers* 7(13); G. Falkner and M. Hartlapp. 2009 "Problems of Operationalization and Data in EU Compliance Research," *European Union Politics* 10(2): 281–304.

22 See again U. Sedelmeier, 2006 "Europeanization in New Member and Candidate States," cit.

23 Preoccupied with its internal affairs, the EU seemed to lose interest in keeping the promise of a European future for the Western Balkans. As a result it started to lose credibility and influence in a region that experienced the risk of sliding back towards instability. Criticism of the EU's "wait-and-see" approach to the Western Balkans was therefore addressed by academics in J. Marko. 2009. "A Response to the Interview with Michael Leigh, Director-General of the European Commission," *Journal of Southeastern Europe* 33(1); H. Grabbe, G. Knaus, and D. Korski. 2010. "Beyond Wait-and-See: The Way Forward for EU Balkan Policy," *European Council on Foreign Relations.*

2 The elusive essence of the rule of law

The problem of knowledge

Democratic consolidation is intimately linked with the effectiveness of rule of law, but, at the same time, the concepts of democracy and rule of law are not identical. This can be seen from the different historical development of the English common law tradition on the one hand, and continental European civil law traditions on the other.[1] However, as Kochenov describes for the Eastern enlargement process, the structure and substance of the Copenhagen-related documents do not make any distinction between the assessment of democracy and the rule of law. In the course of the pre-accession, the Commission opted for "fusing their assessment,"[2] with the effect that it gained political maneuvering space for more specific policy prescription in the process. Moreover, rule of law as a constitutional principle and institutional mechanism in legal textbook descriptions are quite different from practical requirements with regard to the conceptualization and operationalization of benchmarks for monitoring processes in the SAP, as can be seen from applied research.[3]

Nevertheless, the most recent *Enlargement Strategy and Main Challenges 2015* report in the Communication from the Commission to the European Parliament and the Council spells out that, "Strengthening the rule of law remains a key challenge for most of the countries in the enlargement process, in particular in terms of improving the functioning and independence of the judiciary."[4] Rule of law and the judicial sector reform are again highlighted by recent reports on the negotiations for the accession of the Republic of Croatia to the EU. Turkalj, former member of the Croatian negotiating team for EU accession, highlights Chapter 23 on "Judiciary and Fundamental Rights" as crucial for the outcome of the entire negotiation process.[5] Moreover, the former European Commissioner for Enlargement, Štefan Füle, when presenting the Enlargement Strategy in 2010, underscored that

> the EU expects a convincing track record in the fulfillment of these benchmarks, in particular regarding judiciary and fundamental rights. Accession negotiations do not simply involve ticking boxes about legislative approximation. Countries must build a credible track record of reform and implementation, in particular in the area of rule of law.[6]

The recent documents, as well as the address of the former Commissioner, thus highlight again the importance of rule of law implementation and judicial sector reform for overall progress in the SAP.

Legal bedrock: rule of law and the judicial reform

The rule of law principle has a long common tradition in most influential legal orders, but it has not been precisely defined by any of them. The definition of the rule of law remains legitimately open-ended, and therefore academics and practitioners alike are at liberty to formulate what attributes must be included in its definition. Despite the apparent lack of a universally accepted definition, the EU and various international donors have spent "more than a billion dollars"[7] over the last two decades trying to build the rule of law in countries transitioning to democracy. Hence, instead of going deeper into the quest for the proper definition of the term "rule of law," this study will grasp its core *concept* within the EU context, and more precisely within the field of EU external policy.

To no surprise, the rule of law was not defined by the founding fathers of the EU. It has instead become a predominant organizational model of contemporary constitutional law, a dynamic "meta-principle"[8] providing a firm foundation for an independent and effective judiciary. As such, the rule of law in the context of the EU essentially describes and justifies the "subjection of public power to formal and substantive legal constraints with a view to guaranteeing the primacy of the individual protection against arbitrary or unlawful use of public power."[9] It never appears as a "stand-alone" principle but rather as an "umbrella-principle,"[10] usually accompanied by the principles of liberty, democracy, and the respect for fundamental rights.

Due to the predominance of the legal interpretation of the rule of law principle, it has already been asked whether the principle is not more a "Rule of Lawyers" than a "Rule of Law."[11] The dilemma that this question raises is not one of efficiency or protecting the purity of law, but rather of preservation of the integrity of law, which can only be achieved if the institutional arrangements are capable of dealing reasonably with the dual dangers of anarchy and unrestrained power. The (legal) institutional arrangements alone, however, are not sufficient to complete this task, as they always need "a supporting circumstance,"[12] namely societal and political support, which are often difficult to engineer. More concretely, institutions must fulfill certain conditions in order to be able to restrain the exercise of power. These conditions, on the other hand, depend on other non-legal conditions falling within the scope of sociology and politics. As Krygier writes, "successful attainment of the rule of law [therefore] is a *social* outcome, not a merely legal one."[13] To conclude, if rule of law—this applies even more to EU rule of law– should become an important component in the life of a society, then norms must become socially normative.

Functionally, the rule of law exercises two main functions. The first is to impose restraints on government officials by requiring compliance with the existing law, as their acts must have positive legal authorization and must not contravene a legal prohibition or restriction, and also to impose limits on the law-making power. The second function of the rule of law is to maintain and coordinate behavior and transactions among the citizens. In this regard, we observe that the establishment of a lasting and effective rule of law requires not only a widely shared conviction among the society—citizens and political and economic elites– that people identify themselves with law, but also the presence of an institutionalized, independent, accountable, efficient and effective judiciary, crucial to both aforementioned functions. However, a well-functioning judiciary is not conceivable without the existence of a robust legal profession and a legal tradition committed to the rule of law. This egg–hen situation presupposes the need of the rule of law promoters to dedicate particular attention to the reform of judiciaries around the globe.

Rule of law in the process of EU accession

Article 2 of the EU requires the respect and promotion of the values on which the EU was founded as one of the conditions not only of membership but also of an application for membership.[14] Values on which the Union is founded are "respect for human dignity, freedom, democracy, equality, the rule of law and respect for human rights, including the rights of persons belonging to minorities."[15] In *Partie Ecologiste "Les Verts" vs. Parliament*[16] from 1986, the European Court of Justice (ECJ) for the first time affirmed "that the European Community is a community based on the rule of law" and that the Treaty had to be recognized as its "basic constitutional charter." Based on this seminal ruling, values such as rule of law under the Treaty of Lisbon are "constitutive" of the EU. As such they define the collective identity of the whole organization and thus essentially determine the Union's action in the domestic and international realms as well as the conditions for membership. However, Article 2 EU TL is merely the departure point for the progression of the (potential) candidate countries towards EU accession.

The accession system is only loosely rooted in the EU Treaties. In fact, it is not elaborated in a single working document, but rather in the bulk of Copenhagen-related documents that Kochenov portrays as a "'spider web' of political and legal obstacles"[17] towards capturing the essence of the rule of law accession requirement. He distinguishes between two principal groups of documents pertaining to the rule of law conditionality whereas the first group includes the documents addressed to particular countries such as the Commission's Opinions on the Application for Membership of the EU, Regular Reports on the candidate countries' progress towards accession, Accession Partnerships, Roadmaps, etc. The second group comprises documents of more general application including the Commission's Agenda 2000, yearly Composite Papers and Strategy Papers, Comprehensive Monitoring Reports, etc. Furthermore, both groups of documents frequently reference credentials created by sources falling beyond the scope of EU law, thus effectively including international organizations such as the OSCE and the Council of Europe to indirectly contribute to the assessment of the candidate countries' compliance, particularly in regard to the political criteria of democracy and the rule of law. By providing a variety of influence tools, the Copenhagen-related documents in fact provided the Commission with a "sophisticated system of reform promotion in the candidate countries that allowed it to make practical use of the conditionality principle for the benefit of both the European Union and the candidate countries."[18] Moreover, in the course of the pre-accession, the Commission assesses the rule of law and democracy interchangeably, with the effect that it gained political maneuvering space for more specific policy prescriptions within the process. In essence, both terms—democracy and the rule of law—were left indeterminate to the advantage of the Union, which, "by providing no single list of contents to act as benchmarks, was able to introduce new components under these umbrella terms."[19] Consequently, the Union is able to manipulate these terms in dealing with membership candidate countries.

An additional predicament arises from the difficulty of quantitatively verifying the achieved level of compliance in regard to the Copenhagen political criteria. In contrast to economic reform, which is easily measured against the benchmarks of inflation rate, gross domestic product, inflation, etc., little can be established with great accuracy in the field of the rule of law and democracy due to the very nature of these concepts. Since the political accession criteria are generally not amenable to quantitative verification, EU candidate states are confronted with conditions that appear to them as moving targets. Bearing this in mind, the next task is to systematically conclude which benchmarks the EU uses in assessing rule of law compliance.

Rule of law conditionality as a requirement for judicial reform

The requirements for democracy and the rule of law were first addressed within the accession context in respect to the Mediterranean enlargements of the 1980s for the three post-authoritarian countries acceding to the EU within the wider framework of their respective democratic transitions. These requirements were addressed at the 1978 Copenhagen European Council in its Declaration on democracy. Through the Declaration, member states confirmed their will to safeguard the principles of the rule of law, social justice and of respect for human rights within a political system of pluralist democracy.[20] However, the Direction was primarily aiming at underlining the European Economic Community's position towards future members.[21] As mentioned earlier in this Chapter, the Maastricht Treaty on European Union in its Preamble confirmed the Member States' attachment to the principal of the rule of law. Yet, in the absence of clear EU indicators of the contents of requirement for democracy and the rule of law, in its negotiations with Austria, Finland and Sweden, the Union borrowed external indicators, most notably the Commission on Security and Cooperation in Europe's 1990 Charter of Paris for a New Europe.[22] While the Paris Charter details on the form of representative and pluralist democratic government, it yet again failed to address the rule of law, which continued to be considered as something of "'an umbrella concept' that 'has no determinate meaning'."[23] It was not until the fall of the Iron Curtin and the prospect of Eastern Enlargement that the EU enhanced its rule of law membership requirement. In regard to the Central Eastern European Countries (CEEC), the European Commission defined its political criteria in Agenda 2000[24] as a combination of free and fair elections, political pluralism, freedom of expression and freedom of religion, the need for democratic institutions, and the independent judicial and constitutional authorities. Even so, this approach was criticized for its rather "simplistic sum"[25] of the rule of law, and the lack of "actual substance."[26]

Only with the prospect of enlargement to the SEE did the EU become more aware of the need to provide content criteria, or benchmarks, with which to measure success or failure in fulfilling the principle of democracy and the rule of law.[27] Hence, in its April 1997 Conclusions, the General Affairs Council declared the political criteria SEE countries need to fulfill to conclude a Stabilization and Association Agreement (SAA)—which marks only the beginning of the contractual relationship between the EU and the candidate country. This time the Council made express reference to the rule of law, as it concluded that each SEE country must be ready to demonstrate:

1 the separation of executive, legislative and judicial powers,
2 effective means of redress against administrative decisions,
3 access to courts and the right to a fair trial,
4 equality before the law, and
5 freedom from inhumane or degrading treatment and arbitrary arrest.

Additional clarifications aimed at each potential candidate country individually were voiced by the European Commission in its Progress (previously Regular) Reports. Benchmarking that had direct bearing on the judiciary in the accession countries identified from the content analysis of the Progress Reports prepared for the SEE countries scrutinized in Chapter 5 of this study consists of:

1 rule of law,
2 independence of judiciary,
3 training of judges and judiciary to apply the *Acquis*,
4 human resources and system of infrastructure, and
5 effectiveness of court procedures.

Elusive essence of judicial governance

In addition to the elaborated issue of vagueness of the rule of law criterion *per se*, and within the context of the EU integration, even judicial organizations and judicial and legal systems throughout EU differ from one another, due to the differences in the constitutional systems and legal traditions of European states. Notoriously, the EU's jurisdiction over the judicial systems of its member states, mostly manifested through the institutional autonomy of the Member States,[28] is highly limited and also extremely contested.[29] Furthermore, Member States remain sovereign in shaping the organization of their respective courts system.

With the enlargement of the EU toward the ex-communist East, a remarkable assortment of "standards, recommendations, opinions, peer reviews,"[30] have been developed by the EU and Council of Europe. Although not legally binding, this collection of norms paved a way for the development of a soft power over European judicial governance "based on moral suasion and communicative action, rather than regulation."[31] Currently, various European institutions and expert organizations are contemplating models and templates of judicial governance. These include the European Network of Councils for Judiciary (ENCJ),[32] the Consultative Council of European Judges,[33] The European Judicial Training Network,[34] and the European Judicial Network.[35] Contemporary discourse on judicial reform in the EU is underpinned by the Vilnius Declaration, adopted by the ENCJ in 2011.[36] The Vilnius Declaration had produced a set of recommendations for the judiciaries of Europe on how to respond to the actual challenges and opportunities they are facing due to the "new economic landscape."[37] The recommendations call for the courts to improve their efficiency, to establish alternative dispute resolution, and to promote stronger relations with civil society in order to reinforce public confidence and gain support for necessary reforms. Following on the ENCJ findings, the European Commission has established the EU Justice Scoreboard, "an evolving tool that should assist the EU and its Member States to achieve more effective justice by providing objective, reliable and comparable data on the functioning of the justice systems of all Member States."[38] The EU Justice Scoreboard is a non-binding mechanism operated as part of an open dialogue with the Member States which aims to assist the EU institutions and Member States in defining better justice policies. The first EU Justice Scoreboard concludes that "[w]hatever the model of the national justice system or the legal tradition in which it is anchored, quality, independence and efficiency are some of the essential parameters of an 'effective justice system'."[39] On the basis of the first EU Justice Scoreboard, the Commission is supposed to commence work towards improving national judicial systems in the EU in close collaboration with judges, judicial councils and legal practitioners, as well as with the European Parliament and with EU Member States. Nevertheless, the promotion of European judicial standards remains in its infancy, and current efforts are not sufficient to claim that EU demands in connection to the rule of law conditionality are clear. Therefore, the EU has to distil particular criteria and indicators on which basis countries will be graded.

Concluding analysis

Despite the fact that academic scholarship and democratic politics agree on rule of law as a legitimizing principle for the exercise of state authority, there is no uniform "European standard" for institution-building or monitoring activities by the EU in this area. Hence, the EU rule of law promotion taking part within the accession conditionality process tends to "translate the rule of law into an institutional checklist, with primary emphasis on the judiciary."[40] More precisely, alignment with the *Acquis* is measured up to formal legal and institutional benchmarks. Interchangeable use of the terms *rule of law* and *judicial reform* is common in the field of rule of law promotion, since most of the promotion experts are lawyers, "and when lawyers think about what seems to be the nerve center of the rule of law they think of the core institutions of law enforcement,"[41] i.e. the courts. However, a particular challenge still lies in the fact that the basic concepts—democracy and the principle of rule of law—remain interlocked and characterized by ambiguity and vagueness throughout the accession process.

Notes

1 A number of theoretically informed studies have debated the rule of law concept dilemma; for example, see T. Fleiner, L. R. Basta. 2009. *Constitutional Democracy in a Multicultural and Globalized World* (Berlin, Heidelberg: Springer); L. Pech. 2009. "The Rule of Law as a Constitutional Principle of the European Union," *Jean Monnet Working Paper* 04/09.

2 D. Kochenov. 2008. *EU Enlargement and the Failure of Conditionality: Pre-accession Conditionality in the Fields of Democracy and the Rule of Law* (The Hague: Kluwer Law International): 76.

3 J. Marko, F. Palermo, and J. Woelk. July 2004. "Re-enforcement of the Rule of Law," cit.

4 European Commission. *Enlargement Strategy and Main Challenges 2015. Communication from the Commission to the European Parliament and the Council* (COM [2015] 611) (Brussels: 10.11.2015): 5.

5 Speech by Kristian Turkalj, former member of the Negotiation Team responsible for Chapters 23 "Judiciary and Fundamental Rights" and 24 "Justice, Freedom and Security" in the Ministry of Justice of the Republic of Croatia. K. Turkalj. 29–30 April 2010. "Negotiations for the Accession of the Republic of Croatia to the European Union in the Area of Justice ('State of Play for Chapters 23 and 24')." Paper presented at the Conference "Croatia on the Eve of EU Accession: The Path of Reform" (Zagreb: Croatia).

6 Š. Füle. European Commissioner for Enlargement and Neighbourhood Policy Presentation of Enlargement Package European Parliament – Foreign Affairs Committee (AFET) (Brussels: 9 November 2010). Available online at http://europa.eu/rapid/press-release_SPEECH-10-638_en.htm.

7 R. Kleinfeld. 2006. "Competing Definitions of the Rule of Law," in T. Carothers, *Promoting the Rule of Law Abroad* (Washington D.C.: Carnegie Endowment for International Peace), 31–73, at 31.

8 This term was first used by L. Pech. 2009. "The Rule of Law as a Constitutional Principle of the European Union," *Jean Monnet Working Paper* No. 04/09.

9 Ibid.: 44.

10 P. Leino. 2002. "Rights, Rules and Democracy in the EU Enlargement Process: Between Universalism and Identity," *Austrian Review of International and European Law* 7: 53–80.

11 See a detailed elaboration of this question in F. Kratochwil. 2009. "Has the 'Rule of Law' become a 'Rule of Lawyers'? An Inquiry into the Use and Abuse of an

Ancient Topos in Contemporary Debates," in G. Palombella and N. Walker, *Relocating the Rule of Law* (Oxford: Hart): 171–196.

12 See M. Krygier. 2009. "The Rule of Law: Legality, Teleology, Sociology," in G. Palombella and N. Walker, *Relocating the Rule of Law*, cit.: 51–79.

13 Ibid.: 64.

14 Article 2, Treaty of Lisbon amending the Treaty on European Union and the Treaty establishing the European Community, European Commission (2007/C 306/01), Lisbon 2007. Reference to Article 2 of the EU was first introduced by the 1992 Mastricht Treaty. The list of values, formerly called principles, did not at the time include human dignity and equality.

15 Art. 2 EU TL.

16 Case 294/83 *Les Verts v. Parliament* (1986) ECJ 1339: para. 23.

17 See in D. Kochenov. 2008. *EU Enlargement and the Failure of Conditionality*, cit.: 78.

18 Ibid.: 84.

19 F. A. Tatham. 2009. *Enlargement of the European Union* (Kluwer Law International: Alphen aan den Rijn): 210.

20 European Council. 7–8 April 1978. "Declaration on Democracy." Copenhagen. Bull. EC 3–1978: 6.

21 See in F. A. Tatham. 2009. *Enlargement of the European Union.*

22 Commission on Security and Cooperation in Europe. 1990. *Charter of Paris for a New Europe*. Bull. EC 11–1990.

23 F. A. Tatham. 2009. *Enlargement of the European Union*, cit.: 209.

24 European Commission. 16 July 2007. *Agenda 2000: For a Stronger and Wider Union* [COM(97) 2000]. Brussels.

25 F. A. Tatham. 2009. *Enlargement of the European Union*, cit.: 209.

26 P. Leino. 2002. "Rights, Rules and Democracy in the EU Enlargement Process: Between Universalism and Identity," cit.: 53–80.

27 D. Smilov. 2006. "EU Enlargement and the Constitutional Principle of Judicial Independence," in W. Sadurski, A. Czarnota and M. Krygier (eds), *Spreading Democracy and the Rule of Law?: The Impact of EU Enlargement for the Rule of Law, Democracy and Constitutionalism in Post-Communist Legal Orders* (Dordrecht: Springer).

28 The term itself is misleading as this autonomy can indeed be limited by EU rules, see as early as 1983, European Court of Justice case 205/82 Deutsche Milchkontor, Rec 1983, 2633 [procedural autonomy].

29 Recently the European Court of Justice has been criticized for its judicial activism by leading politicians, national judges and scholars mostly, but not only, from Germany, Austria, Denmark and Sweden. Concretely, the Court was contested for overstepping its jurisdiction to the judicial autonomy of the member states. See, H.W. Micklitz and B. De Witte. 2012. *The European Court of Justice and the Autonomy of the Member States* (Cambridge: Intersentia).

30 D. Piana. 2010. "Beyond Judicial Independence: Rule of Law and Judicial Accountabilities in Assessing Democratic Quality," in L. Morlino and G. Palombella (eds), *Rule of Law and Democracy: Inquiries Into Internal and External Issues* (Leiden: Koniklijke Brill): 65–93, at 82.

31 Ibid.

32 In 2011 the European Network of Councils for the Judiciary adopted the Vilnius Declaration, which lists a set of recommendations for the judiciaries of Europe on how to respond to the actual challenges and opportunities they are facing due to the new economic landscape.

> The recommendations call for the development of long-term policies that include necessary reforms of the judiciary. Courts should improve their efficiency, alternative dispute resolution should be promoted, and the judiciary should

develop stronger relations with civil society in order to reinforce public confidence and gain support for the necessary reforms. Councils for the Judiciary should take the lead in the reform process involving judges and courts.

(Taken from www.encj.eu)

33 The Consultative Council of European Judges (CCEJ) is an advisory body of the Council of Europe on issues related to the independence, impartiality and competence of judges. It is the first body within an international organisation to be composed exclusively of judges, and in this respect, it is unique in Europe. The CCJE adopts Opinions for the attention of the Committee of Ministers on issues regarding the status of judges and the exercise of their functions. It addresses topical issues and, if necessary, visits the countries concerned to discuss the ways of improving the existing situation through developing legislation, institutional frameworks and/or judicial practices.

(Taken from www.coe.int/t/DGHL/cooperation/ccje/default_en.asp)

34 The European Judicial Training Network (EJTN) was established in 2000 as the principal platform and promoter for the development, training and exchange of knowledge and competence of the EU judiciary. EJTN develops training standards and curricula, coordinates judicial training exchanges and programmes and fosters cooperation between EU national training bodies.

35 The European Judicial Network (EJN) was established in 1998 as a network of national contact points for the facilitation of judicial cooperation in criminal matters. See more at http://www.ejn-crimjust.europa.eu/ejn/EJN_StaticPage.aspx?Bread=2.

36 *The Vilnius Declaration on Challenges and Opportunities for the Judiciary in the Current Economic Climate*. European Network of Councils for Judiciary (Vilnius: 2011). Available online at http://www.encj.eu/images/stories/pdf/GA/Vilnius/encj_vilnius_declaration.pdf.

37 Ibid.

38 P. Mc Namee (ed.). May 2013. *Council of Bars and Law Societies of Europe-INFO*, No. 33, (European Lawyers Promoting Law and Justice: Brussels): 9. Available at http://www.uianet.org/sites/default/files/Newsletter_33_2013_EN_0.pdf.

39 Directorate-General for Justice. The EU Justice Scoreboard: A tool to promote effective justice and growth. Communication from the Commission to the European Parliament, the Council, the European Central Bank, the European Economic and Social Committee and the Committee of the Regions, European Commission. COM (2013) 160 final (Brussels: 2013): 3. Available at http://ec.europa.eu/justice/effective-justice/files/justice_scoreboard_communication_en.pdf.

40 T. Carothers (ed.). 2006. *Promoting the Rule of Law Abroad*, cit.: 20.

41 Ibid.

3 Theory

Europeanization by rule of law implementation

Europeanization

One of the basic functions of the EU is to "provide rules and mechanisms to regulate the behavior of public and private actors across integrated policy areas."[1] In this context, Europeanization can be understood as an internal impact of European governance in the EU member states in which member states are both contributors to and products of EU integration.[2] Alternatively, a more encompassing definition of Europeanization is offered by Radaelli who claims that this process consists of

> (a) construction (b) diffusion and (c) institutionalization of formal and informal rules, procedures, policy paradigms, styles, "ways of doing things" and shared beliefs and norms which are first defined and consolidated in the EU policy process and then incorporated in the logic of domestic (national and subnational) discourse, identities, political structures and public policies.[3]

However, as discussed earlier, this "top-down" process of Europeanization is as of recently affecting not only the old and new members of the EU, but also third countries. Since the 1990s the EU began to use the attractiveness of its membership incentive for the post-communist countries to promote "the external projection of internal solutions,"[4] manifested in a broad range of political and economic membership criteria. The concern of scholars of EU integration thus shifted towards evaluation of rule transfer from the EU to the candidate countries and the variation in its effectiveness. This led to the creation of the Europeanization of candidate countries as a separate sub-field of the Europeanization agenda.

This literature review will consider a recent strain of studies that looks at the instruments and the degree of EU impact on domestic politics and policies in candidate countries. Europeanization scholars have identified a number of important elements shaping the democratic transitions, such as initial conditions, institutional choices and timing of reforms, communication and quality of policies, the strengths of state apparatus, ethnic composition, and external support. The aim of this review is to assess the causal connection between these elements and the domestic dynamics in the WB in the context of the European integration. Particular attention will be dedicated to the impact on the rule of law norms diffusion against the background of the EU accession process.

Europeanization in candidate countries

Volumes aiming to bring these tracks together do all begin with the scientific assumption that there is an impact on the new democracies of Eastern Europe based on their associations with the "objects desire"—EU membership. Authors have raised the following questions: Have candidate countries had to act in certain ways, develop certain institutions and implement certain laws? How did the EU make use of the apparent leverage in relation to the SEE states? What difference did the decision to join make in these countries' political institutions, legal order, and legal institutions? Under what conditions are the EU's attempts to influence candidate countries effective? In sum, scientific interest in Europeanization of candidate countries contains two facets: an empirical assessment of the extent to which the EU has a domestic impact, and an analysis of what factors account for this impact (or the lack thereof). Therefore, literature on the Europeanization of candidate states does not only look at the instruments and the degree of EU impact on domestic politics and policies, but also analyzes how this impact takes place and how compliance with the EU norms can be induced.[5]

The EU–candidate relationship is one of obvious asymmetry of interdependence. On one side the EU has the benefits of trade, aid[6] and finally accession to offer, while by contrast, given their tiny economic size, candidate countries have little to offer to the EU. Also, the candidate countries, or at least their political elites, show a strong desire to join the EU, which decreases their bargaining power. In sum, this allows the EU to set the rules that through the process of Europeanization shape the public policy making in the candidate countries.

Informed literature can be seen as arriving at two principal explanations about why candidate countries adjust to the EU norms, namely the "logic of consequentiality" based on the "rationalist institutionalism," and the "logic of appropriateness" based on the "constructivist institutionalism."[7]

Logic of consequentiality

Rationalist institutionalism presupposes cost–benefit calculations by both EU institutions and domestic elites. It deals with particular questions such as the clarity of EU demands which is particularly problematic in the field of rule of law, as mentioned above, and the credibility of conditionality in general. It assumes that actors choose the behavior that maximizes their utility under the circumstances. The "logic of consequences" goes on to claim that the cost–benefit calculations of the candidate country can be successfully manipulated by the EU through external incentives (sanctions and rewards).

The predominant mechanism for the Europeanization of candidate countries is conditionality based on the strategy of reinforcement by reward.[8] In other words, the EU pays the reward to governments that comply with their demands, and alternatively withholds the reward from those that do not. The most powerful conditionality tool with any candidate country is "gate keeping" during the different phases of the EU accession process—particularly achieving candidate status. Although the biggest, full membership is often a distant reward on a "rocky road"[9] toward accession. As the success of conditionality largely depends on the size and speed of reward, the use of intermediary rewards—such as market access, enhanced financial aid, or visa liberalization—is unusually important as part of this mechanism. Moreover, the candidates must be assured that they will receive promised rewards after complying with the EU demands, but at the same time they need to know that the reward will follow only after fully completing the compliance process.[10] Thus, credibility of conditionality depends on a reliable, merit-based application of conditionality by the EU. Lack of clearly elaborated conditions may further influence the cost–benefit calculations of Europeanization actors. Particular traps for uncertainty may be found in the ever-growing body of EU law, or absence of a single EU model in many policy areas, including the rule of law. Next, if the adoption cost of complying with the EU demands for the candidate country is greater than the benefit of the EU reward, it is likely that Europeanization will fail or at best suffer a significant setback. Finally, the likelihood of the effectiveness of the conditionality decreases with the number of veto players incurring net effective power losses from compliance.[11] The number of actors opposed to the EU's conditions is likely to increase in matters that are connected to strong institutional legacies. Alternatively, the likelihood of compliance to the EU demands may sometimes be lessened by the low density of administrative capacities in the target country.[12]

Logic of appropriateness

Constructivist institutionalism, on the other, deals with the process of "norm socialization," in which domestic elites and populations at large internalize EU norms which they regard as legitimate. Instead of directly manipulating or indirectly influencing the cost–benefit calculations of the candidate countries, candidate countries are motivated by "internalized identities, values, and norms [so that] among alternative courses of action they choose the (most) appropriate or legitimate one."[13] According to the theory of constructivist institutionalism, rule transfer can only be effective if elites and populations in candidate countries identify with the EU and are thus open to behavioral change by "social learning" through "soft" mechanisms for the EU's domestic impact—socialization and persuasion.[14] Thus, Europeanization in this case works when the domestic actors are convinced of the legitimacy and appropriateness of EU demands.

According to this logic Sedelmeier identified a number of facilitating factors that increase the likelihood that socialization and persuasion will be effective. Since the candidate country does not take part in setting the conditions and making the rules, but is rather asked for unilateral adjustment, the EU "legitimacy [would be] increased if it used soft tactics rather than overt pressure, and with a 'low density of EU demands,' which allows domestic actors to engage in relatively unpressured learning."[15] Furthermore, EU demands are more likely to be perceived as legitimate if they are part of the *Acquis Communautaire*, and if they are not more burdensome than for the existing member states.[16] Finally, rule adoption will be facilitated in the case of resonance between traditional domestic rules and EU norms.

Europeanization by rule of law implementation—missing links

While the EU's impact on democratic transformation and fundamental rights has become a well-established subfield of research, studies on Europeanization of the judiciary in candidate countries remain rare. Zubek and Goetz for example assert that the EU had a strong impact on the state institutions of CEEC—executives, legislatures and judiciaries.[17] However, they attribute the impact on the judiciary reform to the internal pressures stemming from the requirement to formulate a negotiating position with the EU, rather than from an intentional effort by the EU to modify its structure. Dimitrova and Toshkov again highlight the role of the domestic elites by disclosing the direct correlation between far-reaching changes of national executives and judiciaries' organizational structures with the change of the governments in Romania.[18] Grasping the results of the 2004 enlargement round, Piana confirms that EU pressure had an impact on the governance of the courts in Poland, the Czech Republic and Hungary.[19] Dallara analyzed the explanatory factors of different EU trajectories and outcomes of judicial reforms in Slovenia, Romania, Croatia and Serbia. She has accounted domestic factors, namely the legacies of the past and high number of veto players (political and judicial actors) as chief obstacles to judicial reforms.[20] She concludes that in an absence of a clear institutional model by the EU, such deviating outcomes of the judicial reform across the case study countries reflect the pre-existing distribution of power in the domestic constellation. Alternatively, in a study on impartiality and capacity of the courts, Mandelski looks at the supply side of rule of law export in his assessment of a"politicized, uncoordinated and incoherent reform approach"[21] in Serbia.

The mushrooming literature on the Europeanization of EU candidate countries confirms that credible conditionality has indeed played a significant role in the EU integration process, as it has successfully induced pressure on candidates.[22] At the same time, the overall success of conditionality remains dependent on the level of adoption costs for domestic authorities. Alternatively, other instruments for promoting EU norms, such as socialization of domestic elites and persuasion, do not appear to have been "consistent and effective substitutes"[23] for political accession conditionality, even though they are described as unique EU strategies.

Second, EU norms and policies are generally transferred in a top-down mode to the external states. In their relations with candidate countries the EU mostly depends on intergovernmental bargaining, while privileging central governments and charging them with implementing EU norms.[24]

Third, empirical findings show that although the *Acquis Communautaire* is at the core of Europeanization in candidate countries, the contents of Europeanization are "of a more general character."[25] This particularly relates to the core goals of Europeanization, such as stability, security, democratization, rule of law, etc.

Fourth, the Europeanization literature concludes that the "EU's impact is differential across countries and issues"[26] and therefore is unable to provide all-out recommendations for the use of Europeanization in future waves of enlargement. Namely, while the EU's enlargement policy has "considerably contributed to the political transformation process [...] by promoting the rule of law"[27] in CEE, recent political developments in the Western Balkans raise concerns about the effectiveness of the EU's mechanisms to influence the present wave of enlargement.[28] Unlike in CEE, the "national identity"[29] of the Western Balkans countries is shaped by problems of limited statehood, state capture and difficult legacies of ethnic conflict. This observation is important since EU's incentive-based Europeanization instruments only trigger democratic change if national identity does not run counter to EU requirements. In addition, previous research with regard to CEE[30] has already established the strong legacy of communist rule, in particular in the administrative sphere, and the high adjustment costs, meaning that domestic cultural understanding and informal institutions are "key mediating factors determining whether domestic actors engage in a social learning process in which EU rules redefine their interests and identities."[31]

Next, the theoretical reflection on Europeanization literature points to the conclusion that the EU's impact on the rule of reforms in present day candidate countries depends on the resonance between EU demands and domestic rules. However, the existence and an analysis of such resonance remains untested in the Western Balkans.

Finally, empirical research investigating the EU's "transformative power"[32] with regard to the effectiveness of rule of law and judicial sector reform is only in its infancy, whereas for the SEE there is only limited bibliography available, so that comprehensive, comparative and interdisciplinary research with a strong focus on rule of law is *still* missing.

These are precisely the gaps that this book will attempt to fill up.

Notes

1 F. Schimmelfennig. 2010. "Europeanisation beyond the Member States," *Zeitschrift für Staats- und Europawissenschaften* 8(3): 319–339, at 319.

2 F. Trauner. 2011. *The Europeanization of the Western Balkans: EU Justice and Home Affairs in Croatia and Macedonia* (Manchester: Manchester University Press).
3 C. Radaelli. 2003. "The Europeanization of Public Policy," in K. Featherstone and C. Radaelli (eds.), *The Politics of Europeanization* (Oxford: Oxford University Press): 30.
4 S. Lavenex. 2004. "EU External Governance in 'Wider Europe'," *Journal of European Public Policy* 11(4): 695.
5 See for example: F. Schimmelfennig. 2010. "Europeanisation Beyond the Member States," 319; D. Jano. 2010. *The Europeanization of Western Balkans: A Fuzzy Set of Qualitative Comparative Analysis of the New Potential EU Member States* (Saarbrücken: VDM Verlag); F. Trauner. 2011. *The Europeanization of the Western Balkans*; U. Sedelmeier. 2011. "Europeanization in New Member and Candidate States," *Living Reviews in European Governance* 6(1); F. Schimmelfennig. 2012. "Europeanization beyond Europe," *Living Reviews in European Governance* 7(1); T. Börzel. 2011. "When Europe Hits Limited Statehood. Europeanization and Domestic Change in the Western Balkans," *KFG Working Papers No. 30*. Research College "The Transformative Power of Europe," Berlin: Freie Universität Berlin; T. Börzel., T. Risse. 2012. "From Europeanisation to Diffusion. Introduction," *West European Politics* 35(1): 1–19; Elbasani, A. (ed.) 2013. *European Integration and Transformation in the Western Balkans: Europeanization or Business as Usual?* (New York: Routledge); F. Schimmelfennig. 2015 "EU Enlargement," in J. Richardson and S. Mazey (eds.), *European Union: Power and Policy-Making* (London: Routledge): 261–282; U. Sedelmeier. 2015. "Enlargement: Constituent Policy and Tool for External Governance," in H. Wallace, M. Pollack and A. Young (eds.), *Policy-Making in the European Union* (Oxford: Oxford University Press): 407–435.
6 Technical assistance provided by the EU for the reform of the judiciary in the WB over the past 15 years is comprised of European Agency for Reconstruction (EAR) assistance, structural development programs of the EU embodied in the Technical Assistance and Information Exchange (TAIEX) assistance, and twinning programs.
7 J. G. March and J. P. Olsen. 2004. "The Logic of Appropriateness," *Arena Working Papers* 04/09 (Oslo).
8 F. Schimmelfennig. 2010. "Europeanization beyond the Member States"; F. Schimmelfennig. 2010. "The Normative Origins of Democracy in the European Union: Towards a Transformationalist Theory of Democratization," *European Political Science Review* 2(2): 211–233.
9 C. Pippan. 2004. "The Rocky Road to Europe: The EU's Stabilisation and Association Process for the Western Balkans and the Principle of Conditionality," *European Foreign Affairs Review* 9(2): 219–245.
10 See for example in H. Grabbe. 2006. *The EU's Transformative Power: Europeanization through Conditionality in Central and Eastern Europe* (London: Palgrave Macmillan).
11 F. Schimmelfennig and U. Sedelmeier (eds.). 2005. *The Politics of European Union Enlargement: Theoretical Approaches* (UK; New York: Routledge).
12 D. Toshkov. 2008. "Embracing European Law: Compliance with EU Directives in Central and Eastern Europe," *European Union Politics* 9(3): 379–402.
13 S. Bailer, R. Hertz and D. Leuffen. 2009. "Oligarchization, Formalization, Adaptation? Linking Sociological Theory and EU Enlargement Research," *Journal of European Public Policy* 16(1): 162–174.
14 J. T. Checkel. 2005. "International Institutions and Socialization in Europe: Introduction and Framework," *International Organization* 59(4): 801–826.
15 U. Sedelmeier. 2006. "Europeanization in New Member and Candidate States," cit.
16 T. Freyburg and S. Richter. 2010. "National Identity Matters: The Limited Impact of EU Political Conditionality in the Western Balkans," *Journal of European Public Policy* 17(2): 262–280.

17 R. Zubek and K. H. Goetz. 2010. “Performing to Type? How State Institutions Matter in East Central Europe,” *Journal of Public Policy* 30(1): 1–20.

18 A. Dimitrova and D. Toshkov. 2009. “Post-accession Compliance between Administrative Co-ordination and Political Bargaining,” *European Integration Online Papers*. Special Issue: 2–13.

19 See D. Piana. 2011. “In Search of A New Judicial Professionalism: Intertwining Legal and Extra-Legal Values in Post-Authoritarian Training Programs,” *Web Journal of Current Legal Issues* 2.

20 C. Dallara. 2014. *Democracy and Judicial Reforms in South-East Europe* (Springer: Bern).

21 M. Mandelski. 2013. “They Have Failed Again! Donor-driven Promoting of the Rule of Law in Serbia,” *Südosteuropa* 61: 79–113.

22 Radeljić, B. 2013. “Democratising and Europeanising the Western Balkans: Contexts, Challenges and Prospects,” *East European Politics* 29(2): 245–251; Keil, S. 2013. “Europeanization, State-building and Democratization in the Western Balkans,” *Nationalities Papers* 41(3): 343–353; Economides, S. and Ker-Lindsay. J. 2015. “‘Pre-Accession Europeanization’: The Case of Serbia and Kosovo,” *JCMS: Journal of Common Market Studies* 53(5): 1027–1044, September.

23 U. Sedelmeier. 2006. “Europeanization in New Member and Candidate States,” 11.

24 H. Grabbe. 2006. *The EU’s Transformative Power: Europeanization through Conditionality in Central and Eastern Europe*, cit.

25 F. Schimmelfennig. 2012. “Europeanization beyond Europe,” *Living Reviews in European Governance* 7(1): 22.

26 Ibid.

27 T. Freyburg and S. Richter. 2010. “National Identity Matters: The Limited Impact of EU Political Conditionality in the Western Balkans,” 263.

28 G. Noutcheva. 2012. *European Foreign Policy and the Challenges of Balkan Accession: Conditionality, Legitimacy and Compliance* (London: Routledge).

29 T. Freyburg and S. Richter. 2008. “National Identity Matters: The Limited Impact of EU Political Conditionality in the Western Balkans,” cit.

30 U. Sedelmeier. 2006 “The EU’s Role as a Promoter of Human Rights and Democracy: Enlargement Policy Practice and Role Formation,” in O. Elgstrom, M. Smith (eds.), The European Union’s *R*ole in *I*nternational *P*olitics: *C*oncepts and *A*nalysis (London: Routledge): 118–135; O. Treib, H. Bähr and G. Falkner. 2007. “Modes of Governance: Towards a Conceptual Clarification,” *Journal of European Policy* 14(1): 1–20; A. L. Dimitrova. 2010. “The New Member States of the EU in the Aftermath of Enlargement: Do New European Rules Remain Empty Shells?,” *Journal of European Public Policy* 17(1): 137–148; D. Jano. 2010.*The Europeanization of Western Balkans: A Fuzzy Set of Qualitative Comparative Analysis of the New Potential EU Member States*, cit.

31 U. Sedelmeier. 2006. “Europeanization in New Member and Candidate States,” 11.

32 H. Grabbe. 2006. *The EU’s Transformative Power: Europeanization through Conditionality in Central and Eastern Europe*, cit.; H. Grabbe. 2014. “Six Lessons of Enlargement Ten Years On: The EU’s Transformative Power in Retrospect and Prospect,” *Journal of Common Market Studies* 52(Supplement S1): 40–56.

4 Research design

Cases and methods

The analytical framework

"Europeanization" is the key concept in the exploration of the impact that EU integration has on democratic consolidation in the Western Balkans. In line with previously analyzed scholarship on "Europeanization," this phenomenon can be understood as a *politically* driven process by which EU institutions, rules and policy-making processes impact the legal systems, institutional mechanisms and collective identity formation of non-EU member states. Democratic consolidation, including the establishment of an effective system of rule of law as part of the more general "top-down" process of "Europeanization," however, does not only affect the old and new members of the EU. The concern of a third generation of scholars of EU integration is the evaluation of the influence of EU institutions, rules and policy-making processes and their impact on the laws, institutions and identities of "third" (non-EU) countries. Therefore the study of EU external relations is not only understood as a foreign policy approach in the context of international relations, but also as a form of "governance export"[1] and "norm diffusion."[2]

Hence, the central research focus with regard to a multifactor analysis remains the same for this book: the existence and kind of influence the EU institutions have as the independent variable, so that the EU institutions and the countries of South East Europe selected for comparative purposes—namely Bosnia-Herzegovina, which has concluded a Stabilization and Association Agreement; Kosovo, which is a potential EU candidate; Macedonia, which is enjoying candidate status but also experiencing serious problems in the stability of its institutions; Montenegro, which is currently in the phase of accession negotiations; and Serbia, which is set to open its first accession chapter in 2015—form the basic units of analysis. From this basic analytical framework, a subset of more concrete research questions follows: How much pressure has been put by EU institutions on domestic political elites? Which incentives are given? Under which conditions are EU rules adopted? How and when does "formal change" through legal transposition of the EU *Acquis Communautaire* onto national legal systems, i.e. rule adoption, not only mean lip-service to EU requirements, but also triggers rule implementation and norm socialization, i.e. behavioral changes?

In contrast to the previous "southern enlargement," when Greece, Spain and Portugal became full members on the basis of a feeling of "solidarity" with those countries' efforts to stabilize new democratic regimes, the well-known Copenhagen and Madrid Council's criteria from the early 1990s linked accession and membership in the EU to "political" conditionality as concerns the stability of institutions guaranteeing democracy, rule of law, and protection of human and minority rights. These criteria are seen both as legal principles stemming from EU primary law, but also as core values of the EU and prerequisites in the formation of a post-national European identity. In addition, the ability to fulfill the obligations of membership by implementation of the EU legal order, i.e. the *Acquis Communautaire*, is basically seen—in legal discourses– as a "technical"[3] conditionality requirement.

However, when examining the specific strategies and instruments used by the EU and posing the question which of them are most effective, as this book seeks to do, it becomes obvious that rule adoption and the implementation of the *Acquis Communautaire* is not only a technical matter, but a highly political affair. The *Acquis* is not only a formal body of law, but a "framework in which shared policies and values are established and through which they are implemented."[4] Since—with regard to the proposed unit of analysis—non-EU member states' elites have no say in the formulation and decision-making process of EU institutions, and due to the asymmetric power the EU exercises through the Copenhagen/Madrid conditionality in rule transfer, not only has the EU been characterized as an "imperial hegemon"[5] or a "cooperative empire,"[6] but the question has arisen of why—with the exception of Montenegro and perhaps even Serbia—political and economic elites in the countries of concern for this research should give in to external pressure, if membership as the main incentive is uncertain or attainable only in a more distant future?[7] One of the main foci of this research project is thus to explore which strategies and conditions can facilitate the effectiveness of the Europeanization process within the SAP. Must "membership conditionality," if it is no longer fully credible, simply be supplemented by a more short-term oriented "policy conditionality,"[8] as Trauner recommends? Or does this approach remain trapped in the logic of intergovernmental negotiations following from a "realist" international relations approach?

This question raises a more theoretical problem. Several scholars—based on March/Olsen's seminal distinction of the "logic of consequentiality" versus the "logic of appropriateness"[9]—have already created a theoretical framework with two analytically distinct approaches, namely "rationalist institutionalism" and "constructivist institutionalism."[10] Rationalist institutionalism, based on "cost–benefit calculations"[11] by both EU institutions and domestic elites, will thus deal with particular questions, such as the "normative clarity"[12] of EU demands, which is a special problem in the field of rule of law as mentioned above, and the credibility of conditionality in general. Several scholars have already observed from studying previous enlargements that the *Acquis* as a strategic instrument remains exclusively in the hands of the EU institutions, and that this allows "strategic content adjustment" with regard to the "scope, determinacy, and flexibility" of the *Acquis*, resulting in the accusation on the part of these scholars that the EU practices a strategic game of conditionality stretching or "moving the goal posts."[13] This suggestion will, of course, play into the hands of domestic "gatekeeper elites"[14] who are not interested in quick EU membership, such as economic elites who are content with a quick profit-maximizing logic against EU rules enforcing more competition, or political elites, both in power and opposition, who will avoid rule adoption and implementation if they fear negative consequences for their support in the next elections.

Constructivist institutionalism, based on the "logic of appropriateness," deals with the process of "norm socialization," in which domestic elites and populations at large internalize EU norms which they regard as legitimate. The constructivist approach regards the use of "soft instruments" as of primary importance in order to persuade and to socialize domestic ruling elites.

Research focus

Following from the theoretical explanations of the processes of Europeanization, the first hypothesis this book attempts to test is that rule transfer is more effective if domestic elites and populations "identify" with the EU and are thus open to "norm socialization" through persuasion and norm internalization: in other words how the interplay between rationalism and constructivism influences the end goal of Europeanization by rule of law implementation in the Western Balkans, and more specifically, how it affects the internalization of the rule of law norms. Secondly, from the previous analysis arises the second hypothesis that the current EU approach to the rule of law reform in candidate countries does not yield results because it does not work beyond the critical point of norm adoption.

Whether EU rules will be successful in redefining the interests and identities of domestic actors engaged in a social learning process depends on a number of independent variables, including the persistence of the legacies of communist and authoritarian rule, the price of the adjustment cost, and the role of the domestic elites. This is also highlighted by recent explorative research on the ex-Yugoslav republics. Based on a literature review of domestic sources, Džihić/Segert[15] hypothesize that the problems of "enclave democracies" or "electoral authoritarianism" in some of the ex-Yugoslav republics remain persistent not only as a result of ongoing ethno-nationalist mobilization of the population by interwoven economic and political elites interested in the preservation of political power for their private economic interests, but also because of the (wrong) perception that external support is the key for the solution to overcome "frozen democratic consolidation" in those countries. They argue that both actors, the EU institutions and the domestic elites, but also populations are trapped in "unrealistic expectations, hegemonial interests, wrong perceptions and mimicry on both sides."[16] In conclusion, they require from future research on Europeanization in the WBCs to take the "cardinal problem" into account that external support for democracy and rule of law promotion is not seen as politically neutral by both elites and the population at large, so that Europeanization might end up in "cultural alienation" instead of an internalization of European values.

Seen from these perspectives and against previous hypotheses,[17] it can be assumed that rationalist and constructivist institutionalism do not necessarily exclude each other, but are not necessarily complementary either. But this has not yet been empirically tested in a comprehensive and comparative way.

Reconceptualization of the "spiral theory"

Hence, the first task of this study is to re-conceptualize the dichotomy of "rationalist" and "constructivist" institutionalism by reframing the political processes within a comprehensive analytical framework for the assessment of the dialectics of these two logics for the entire process of (1) rule transfer, (2) rule adoption, (3) rule implementation and (4) norm socialization, directly leading to political and social change, and indirectly reaching the goal of EU membership (see Figure 4.1). For this purpose this study makes use of the "spiral theory,"[18] originally elaborated by Risse, Ropp and Sikkink for the analysis

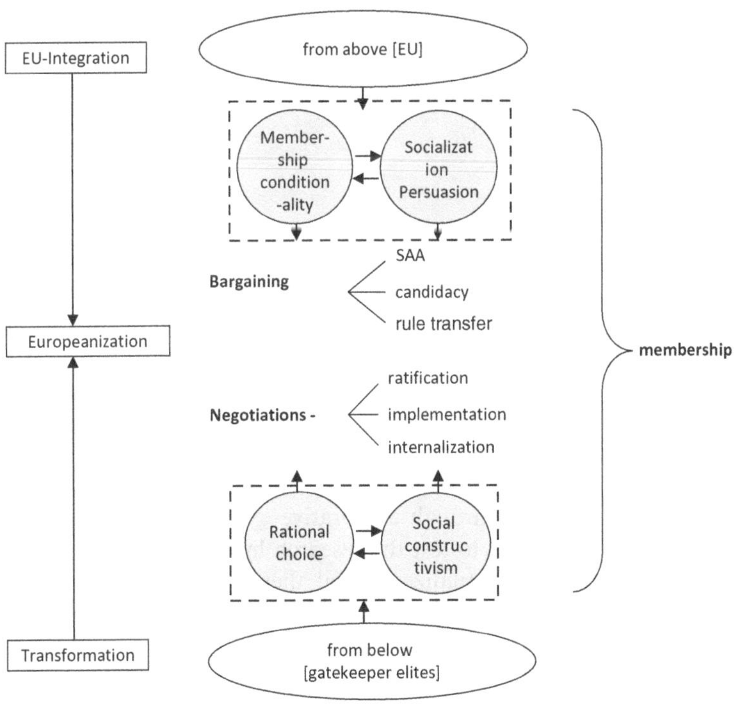

Figure 4.1 Europeanization theory

of human rights compliance, as well as their differentiation of "phases." The goal of this exercise is to elaborate more detailed research questions for the identification of the interplay between the logic of consequentiality and the logic of appropriateness. In other words, what interests us is when and how will "rational" interests based on cost–benefit calculations be transformed into common values and attitudes; i.e., when and how will intergovernmental "bargaining," based on the perception of different interests according to the logic of a zero-sum game, be transformed into negotiations in preparation for EU membership based on the perception of a common goal, thereby transcending the "us versus them"[19] feeling as a prerequisite for norm socialization by Europeanization?

The interests of political and economic elites as possible "veto players" and units of analysis is under-researched. Previous studies[20] clearly demonstrate that the EU has almost no leverage if regime change through democratic consolidation or revolutions is not successful, because illiberal elites have come into power through democratic elections (Slovakia under Mečiar, Croatia under Tuđman), resulting in a situation in which they and the winners of privatization form a "predatory elite" that has to fear the application of, for instance, EU competition law and restrictions on state aid.[21] Hence, the EU methodology applied by a top-down legalistic and technocratic approach to promote reforms,[22] accompanied by regular monitoring, financial and technical assistance and the development of socialization through technical committees, twinning, and selective participation in EU programs may have its limits, depending on the phases from bargaining to norm internalization.

Cases and methods

The entire book is based on a "neo-institutional approach,"[23] which attempts to overcome the separation of research by EU legal scholars, lawyers, and political scientists and to re-integrate the different aspects of legal and political analyses through the logic of functional interdependence. Hence, the normative and empirical analyses have used the same written documents, i.e. legally binding and non-binding EU law, "soft law," declarations, etc., while applying their respective methods of description, analysis and interpretation not only to texts, but also to the empirical results of research. In addition, qualitative empirical analysis required not only the identification of all relevant texts, but also actors through explorative expert interviews and in-depth interviews with these actors to test the research hypotheses following from the framework of the re-conceptualized spiral theory for Europeanization. The empirical analyses of Europeanization are elaborated by in-depth interviews based on a semi-structured questionnaire, with representative samples comprised of a total of 52 representatives of the political elites, economic elites, EU experts, and rule-of-law enforcement officers of the respective countries of concern.

With regard to the comparative method applied, to begin with this study makes a selection of countries according to their status in the EU accession process. Hence, the sample for comparison includes a selection of countries according to their status in the accession process, namely (1) Bosnia-Herzegovina, which have signed Stabilization and Association Agreements, but also have serious problems with state institutions' stability due to the unresolved statehood and nationality issues; (2) Kosovo, as a potential candidate country, still not recognized by five EU member states; (3) Macedonia, which is a candidate for EU accession but with no date set for commencing accession negotiations; (4) Montenegro as a candidate country in the process of accession negotiations; and (5) Serbia, which formally started accession negotiations in January 2014.

During the process of selection of case study countries, this book does not exclude countries that can be characterized as non-consolidated democracies, namely, Bosnia-Herzegovina, which is still under international control by a High Representative who is politically responsible to an international Peace Implementation Council and regularly reports to the UN Secretary General on progress in the implementation of the Dayton Peace Agreement.[24] Almost the same holds true for Kosovo, which has been under international territorial administration since 1999 following UN-Security Council Resolution 1244. Despite Kosovo's having unilaterally declared independence in 2008[25] and adopted a constitution,[26] international supervisory mechanisms such as the United Nations Mission in Kosovo (UNMIK), under the leadership of the Special Representative of the Secretary General (SRSG), and the European Union Rule of Law Mission (EULEX) are still in place and exercise full monitoring powers. Without having to clarify the "statehood question"[27] from the perspective of public international law, it is, however, of special interest for this research to study the role of the EU in an internationally administered framework both in Bosnia-Herzegovina and under UNMIK and, in particular, the role of the EULEX mission since 2008, in order to gain more knowledge of problems facing the development of policy strategies for rule of law promotion and lessons to be learned for other conflict areas with no prospect of membership, such as the Caucasus and the European Neighbourhood Policy (ENP). Finally, this study focuses on hard cases where problems of the legacy of post-communism and nationalist fractures entrench

Table 4.1 Case study countries

Category country	*Case study country*
SAA country	Bosnia-Herzegovina
Potential candidate country	Kosovo
Candidate county without date	Macedonia
Negotiating candidate	Montenegro
Negotiating candidate	Serbia

strong veto players in the domestic system, which poses equal challenges to the rule of law reforms promoted by the EU.

Secondly, the comparative method also helps to identify and to specify the independent variables both in the normative and empirical analyses. This will help to identify the "misfit"[28] between EU law, the laws adopted by the parliaments of (potential) candidate countries and the rule implementation by executives and judiciaries, which shall be achieved by content analysis of legal rules, administrative regulations and decisions. By comparing "vetos" and "veto players" in the different phases of the norm socialization process also from the empirical level, this study will show when, how and why the "logic of consequences" gives way to a "logic of appropriateness" or might be reversed again, so that neither "norm socialization" at the domestic level, nor learning processes on the side of the EU take place.

Notes

1 A. Magen. 2007. "Transformative Engagement through Law. The Acquis Communautaire as Instrument of EU External Influence," *European Journal of Law Reform* 9(3): 361–393.
2 F. Schimmelfenning. 2000. "International Socialization in the New Europe: Action in a Rational Institutional Environment," *European Journal of International Relations* 6(1): 109–139.
3 D. Kochenov. 2008. *EU Enlargement and the Failure of Conditionality*, cit.
4 A. Magen. 2007. "Transformative Engagement through Law," cit.: 363.
5 Ibid.
6 J. Zielonka. 2006. *Europe as Empire. The Nature of the Enlarged European Union* (Oxford: Oxford University Press).
7 F. Schimmelfenning and A. M. Cirtautas. 2010. "Europeanization Before and After Accession: Conditionality, Legacies, and Compliance," *Europe-Asia Studies* 62(3): 421–441.
8 F. Trauner. 2009. "From Membership Conditionality to Policy Conditionality: EU External Governance in South Eastern Europe," *Journal of European Public Policy*: 774–790.
9 J. G. March and J. P. Olsen. 2004. "The Logic of Appropriateness."
10 Sedelmeier first developed such an analytical framework in U. Sedelmeier. 2006. "The EU's Role as a Promoter of Human Rights and Democracy."
11 F. Schimmelfennig and U. Sedelmeier (eds.). 2005. *The Europeanization of Central and Eastern Europe* (New York: Cornell University Press).
12 E. V. Towfigh. 2009. "Complexity and Normative Clarity – Or: Legal Statutes are Made for Lawyers," *Der Staat* 48(1): 29–74.
13 D. Kochenov. 2008. *EU Enlargement and the Failure of Conditionality,* cit.; A. Magen. 2007. "Transformative Engagement Through Law," cit.
14 J. Tolstrup. 2010. "When Can External Actors Influence Democratization? Leverage, Linkages, and Gatekeeper Elites," *CDDRL Working Papers* 118: 1–31.
15 V. Džihić and D. Segert. 2009. "Das jugoslawische Rätsel: Enklavendemokratie, Staatsschwäche und Probleme externer Demokratieförderung," *Südosteuropa Mitteilungen* 03–04: 51–63.
16 Ibid.: 62.
17 T. A. Börzel and T. Risse. 2000. "When Europe Hits Home: Europeanization and Domestic Change," *European Integration Online Papers (EIoP)* 4(15). Available at http://eiop.or.at/eiop/pdf/2000-015.pdf.

18 T. Risse, S. Ropp and K. Sikkink. 1999. *The Power of Human Rights* (Cambridge: Cambridge University Press).
19 P. L. Berger and T. Luckmann. 1966. *Die gesellschaftliche Konstruktion der Wirklichkeit* (Frankfurt am Main: Fischer).
20 A. Mungiu-Pippidi. 2014. "The Transformative Power of Europe Revisited," *Journal of Democracy* 25(1): 20–32; Vachudova, M.A. 2014. "EU Leverage and National Interests in the Balkans: The Puzzles of Enlargement Ten Years On," *Journal of Common Market Studies* 52(1): 1–17.
21 S. Fisher. 2006. *Political Changes in Post-Communist Slovakia and Croatia. From Nationalist to Europeanist* (London: Palgrave).
22 A. Magen. 2007. "Transformative Engagement Through Law," cit.: 388.
23 J. Marko. 2008. "The Law and Politics of Diversity Management: A Neo-Institutional Approach," *European Yearbook of Minority Issues* 6. 2006/07 (Leiden: Brill): 252–279; J. Marko and M. Handstanger. 2009. "The Interdependence of Law and Political Science: About the 'Essence and Value' of a 'Juristenpolitologie'-Approach: Wolfgang Mantl for his 70th Birthday," *Vienna Online Journal on International Constitutional Law* 3(2).
24 F. Bieber. 2010. "Bosnia and Herzegovina since 1990," cit.: 311–328.
25 R. Muharremi. 2008. "Kosovo's Declaration of Independence: Self-Determination and Sovereignty Revisited," *Review of Central and East European Law* 33: 401–435.
26 J. Marko. 2008. "The New Kosovo Constitution in a Regional Comparative Perspective."
27 M. Weller. 2009. *Contested Statehood: Kosovo's Struggle for Independence.*
28 G. Falkner. 2003. "Comparing Europeanisation Effects: From Metaphor to Operationalisation," cit.

Part II

5 Legacies of the past as obstacles to the EU rule of law promotion

Introduction

Before proceeding with an empirical analysis of the reform of judiciaries in five countries under scrutiny, it is necessary to provide a historical overview of the evolution of the judiciary branch in the region. The aim of this exercise is to establish if and what kind of fundamental cultural predispositions play a role in the current reform of the judiciary branch and, consequently, shape the relationship between SEE countries and the EU, in this regard. As already mentioned, previous research related to the CEECs has already established the strong legacy of communist rule in the administrative sphere, so that the domestic cultural understanding and informal institutions are key mediating factors in determining whether domestic actors engage in the process of Europeanization.[1] In addition to this common characteristic, the SEE region has suffered from the more recent consequences related to the 1990s armed conflicts that influenced both human and technical capacities of the existing judiciary. Furthermore, the lack of absorption capacity, on the side of domestic administration, also needs to be addressed from the historical legacies perspectives. Namely, administrative and technical capacities, budgetary constraints, and levels of societal mobilization that interplay with unfavorable historic legacies can influence compliance with EU demands. Finally, legacies constitute obstacles in compliance, even in cases where the candidate countries remain dedicated to socializing EU norms.

Following more than five centuries of rule by the Ottoman and Austro-Hungarian empires over the territories which comprise the present day Southeastern Europe, the judiciary and embryos of constitutionalism in contemporary Bosnia and Herzegovina, Kosovo, Macedonia, Montenegro and Serbia had its roots in the emergence of national independence movements throughout the most of the nineteenth and early twentieth century. The initial development of the judiciary branch of government, in these countries, was influenced mostly by the legal traditions of Austria, Germany, Hungary and France, which were introduced to the region by the returning young scholars after completing their education at the prestigious European law schools. For example, the 1844 Serbian Civil Code was based closely on the French Code

Civil along with the admixture of German and Austrian law, while in today's Vojvodina Hungarian customary law is utilized.

Ever since the establishment of the national judicial apparatus in South Eastern Europe, the judiciary has been exposed to a perpetual flux between the tendencies to create an independent and moderate judicial system on one hand, and counter pressure coming from the local authoritarian rulers attempting to impose political hegemony over state institutions, on another.[2]

Legacies of the socialist legal culture

The most significant and long-lasting influence on the WB judiciary is the legacy of the 40 year long communist rule in Socialist Federal Republic of Yugoslavia (SFRY),[3] which was the common state for all countries under research, or more precisely, all the remaining South East European states that are still not part of the EU, excluding Albania. The role and functioning of the judiciary was neglected in research in the former Communist countries. Most of the contemporary studies treated the judicial behavior simply as an "auxiliary and highly manipulated aspect of overall party control,"[4] which therefore did not require any systematic legal analysis. Furthermore, scholastic attention was diverted from substantive analysis of legal and judicial developments in Eastern Europe due to the perception of the judiciary as a political instrument in the hands of the regime during the mobilization phase of Communist parties. The Yugoslav legal system was no exception, despite its early departure from the Marxist-Leninist model of judicial development. Finally, several other original features of the Yugoslav communist system, such as self-management, federalism, the nonalignment movement etc., additionally dispersed contemporary scientific attention from the analysis of the judiciary.

The analysis of the judiciary during communist Yugoslavia followed the dynamics of the country's structural reorganization and decentralization based on the gradual progress of the economy. Although economic changes were the root cause of Yugoslavia's constitutional changes, from 1946 until 1974 important innovations introduced in the field of the judiciary could be observed as well.[5]

In the aftermath of World War II, the emerging communist leadership was faced with the legal vacuum caused by the change of the political system and revolutionary change of government. In a swift response to establish its own legal structure, the regime had established People's Courts at the level of local self-government units. The judicial structure above these courts was a simple hierarchy of criminal and civil courts; each succeeding higher court played a supervisory role over the subordinate courts. Formed with the goal of administering post-revolutionary communist justice, these courts often ruled based on the "values of the national liberation struggle,"[6] [tekovinama narodno oslobodilačke borbe] rather than on the positive law or even principles of natural law. During this period laws and lawyers were perceived as "an obstacle to direct revolutionary action [because] law with its criteria for equality and long procedures hinders the revolutionary élan."[7] Furthermore, while the only formal criteria for the election of judges was the possession of the active voting right, in practice People's Courts were composed of Communist Party members without proper legal training and skills.

Still, unlike in the Soviet legal system, where judges were elected for only a limited term in office, Yugoslav judges were elected for an indefinite period of service. Perhaps the most important characteristic of the initial period of the communist rule was an unprecedented power vested in the office of the Public Prosecutor, and tightened interference of the Department for the Protection of the People[8] in judicial procedures. The Public Prosecutor's office functioned as a highly centralized and hierarchical system that, among other broadly set competences, exercised the control of the administrative application of laws and "the right of intervention during judicial and administrative proceedings."[9]

After breaking political ties with the Soviet Union in 1948, Yugoslavia had gradually opened itself to the West and developed its own *sui generis* Socialist regime, which was characterized with a more liberal approach to fundamental rights accompanied with a system of individual and collective self-management.[10] The 1954 enactments of the Law on Courts[11] and Law on Financial Courts[12] were the first attempts to reform the judicial system in order to overcome the arbitrariness and lawlessness in the administration of justice. The newly established Federal Supreme Court was entrusted with supervising all of the other regular courts in the judicial system, but without the mandate to directly interfere in the judgments of the lower courts. The 1954 Law on Courts made it a punishable offence to subject judges to any extra-judicial pressures, while dismissal from office was only permissible in accordance with the legally specified exemptions. However, by empowering the federal legislative bodies with the election of new judges, the 1954 Law had indirectly maintained *de facto* party control over the judicial system. Hence, official figures presented at the Congress of the Communist Party of Yugoslavia in 1951 warned of the need to undertake the professionalization of the judiciary. As Aleksandar Ranković revealed to the delegates of the Fourth Meeting of the Central Committee of the Yugoslav Communist Party, "110 out of 184 judges in Bosnia and Herzegovina had no legal training. In Serbia two judges of a district court had only finished elementary school, while in Kosovo 65 judges [almost the entire judiciary], had only completed elementary school."[13] Article 46 of the 1954 Law on Courts addressed this problem by prescribing that judges must be professional jurists with an academic degree on law. Gradual professionalization of the judicial staff was accompanied by a similar process among the public prosecutors, whose competences were primarily reduced to criminal prosecution of criminal acts and the perpetrators of economic violations.[14]

As the Yugoslav economic and political system continued to evolve in the innovative direction of self-management socialism in the 1960s, the new Constitution was promulgated in order to foster the decentralization of the country.[15] Changes introduced into the Yugoslav judicial system were, at this time, the primary result of a political climate influenced by the decision of the communist leadership to play a less direct role in the political system. However, as Cohen concludes, innovations introduced with the 1963 Constitution did not eliminate the interference of state authorities in the judicial system; rather, they made it "more indirect, selective, and focused upon certain areas of political opposition."[16] Continuous politicization of the judiciary, during the early 1960s, was clearly illustrated by the politically motivated cases against Milovan Đilas and Milovan Dedijer, prominent Yugoslav dissidents.[17]

The greatest innovation introduced by the Constitution of 1963 was the establishment of the Yugoslav Constitutional Court as the highest legal authority. This was followed by the establishment of the republics' and provinces' Constitutional Courts one year later. It is interesting to note that the Federal Constitutional Court did not exercise any supervisory functions over the lower level constitutional courts, but functioned more as a complex political-legal body that would decide on the conflicts of self-management, litigations of public bodies, and legal disputes between the federation and its constituent units.[18] Two additional requirements were set for the appointment to a judiciary position: 1) completion of the judiciary exam, and 2) the fulfillment of moral and *political* criteria for the role of a judge. Judges were elected for a period of eight years with no restriction on re-election, which effectively jeopardized the permanence of their positions.

The 1974 Constitution had, for the first time, introduced a formal guarantee for the independence of judges.[19] According to Article 210, "courts shall be independent in the performance of their judicial functions and shall administer justice in accordance with the Constitution, statutes, and self-management enactments." Independence of the judiciary is further reinforced by Articles 230 and 231, which read that judges are elected and recalled from their positions in a manner that shall "ensure judicial independence," and guarantee judges immunity for their expressed opinions given in the process of judicial decision-making. One of the main innovations of the 1974 Constitution was the full equalization of the institutions of the Federal Republics and the Autonomous Provinces of Kosovo and Vojvodina. As part of their institutional structure, Autonomous Provinces gained, *inter alia*, full-fledged judicial systems of ordinary courts (Article 237), supreme courts (Article 390), and constitutional courts (Article 372).

Before the dissolution of the SFRY in 1991, the Yugoslav judicial system underwent a profound transformation, from an arbitrary application of "revolutionary justice" by a staff that often lacked fundamental legal education, to a professionalized apparatus that administered justice in a modern and complex environment. Nevertheless, despite modernization, professionalization and legal guarantees for independence, political interference was extremely pronounced throughout the history of Communist Yugoslavia. Here, the judiciary remained an integral component of the communist power structure.[20] Despite the explicit constitutional provisions, which guaranteed judicial independence, judges could not rule without regard for the "socio-political system."[21] Perhaps, this is best portrayed by Trajković who wrote about the extreme importance of the relationship between politics and the judiciary in Yugoslav society. He explains that "[a]lthough not a political office, the judiciary is 'the greatest political institution' because it implements and applies the law which is in fact a concentrated expression of politics."[22] The main factors that limited normative guarantees for the independence of the judiciary also remained the political considerations for election and the re-election of judges. First, the legislative branch of government played an important role in the recruitment of future judges. Furthermore, the "moral-political suitability" criteria for the election and re-election provided party members' with considerable influence over the judicial bureaucracy. In practice, membership in the Communist Party constituted a criterion for election. Consequently, in 1979, almost 90 percent of the judges were members of the party, while the percentage was higher among public prosecutors (93.7%).[23] A particularly contested issue was the high politicization of the constitutional courts.

In conclusion, the justice system in the SFRY was subjected to a complex and subtle "interplay of professional, bureaucratic, political, and other influences,"[24] which successfully prevented it from exceeding the boundaries of acceptable political non-conformism. The declarative adoption of the principles of the separation of powers and the independence of judiciary, was neglected in cases of "higher state interests," which led to the instrumentalization of law by politics. One of the very few quotations of the SFRY's lifelong president, Josip Broz Tito, that remains popular today turned out to be the perfect paradigm of the Yugoslav judicial system—"judges should not keep to the black letter law like a drunken man to a fence."[25]

Post-communist legacies

In 1990, Yugoslavia underwent a political transformation that concluded single-party rule. The success of ethno-nationalist political parties in the first multi-party elections in most of the Yugoslav republics[26] was an introduction to the bloody dissolution of the country.[27] On the other hand, the introduction of the multi-party political system and subsequent disintegration of the SFRY causally meant the evaporation of the single party ideology capture over the judicial sector. Nevertheless, this did not mean the end of political interference in the administration of justice in the newly established successor states of the SFRY. Discontinuity with the former communist elite practically never occurred throughout the 1990s in Serbia, which at the time included Kosovo and Montenegro.[28] Macedonia's democratic transition suffered hardships and stagnation due to the delicate ethnic balance between the Macedonian and Albanian populations. Meanwhile, Bosnia and Herzegovina was torn apart by an ethnic war that ruined the country's institutional setting and led to the complete devastation of the infrastructure, atrocities performed by all parties involved, grave human rights violations, the expulsion of others, and even genocide.[29]

The initial period of regime change in the Western Balkans took place under extreme circumstances of war, nationalistic mobilization and lack of international scrutiny due to international economic sanctions. In addition to that, the UN and EC's 1991 arms embargo that applied to all of the territory of former Yugoslavia "had the perverse effect of subverting the rule of law since, in both cases, states undermined the rule of law by engaging in illegal trade."[30] Finally, throughout the 1990s the vast majority of the Western Balkans population lived in extreme poverty and depended on state aid, which only led to the creation of new forms of clientelism and state-capture. Such a scenario has proved fertile ground for continuing politicization of the state apparatus and disregard for the limitations of power imposed by the rule of law.

Throughout the 1990s, judges operated under conditions of physical and economic "insecurity."[31] Subtle political influence on the judiciary was also performed through the role of the court's presidents, mostly by manipulating the assignments of politically sensitive cases. This practice ensured that courts firmly remained in line with the regimes. Such a situation led to a severe lack of competent judges and other legal professionals. Furthermore, many court facilities, particularly in Bosnia and Herzegovina and Kosovo, were decaying and in a state of disrepair. Srđa Popović, a prominent Yugoslav human rights lawyer, concluded, "in Yugoslavia [there is] a condition of state anarchy [...]. Ten or twenty years ago we were dissatisfied with the legal state, but at least we had one."[32]

Finally, another problem can be observed that remains common for all post-communist countries where, except for the constitutional courts, the majority of courts "continued in their formalist reading of the law,"[33] rather than performing their assumed transitional roles. Both legal academia and the judiciary in these countries interpret the new laws in a textual way. Poorly supported by their legal education, judges often seek the way out of the more difficult legal cases by case dispositions based on purely formalistic grounds. In this way the simplified version of textual positivism and the ideology of bound judicial decision-making were able to survive the process of judicial reform.

Concluding analysis

Legacies of old legal culture, although without connection to the former political system, remain alive, and continue to influence contemporary legal thought in most post-Communist legal orders. In the WB, the judicial culture is shaped by communism, the authoritarian phase following the "second democratic revolution" in 2000. During the era of communism, judges were instructed to serve as a "meaningful subject force" in a society. Being already trained to follow party ideology, judges were easily reprogrammed by the authoritarian regimes of the 1990s to establish new pattern of clientelism. The application of EU law in the WB countries—which are obliged to gradually harmonize their internal norms with EU law—is therefore an unprecedented challenge for the judiciary. In order to account for the *Acquis Communautaire* in its full meaning, judges must not merely consider the "limited law"[34] of the texts for harmonizing legislation, but also the texts of European directives, European Court of Justice jurisprudence, and the case law of the EU member states—including their reasoning and rationale. Cultural predispositions formed over the last decades thus influence Europeanization and, possibly, shape the relationship between the WB countries and the EU.

Only after 2000, which is said to be the *annus mirabilis* for the WBCs, did the region manage to overcome the consequences of ethnic conflict and (re) start democratic consolidation and economic reform processes.[35] Namely, the year 2000 in the WB was marked by the collapse of Slobodan Milošević's regime in Serbia and Montenegro, and the "second" democratic revolution through general elections in Croatia. These events opened the way for democratic consolidation and the economic reform of the region. Furthermore, the EU launched its new WB policy based on the Stabilization and Association Process, which offered the countries the "perspective" of eventual EU membership.[36] This is precisely why the next part of this study will focus on the WB's relations with the EU.

Notes

1 S. Marčić. 2015. "Informal Institutions in the Western Balkans: An Obstacle to Democratic Consolidation," *Journal of Balkan and Near Eastern Studies* 17(1): 1–15.

2 See for example in S. Radić (ed.). 2004. *Dva veka prvog suda u Srbiji* (Judges Association of Serbia: Belgrade).

3 Throughout this study I shall consistently use the term "Yugoslavia" for the Federal People's Republic of Yugoslavia founded in 1945, and its 1963 constitutionally changed name Socialist Federal Republic of Yugoslavia. The state is most commonly referred to by this last full name which it held until the dissolution in 1991.

4 L. J. Cohen. 1989. *The Socialist Pyramid: Elites and Power in Yugoslavia* (Mosaic Press: Oakville): 257.

5 For comprehensive analyses of Yugoslav constitutions see M. Đuričić. 1978. *Ustav Socijalisticke Federativne Republike Jugoslavije: Strucno objasnjenje* (Institute for Political Studies of the Faculty of Political Sciences: Belgrade); J. Đordjević. 1982. *Ustavno pravo* (Savremena Administracija: Belgrade); and M. Strobl, I. Kristan and C. Ribičić (eds.). 1986. *Ustavno pravo SFR Jugoslavije* (Časopisni Zavod Uradni List SR Slovenije: Ljubljana).

6 See for example in N. Baltić, T. Milej. 2007. "Human Rights under the Yugoslav System, Processes of Ethnic Mobilization and EU Crisis Management," *MIRICO Working Papers*, Bolzano: 9.

7 H. Modić. 1957. "Pravo v prehodnem razdobju," *Ekonomski Zbornik II.*: 91, quoted in L. J. Cohen. 1989. *The Socialist Pyramid: Elites and Power in Yugoslavia*, cit.: 266.

8 Better known under acronym OZNA and as of 1946 UDBA.

9 Constitutional Assembly of the Federal People's Republic of Yugoslavia. (Belgrade: 1946). Constitution of the Federal People's Republic of Yugoslavia, *The Official Gazette of the Federal People's Republic of Yugoslavia*, year II, No. 10. Article 124.

10 It needs to be asserted that individual rights in communist Yugoslavia corresponded to duties towards the community, and were practiced within strict limits of the Socialist system.

11 Federal Assembly of the Federal People's Republic of Yugoslavia. (Belgrade: 1954). Law on Courts, *Official Gazette of the Federal People's Republic of Yugoslavia*, 30/54.
12 Federal Assembly of the Federal People's Republic of Yugoslavia. (Belgrade: 1954). Law on Financial Courts, *Official Gazette of the Federal People's Republic of Yugoslavia*, 31/54.
13 A. Ranković. 1951. 4 June. "Za dalje jačanje pravosuđa i zakonitosti," *Četvrti plenum centralnog Komiteta Komunističke partije Jugoslavije*: 22, quoted in L. J. Cohen. 1989. *The Socialist Pyramid: Elites and Power in Yugoslavia*, cit.: 269.
14 Federal Assembly of the Federal People's Republic of Yugoslavia. (Belgrade: 1954). Law on Public Prosecutors, *Official Gazette of the Federal People's Republic of Yugoslavia*, 51/54.
15 Federal Assembly of the Socialist Federal Republic of Yugoslavia. (Belgrade: 1963). Constitution of the Socialist Federal Republic of Yugoslavia, *Official Gazette*, 14/63.
16 L. J. Cohen. 1989. *The Socialist Pyramid: Elites and Power in Yugoslavia*, cit.: 270.
17 See for example in M. Đilas. 1985. *Rise and Fall* (Harcourt Brace Jovanovich: New York).
18 For more detail see C. Höcker-Weyand. 1978. *Verfassungsgerichtsbarkeit in Jugoslawien* (Bundesinstitut für Ostwissenschaftliche und Internationale Studien: Cologne).
19 Federal Assembly of the Socialist Federal Republic of Yugoslavia. (Belgrade: 1974). Constitution of the Socialist Federal Republic of Yugoslavia, *Official Gazette*, 9/74.
20 See for example in L. J. Cohen. 1985. "Judicial Elites in Yugoslavia: The Professionalization of Political Justice," *Review of Socialist Law* 11(1): 313–344.; J. Trajković. 1987. "Pravosuđe u sistemu organizacije vlasti i samoupravljanja u društveno-političkim zajednicama" in *Društveno-političke zajednice i njihova organizacije vlasti* (Belgrade: Prosveta): 229–294; and K. Čavoški. 1991. *Tito-Tehnologija vlasti* (Dosije: Belgrade).
21 A. Fira. 1980. "Transformation of Executive and Judicial Functions in Yugoslavia," *Yugoslav Law*, II, Belgrade: 23.
22 J. Trajković. 1984. *The Judicial System of Yugoslavia* (Jugoslovenski Pregled: Belgrade): 19, quoted in L. J. Cohen. 1989. *The Socialist Pyramid: Elites and Power in Yugoslavia*, cit.: 291.
23 L. J. Cohen. 1985. "Judicial Elites in Yugoslavia: The Professionalization of Political Justice," cit.: 329.
24 Ibid.: 285.
25 This quotation is attributed to Tito's reaction to the trials in connection to both liberal and nationalist movements in Yugoslavia in 1971.
26 In Slovenia, Croatia, Bosnia and Herzegovina, and Macedonia the communists were defeated by center-right parties in 1990 multi-party elections, while in Serbia and Montenegro former communist elites newly labeled as socialists retained power based on their nationalistic political program.
27 Historical, mythological, and legendary forms were re-activated and amplified by ethno-nationalistic elites at the start of the mobilization processes along ethnic lines which eventually brought hatred between Yugoslav nations. In its last and most intensive phase, ethnic-mobilization in former Yugoslavia turned into a series of armed conflicts which effectively led to the dissolution of the country, more than 200.000 deaths, and more than a million refugees and internally displaced persons.
28 The Socialist Party of Serbia ruled Serbia until 2000, while the winner of the first Montenegro multi-party elections held in 1990 was the League of Communists of Montenegro. In 1991 the League was renamed Democratic Party of Socialists of Montenegro (DPS) and has, despite fractionalization, ever since been the ruling political party in Montenegro.

29 In a 26 February 2007 decision in the case of the Application of the Convention on the Prevention and Punishment of the Crime of Genocide, the International Court of Justice determined that genocide had in fact occurred in the municipality of Srebrenica. See ICJ, Bosnia and Herzegovina v. Serbia and Montenegro, Case 91, Judgment of 26 February 2007.

30 D. Dolenec. 2013. *Democratic Institutions and Authoritarian Rule in Southeast Europe* (ECPR Press: Essex): 190.

31 See for example in V. Vasilijević. "Ko sudi sudijama?" *NIN*, No. 2016 (20 August 1990): 25–26 and L. Kujundžić. "Naručene sudije," *NIN*, No. 2586 (20 July 2000): 16–17.

32 S. Popović. "Ideja suvereniteta je luda" *Stav*, No. 66 (16 November 1990): 26–29.

33 Z. Kuhn. 2011. *The Judiciary in Central and Eastern Europe* (Martin Nijhoff Publishers: Leiden): 166.

34 Ibid.

35 Notwithstanding the fact that in 2001 interethnic contestation led to an armed conflict in Macedonia, and 2004 violent unrest in Kosovo.

36 The European Union sought to account for the region's particularities with the Stabilization and Association Process which requires (I) that the candidate country has achieved stability of institutions guaranteeing democracy, the rule of law, human rights and respect for and protection of minorities, (II) the existence of a functioning market economy, (III) the ability to fulfill the obligations of membership in the implementation of the EU legal order, i.e. the *Acquis Communautaire.*

6 Western Balkans in the EU's waiting room

State of play: Western or "Restern" Balkans

At the Thessaloniki summit in 2003, the European Council declared, "the future of the Balkans is within the European Union."[1] This political commitment of the heads of state and prime ministers of the EU countries was understood as a strong incentive and a promise that the future of the region, within the EU, will be stable and prosperous.

At present, the Western Balkan region has experienced more than a decade of peace. The region has become relatively stable, with no military conflicts, and free, if not always fair, elections. In the meantime, the international community has invested significant amounts of financial assistance and human resources in the Western Balkans.[2]

Despite the initial steps taken, reconciliation after the violent conflicts from the 1990s has still not been fully achieved. In some cases a climate of revenge, fear and hatred still drives the decision-making of political elites along old ethno-national lines and, more importantly, continues to influence attitudes of common people. Past violence has not only left deep scars in terms of deaths and displacement, but has also had the consequence of delaying the region's ability to overcome historical controversies through political debate. Furthermore, the region has also been delayed in terms of democratization and catching up with the rest of Europe.[3]

After the region lost the initial momentum of change gained following the democratic revolution in Serbia and the second democratic revolution in Croatia in 2000, the current situation can best be described as the consolidation of unconsolidated democracies. The latest edition of the Nations in Transit report presents a record of backsliding and stagnation in all key governance indicators across all the countries of the region.[4] While liberal democratic Western Balkan governments seem to identify with the EU, they often remain overshadowed by the high number of domestic formal and informal "gate keeper" elites that continue to control the state in an effort to preserve their private economic interests and their grip on political power.[5]

As a result, of the Western Balkan countries, only Croatia managed to join the EU in 2013, 13 years after the launch of its Stabilisation and Association

Process (SAP). The rest of the region remains excluded with no foreseeable accession date in sight. In addition to the challenges of political and economic transformation, Albania, Bosnia and Herzegovina, Kosovo, Macedonia, Montenegro, and Serbia remain weak states with dysfunctional institutions, notwithstanding the considerable diversity among them.

Despite rapid growth in the early 2000s, effective economic reform has often been delayed due to the fact that the Western Balkan economies are incapable of withstanding the competitive pressures of the EU common market. Throughout much of the region, economies have remained undeveloped, dependent on aid, loans and remittances, and prone to high levels of state intervention. Western Balkan economies also have poor institutional compatibility with the EU market.

In most Balkan countries, the private sector remains underdeveloped while the majority of the working population continues to be employed by state owned enterprises or state administration. The structural changes that have taken place have primarily favored the expansion of the service industry over production. Considering the role of institutional framework, developed during the transition period, the 2008 global financial and economic crisis has only worsened the existing economic problems in the region by adding two further external shocks: reduced influx of capital from abroad and the collapse of export demand. While the entire region experienced a rather modest decline in GDP during the crisis, in most countries, industrial production and exports fell steeply. Additionally, unemployment in the region is very high: 18% in Albania, 27.5% in Bosnia and Herzegovina, 30% in Kosovo, 28% in Macedonia, 19% in Montenegro, and 17.6% in Serbia.[6] Statistics are even more worrisome when it comes to unemployment rates among young people, aged between 15 and 24, as they show that in Bosnia and Herzegovina (57.5%), Kosovo (60%), Macedonia (55.3%), and Serbia (50.9%) more than half of the youth population is unemployed.[7] It is interesting to observe, however, that the issue of unemployment still does not feature significantly in the outcome of elections throughout the region. The 2008 global and European financial and economic crisis has only worsened the existing economic problems in the region by adding two additional external shocks: a reduced influx of capital from abroad and the collapse of export demand.[8] Furthermore, the crisis has also had a negative social impact, resulting in increased poverty and lower living standard, as reflected in the 2014 protests in Bosnia and Herzegovina. Consistently weak investments in education, innovation, research and development, and culture, characteristic for most of the region, exacerbate this situation even further.

The enlargement of the Western Balkans is also endangered from within the EU itself.[9] EU institutions are increasingly preoccupied with the effects of the Eurozone financial and economic crises, while the EU is suffering from enlargement fatigue.[10] In addition, many EU member states seemingly pay lip service to enlargement, while making use of their veto powers to delay the accession process. Opinion polls, which also serve as an important guide for political decision-making, display growing scepticism among European citizens in many member states towards further widening. The latest Eurobarometer polls which investigated the support for further EU expansion in the spring of 2013, show that more EU citizens (53% to 37%) were against than in favour of enlargement. The highest levels of skepticism were found in Austria, the Netherlands, Finland, France and Germany, where three quarters of the population opposed enlargement.[11] This sentiment reflects the member states' internal political debates. The perceived high levels of immigration from the states that joined in 2004, as well as refugees and asylum seekers arriving through and from the Western Balkan countries, are additionally shaping Euro-scepticism among EU citizens. It is possible that some of this disapproval is directed at Turkey, also languishing in the EU's waiting room.[12] Finally, reports of legal uncertainty, corruption, and increasing poverty in the Western Balkans affect public perceptions in the EU countries, and these perceptions color internal decision-making regarding potential enlargement.

The three sets of obstacles outlined in this subsection explain the current delay in the democratic and socio-economic transformation, and thus EU integration, in the Western Balkan countries. As a consequence, the phase of accelerated transformation, seen immediately after 2000, has been replaced with a phase of "stagnation and drift"[13] in EU–Western Balkans relations.

This Chapter provides a contextual comparative analysis of the EU integration processes of five countries for this study. Special focus will be dedicated to the development of contractual relationships between the EU and aspiring members, as well as the EU's rule of law conditionality criteria.

EU approach to the enlargement

Against the background of a deeper relationship between the EU and the Central and Eastern European countries (CEECs) in the early 1990s, the well-known Copenhagen and Madrid Council criteria linked accession and membership in the EU to a precisely defined set of economic and political conditions. The "famous" Copenhagen criteria remain the blueprint for accession of the Western Balkans. They require candidates to have stable democratic institutions, a functioning market economy and the capacity to adopt and implement the ever-growing body of the *Acquis communautaire.*[14] These criteria are seen both as legal principles stemming from EU primary law, and as core values of the EU and prerequisites in the formation of a post-national European identity. The ability to fulfill the obligations of membership by the implementation of the EU legal order, i.e., the *Acquis communautaire*, is basically seen—in legal discourses—as a technical conditionality requirement. However, when examining the specific strategies and instruments used by the EU and posing the question of which of them is the most effective, it becomes obvious that rule adoption and the implementation of the *Acquis communautaire* are not only a technical matter, but also a highly political affair.[15] The *Acquis* is not only a formal body of law, but also a "framework in which shared policies and values are established and through which they are implemented."[16] In addition, it has been stressed that the Union's capacity to absorb new members, while maintaining the momentum of European integration, is also an important consideration for enlargement. Each of these conditions has acquired a very precise meaning for the Western Balkan countries by aiming to overcome the specific nature of enlargement to the region. As a result, this has led to a more complex mosaic of EU demands for the region.

First, the EU's overall strategy for the Western Balkans is based on a regional approach that is conceptualized in the Stabilisation and Association Process. The SAP aims to assist each Western Balkan country in meeting the relevant EU conditions for accession. It is structured with a bilateral dimension and a regional dimension. The bilateral component includes matters such as: enhanced trade liberalization, financial assistance, cooperation in Justice and Home Affairs, and the Stabilisation and Association Agreement (SAA). In addition to the fact that the SAA produces a definite perspective on membership, it also provides a contractual framework by which the EU can ensure compliance with more precise conditions outlined for the aspiring Western Balkan countries. The regional dimension, on the other hand, fosters regional cooperation and good neighborly relations between the South East European countries. In addition, the Western Balkan countries are also participating in the work of the Regional Cooperation Council (RCC), which replaced the Stability Pact for South Eastern Europe in 2008.

Second, the Western Balkan aspiring members are facing an additional set of politically sensitive conditions, often colloquially referred to as the "Copenhagen Plus" criteria, which include the requirement of full cooperation with the International Criminal Tribunal for the Former Yugoslavia (ICTY), refugee return, regional cooperation and reconciliation, and the resolution of bilateral disputes or of statehood dilemmas. Additionally, the "Copenhagen Plus" criteria encompass a strong security dimension, which pertains to the respect for and implementation of various political and peace agreements stemming mostly from the armed conflicts of the 1990s, which distorted the region. They include the UN Security Council Resolution 1244, the Dayton, Kumanovo, Ohrid, and Belgrade agreements, and the Agreement on Normalization of Serbia–Kosovo Relations.

Third, the EU has redefined its existing monitoring mechanisms, becoming much more rigorous in the way it applies conditionality. It has introduced new mechanisms, such as intermediary benchmarks and the early screening processes. In addition, the European Commission has devised creative ways to keep the reform process going in situations of domestic or bilateral deadlocks in the Western Balkans. These include the High Level Accession Dialogue with Macedonia, the Structured Dialogue on Justice with Bosnia and Herzegovina, the Structured Dialogue on the Rule of Law with Kosovo, and the High Level Dialogue with Albania. The EU continues to borrow expertise from other international organizations during the monitoring of the implementation of the adopted policies, most notably from the Council of Europe, the

OSCE, international financial institutions, and relevant non-governmental organizations (NGOs).

Fourth, conditionality for the Balkans features an increased focus on "good governance" criteria, particularly the maintenance of the rule of law, an independent judiciary and an efficient public administration. The new EU approach on Chapters 23 and 24, introduced for the first time in the Croatian negotiating process, is now fully integrated into the EU's negotiations with Montenegro and Serbia, and will most likely apply to all future accession talks in the region. In this novel approach, proposed in 2011 by the European Commission[17] and endorsed by the Council, Western Balkan countries are expected to get a head start on the most difficult aspect—rule of law reforms—in order to allow enough time to build solid track records of implementation before opening other negotiating chapters. Furthermore, the "new approach" envisages an interim benchmarking system that would assess the country's preparedness to open and close a negotiating chapter, and introduces safeguard measures, most notably the overall balance clause, as referred to above. The Negotiating Framework for Montenegro's and Serbia's accession places a specific emphasis on Chapters 23 and 24, thus reflecting concerns about matters related to the rule of law, corruption and organized crime.

Despite all the novelties in its approach to enlargement, the EU still follows a strategy of reinforcement by reward in its relations with potential candidate countries from the Western Balkans. This means that the EU rewards governments that comply with its demands and, alternatively, withholds rewards from those that do not. The most powerful conditionality tool is still that of granting or withholding access to the different phases of the accession process, particularly once candidate status is achieved and negotiations begin. Clearly, membership remains the biggest, albeit the most distant, reward for countries that adhere to EU conditions on the rocky road toward accession.[18]

Bosnia and Herzegovina

Bosnia and Herzegovina faced a vicious war, from 1992 until 1995, that saw atrocities from all parties involved, including grave human rights violations, the expulsion of others, and genocide.[19] The conflict did not end until the international community brokered the General Framework Agreement for Peace in Bosnia and Herzegovina.[20] Stemming from the need to create a feasible state within Bosnia and Herzegovina, the Dayton/Paris General Framework Agreement for Peace was envisaged as a constitutional, state-institution engineering platform to which the conflicting parties had to agree. The main task of the Agreement was to preserve a balance of power between three state-forming nations, i.e. "constituent peoples." The Dayton Agreement, therefore, attempted to solve "the most urgent problem in the design of democratic institutions" by providing a model of corporate power-sharing between Muslims, Serbs, and Croats in Bosnia and Herzegovina, which was based on the principles of proportional representation in a bi-cameral parliament and Presidency,[21] veto powers,[22] division of powers between the state level and entities,[23] internal and internationally supported mechanisms of coordination to counterbalance the disintegrating tendencies deriving from territorial delimitation, and corporate power sharing.[24]

Effectively, the Dayton Agreement envisaged the administration of justice divided between two constituent entities and the Brčko District,[25] leaving the state institutions without any responsibilities in establishing the judicial system. Hence, Bosnia and Herzegovina is a unique case study with four separate legal systems. Moreover, representatives of the cross-entity judiciaries rarely meet at the state level, except for a very few procedural matters. Finally, keeping in mind that one of the entities, the Federation of Bosnia and Herzegovina, was divided into cantons in 1995, there are a total of 13 different judicial systems within Bosnia and Herzegovina.

Ever since the end of hostilities, the EU has been active in Bosnia and Herzegovina with the process of institution building, the reconstruction of the economy, and the creation of a liberal democratic society, including rule of law. In early 2000, the EU developed a "Road Map" of 18 priority reform steps for Bosnia and Herzegovina, rule of law being one of them. The EU had, at this time, established preliminary conditions in the field of rule of law. These mostly focused on the establishment of new rule of law mechanisms[26] and the allocation of funds for the operations of the Constitutional Court of Bosnia and Herzegovina. Once the Road Map was assessed as "substantially completed" in September 2002, the European Commission initiated the Feasibility Study for Bosnia and Herzegovina as an intermediary step towards the opening of negotiations for a Stabilisation and Association Agreement. Here, the first tangible rule of law conditions for prospective members were set. Conditions set in this Study addressed the independence and effectiveness of the judiciary, particularly calling for the establishment of a single High Judicial and Prosecutorial Council. Similarly, the 2004 European Partnership with Bosnia and Herzegovina[27] reaffirmed this condition and asked for appropriate staff and funding for the State Court—established in 2002—as a short-term condition, and the functioning of these institutions as medium-term priorities.

Since 2005, the European Commission has monitored the annual progress of Bosnia and Herzegovina in its Progress Reports, where more substantive rule of law indicators are being considered. Namely, in its Reports, the Commission has monitored the process of the re-appointment of judges and prosecutors; the independence of the judiciary and the establishment of the High Judicial and Prosecutorial Council (HJPC); the salaries of judges; the establishment of training centers; funding of the judiciary; infrastructure and equipment for the courts; and the backlog of cases.

The signing of the Stabilisation and Association Agreement,[28] on 16 June 2008, marked the beginning of a new phase of negotiations between the EU and Bosnia and Herzegovina. In light of the progress that led to the signing of the SAA, the 2008 Progress Report[29] observed improvement in the judicial system. Particularly, it welcomed the adoption of the "National Strategy for

Development of the Justice Sector."[30] Nevertheless, despite each of the subsequent Progress Reports continually praising limited progress in the implementation of judicial reform, it seems the positive momentum has been lost.

In an effort to overcome the stalemate in the SAP, the European Commission launched the "Structured Dialogue on Justice," in June 2011,[31] for Bosnia and Herzegovina, which has become the first enlargement country to benefit from the new methodology. Basically, the "Structured Dialogue on Justice" aims to assist Bosnia and Herzegovina in the consolidation of rule of law and the establishment of an independent, effective, impartial and accountable judicial system across the whole country. The underlying idea behind this newly established mechanism is to advance structured relations, regarding rule of law, with potential candidates, prior to the beginning of membership negotiations. The goal of the dialogue is to depoliticize the justice sector, as that is seen by the Commission as "the only possible way to secure the independence of the judiciary for good."[32] At the end of each plenary session of the Dialogue, the European Commission issues a set of technical recommendations that serve as interim benchmarks to be implemented between the two sessions.[33]

Nevertheless, at the moment of writing this study, Bosnia and Herzegovina remains distant from EU membership. While even the very survival of the country is regularly challenged by the Alliance of Independent Social Democrats—the ruling political party in the Republika Srpska led by Milorad Dodik—most structural reforms and conditions for closer ties with the EU remain unfulfilled due to uncompromising mono-ethnic political elites.[34] The Stabilisation and Association Agreement with Bosnia and Herzegovina entered into force in June 2015, following the important British-German initiative of late 2014, which was aimed at unblocking the impasse by delaying Sejdić-Finci conditionality to a later stage of EU accession, and the written commitment of 14 political parties to support the reform process in February 2015.

Kosovo

Kosovo declared independence from Serbia on 17 February 2008 following decades of severe ethnic tension between Kosovo's Albanian and Serb populations. Inter-ethnic violence throughout the 1990s, including the Kosovo War of 1999, ended with a NATO-led military intervention. Kosovo is formally recognized by 111 UN member states.[35] Although Serbia recognizes Kosovo's governance of the territory, it continues to claim it as its own Autonomous Province of Kosovo and Metohija.

Despite the EU member states not having a common official position towards Kosovo's legal status, the EU is present in Kosovo through the European Union Office in Kosovo/European Union Special Representative (EUSR), the European Union Rule of Law Mission in Kosovo (EULEX), and 18 EU Member State Embassies and Liaison Offices. EULEX, the largest civilian mission ever launched under the European Security and Defence Policy, was deployed to ensure a continuation of international civil presence in Kosovo. The goal of the mission is to provide assistance and support to the Kosovo authorities in areas of rule of law, specifically police, judiciary and customs.

Prior to the declaration of independence, the EU announced the European perspective for Kosovo with its 2005 strategic document entitled "Communication from the Commission—A European Future for Kosovo."[36] The European Commission has pledged to provide political contributions for ensuring Kosovo's stability and institution building via the Stabilisation and Association Process Tracking Mechanism (STM), a forum for discussing the country's progress in the implementation of the European Partnership. The Commission's strategy for fostering capacity building in Kosovo's public administration and judiciary was based on the plan for closer cooperation with Kosovo's institutions with the EU; mostly through the establishment of the Technical Assistance Information Exchange Office (TAIEX), and the allocation of EU funds to assist local institutions in drafting legislation that conforms with EU standards and assists in its implementation and enforcement.

In November 2009, Kosovo–EU relations were elevated, by the Stabilisation Association Process Dialogue (SAPD), based on the European Commission Communication to the European Council and Parliament titled "Kosovo*—Fulfilling its European Perspective."[37] Nevertheless, the EU has not elaborated on what the rule of law benchmarks for Kosovo are, despite a number of declarations and strategic papers, and without a clear membership perspective.

The Brussels agreement of principles governing the normalization of relations between Belgrade and Pristina of April 2013 has, at least formally, resolved the issue of a separate Serb administration in the North of the country. The agreement primarily focuses on the establishment of the Association/Community of Serb majority municipalities, the police force, the justice sector and elections. Pertaining to the justice sector, the Agreement mandates that all judicial authorities must integrate and operate within Kosovo's legal framework. More importantly, it mandates that the Appellate Court in Pristina establishes a panel of judges with a Serb majority "to deal with all Kosovo Serb Majority municipalities." This Panel will sit permanently in the Mitrovica District Court building in Northern Mitrovica. While the dynamics of the EU integration process seem to have introduced a new phase of political relations for both countries, recent worsening of Serbian–Albanian relations overburdened by historical legacies,[38] give the impression that a relapse into the doctrines of the ethnically pure state, and ethnic extremism, is still possible.

Still, the greatest problem in terms of Kosovo's EU integration perspective remains the fact that five EU member states—Cyprus, Greece, Slovakia, Spain and Romania—have not recognized Kosovo's independence. As a result, Kosovo's membership perspective remains elusive, and the European

Commission refers only to "Kosovo*,"[39] with the asterisked footnote containing the text agreed upon during the Belgrade–Pristina negotiations.

Thus, the entry into force of Kosovo's SAA, which is expected to take place in 2016, remains uncertain. Bearing in mind that Kosovo cannot expect to become an EU member state in a foreseeable future, it is evident that the EU conditionality mechanism alone will not effectively guide the politically sensitive rule of law reform in Kosovo. In an attempt to strengthen institutional ties between the EU and Kosovo, and in an absence of contractual obligations between them, the EU proposed the launch of the Structured Dialogue on the Rule of Law, which was announced in the 2011–2012 Enlargement Strategy.[40] The Structured Dialogue commenced on 30 May 2012. It is envisaged to include high-level rule of law meetings and discussions focused on the main rule of law priorities for Kosovo. However, it has a broader scope of targets, as it regularly assesses Kosovo's progress on three issues: the judiciary, the fight against organized crime and the fight against corruption. The Dialogue is supposed to serve as a high-level forum that should encourage judicial reform to further strengthen independence, impartiality and transparency, as well as to address reducing the backlog of cases, ensuring a sufficient budget for the proper functioning of the courts, the restructuring of prosecutorial offices, and equal representation of minorities in judiciary institutions.[41] It is expected that the Structured Dialogue on Rule of Law will strengthen the coordination and monitoring mechanisms necessary to maximize implementation, sustainability and progress in the field of rule of law reform.

Macedonia

Macedonia became an independent state in 1991. It managed to avoid a full-scale war, and reduced inter-ethnic tensions with the mostly successful implementation of the Ohrid Framework Agreement of 2001. As a result, Macedonia was the first country from the region to enter into contractual relations with the EU by signing the SAA back in 2001.[42] The SAA with Macedonia contained a future development clause in its preamble, thus confirming the country's status as a potential candidate for EU accession. The main aspects of the SAA include accords on cooperation and good, neighborly relations with the other countries of the region; creation of a free trade area between the countries linked to the EU by an SAA; and political and economic aspects of approximation with EU law.

However, despite gaining candidate status already in 2005, the country's Euro-Atlantic integration has since been consistently vetoed by Greece, due to the acrimonious name dispute. More than 20 years since the beginning of the efforts for the resolution of the name dispute led mostly by the United Nations (UN), a mutually acceptable solution seems as distant today as it was at the start of the process. In the meantime, the ruling VMRO-DPMNE party turned to authoritarian policies, misusing its position of power in order to mobilize citizens along nationalist lines via projects such as the controversial

"Skopje 2014." Politics of state capture led to growing tensions in Macedonia, which resulted in the complete breakdown of legitimate institutions and enormous political polarization.[43]

In the meantime, the EU developed a new platform for advanced cooperation with Macedonia in 2012. The High-Level Accession Dialogue (HLAD) takes into consideration recent developments, and the repeatedly recommended, but unopened, membership negotiations.[44] Basically, the HLAD does not supplement accession negotiations, but serves as a bridge toward negotiations. At the same time, it raises the visibility of the EU integration progress. One of the focal points of the HLAD is the Rule of Law reform that addresses the reform of the judiciary, the fight against corruption and fundamental rights. At four HLAD meetings, a set of measures was discussed that aimed to improve the independence, accountability, efficiency and effectiveness of the judiciary. As concluded in the 2013 Commission Progress Report, the HLAD has already produced tangible results in terms of the retreatment of new cases in Macedonian courts.

Nevertheless, in the absence of official negotiations, the credibility of the EU's conditionality is in question. In addition to blocking the official start of accession negotiations, the Greek veto blocks the beginning of the screening process during which the EU compares the compatibility of the laws of a candidate with the *Acquis*. Following the experience of Montenegro and Serbia—where the screening process commenced ahead of the opening of official membership negotiations—the starting of this process in Macedonia would clearly demonstrate a commitment to the European perspective of the country.

Montenegro

Having gained independence in 2006, Montenegro has nearly completed its state-building processes. However, the country's newly achieved independence did not result in the swift resolution of key challenges that Montenegro still faces today—weak governance and widely perceived corruption in the polity. Moreover, the country has never witnessed an alternation of power. The current Prime Minister Milo Djukanović has been in a position of power since 1991, surviving numerous political affairs, including an international criminal investigation. Nonetheless, Montenegro is the regional frontrunner in European integration, as it is the only Western Balkan country participating in the accession negotiations process with the EU at the moment. On 15 November 2015, Montenegro had opened 20 out of 33 negotiating chapters, two of which have been provisionally closed.

The biggest innovation introduced within the framework of Montenegro's accession negotiations process is the inclusion of safeguards and corrective measures, most notably an "overall balance clause" intended to stop negotiations on other chapters if progress on the most difficult chapters, such as "Judiciary and fundamental rights" and "Justice, freedom and security," begins to lag behind.[45] The overall balance clause, and other safeguard measures, will be applied to all other Western Balkan countries as well.

In the meantime, EU integration remains a cornerstone of the Montenegrin government's foreign and domestic policy. On its path to accession, Montenegro has committed to judiciary reform as part of the Copenhagen conditionality related to rule of law. The 2015 European Commission Progress Report observes that despite the good progress on strengthening the legislative framework to increase the independence, accountability and professionalism of the judiciary, the judiciary in Montenegro still has to demonstrate its independence, accountability and efficiency implementation in practice.

Serbia

After the dissolution of the common state with Montenegro in 2006 and Kosovo's declaration of independence in 2008, Serbia is currently in the hands of "reformed" Milošević allies who have turned pro-European. Although none of the euro-skeptic political parties managed to pass the five percent threshold to enter the National Assembly in the elections, Serbia's political elites are still searching for a way to escape the dilemmas over state and nationhood issues.

Serbia's accession path has been fraught with difficulty, as it has been shaped by state dissolution and a legacy of violent conflict. These multiple challenges stand at the core of the explanation of Serbia's slow start in the EU integration process. Nevertheless, as a result of improved cooperation with the International Criminal Tribunal for Former Yugoslavia (ICTY), Serbia signed the SAA[46] in April 2008. As the result of a positive track record in the implementation of the obligations of the SAA, the European Council granted Serbia the status of candidate country, on 1 March 2012.[47]

The mediated dialogue between Belgrade and Pristina, which resulted in the *First Agreement of Principles Governing the Normalization of Relations*[48] from April 2013, allowed the European Council to endorse the Council of Ministers' conclusions and recommendations to open accession negotiations with Serbia. Screening of the *Acquis,* with Serbia, started on 25 September 2013. It has concluded that considerable efforts are needed regarding Chapters 23 and 24, which deal with Judiciary and Fundamental Rights, and Justice, Freedom and Security, respectively. The first Intergovernmental Conference was held on 21 January 2014 at the European Council in Brussels, thus marking the beginning of the official membership negotiations between Serbia and the EU.[49] Yet, despite being internationally praised for achieving progress in the normalization of relations between Belgrade and Pristina, the government of Prime Minister Vučić faces frequent criticism for its domestic authoritarian tendencies, particularly those concerning the control of the media and the judiciary.[50]

Beyond the autopilot mode?

With Croatia joining the EU, Montenegro and Serbia opening accession negotiations, Albania gaining candidate status, and the 2013 Kosovo–Serbia agreement, it appears that EU integration remains a successful transformative tool. Indeed, so far, the prospect of European integration has played an important role in driving the Western Balkan countries to reconstruct post-war institutions and societies, to begin the process of reconciliation between states and people, and to start the process of democratic consolidation. Novelties in the EU approach to the region have brought into focus significant political issues, such as the reform of the system of rule of law. Equally important is the establishment of political dialogues with countries not yet able to start accession negotiations.

However, some 16 years after the launch of the SAP with the EU, Western Balkan accession countries are still far away from EU accession. The combination of aforementioned innovations in the EU approach to the integration of the Western Balkans has created an ever more complex assortment of EU demands, followed by inflexible monitoring of the implementation of membership conditionality. The paradox of the current approach is that it foresees that the countries which have experienced the most difficult democratic and economic transformation process as a consequence of the ethnic conflicts of the 1990s and authoritarian regimes need to overcome higher hurdles in order to join the EU than countries from earlier enlargement rounds. Many politically sensitive reforms are demanded at the early "pre- pre-accession phase" of the accession process. Before the opening of official negotiations with candidate countries, the EU's leverage is not strong, and candidate countries are not motivated to comply with such difficult demands. Thus, this format brings the risk that non-compliance at an early stage can jeopardize the overall accession process. Particularly worrisome is the trend whereby the EU overlooks important structural reforms and core EU conditions on account of its pursuit of the resolution of outstanding political issues, such as the normalization of relations between Serbia and Kosovo. In addition, the involvement of member states in the EU accession talks by way of imposing bilateral conditions is additionally threatening the already fragile credibility of EU conditionality.

This brings us to the greatest limit of the current EU approach to enlargement, namely the lack of transformative leverage for the current laggards of the accession process—Bosnia and Herzegovina, Macedonia, and to a certain degree Kosovo.[51] As already mentioned, ever since Macedonia received candidate country status back in 2005, it has been unable to further progress in its EU integration due to the Greek veto and Bulgaria's threat to use its veto because of bilateral issues. In the meantime, Macedonia has seen a rise of nationalism, a breakdown of democratic consolidation, and an EU-led mediation of its internal political crisis.

Despite achieving little progress in most policy areas, apart from the recent breakthrough agreement with Serbia, Kosovo signed the SAA with the EU in

October 2015. As Kosovo is the first country to sign the SAA after the Lisbon Treaty, which conferred a legal personality to the EU, its SAA will be an exclusive competency of the EU, thus avoiding ratification by all individual member states, which would be impossible due to the lack of recognition by Cyprus, Greece, Slovakia, Spain and Romania. As long as EU member states de facto block Kosovo's membership perspective, the potential for destabilization and regression should not be underestimated.

Finally, the case of Bosnia and Herzegovina is specific since even the EU itself practically acknowledged that its conditionality toolbox has not functioned. For nine years, the EU has been unable to move this country forward, mostly due to the incapability of uncompromising domestic political elites to agree on any reform policies. As the question of how to proceed with Bosnia and Herzegovina became ever more relevant, the British-German initiative of late 2014 aimed at unblocking the stalemate by delaying the implementation of the Sejdić-Finci ruling to a later stage of the accession process. This was done in exchange for a written commitment to reforms by the country's leading politicians. In February 2014, Stefan Füle, the former enlargement commissioner, said that implementing the European Court of Human Rights (ECHR) ruling of the Sejdić-Finci case constitutes "an international obligation of Bosnia and Herzegovina that, following the will of the [EU] member states, is now a key to progress on the EU path."[52] When the SAA with Bosnia entered into force one year later, the EU de facto admitted that its conditionality does not always work, and decided to delay this condition in order to move the accession process forward. Now, it should be stressed that the revamped member states' political will to engage with Bosnia and Herzegovina represents good news. The previous status quo could only have led to more hostile political disputes and a worsening economic situation, with considerable frustration among Bosnian citizens. This is why the EU's policy innovation in Bosnia and Herzegovina deserves to be praised.

However, the point here is that the transformative effect of the "current EU approach" for the Balkans appears to be insufficient. In a nutshell, conditionality works well if membership criteria are clear, if the same criteria are applied to all applicants, if they are strictly but fairly monitored, if the findings are transparently communicated, and if there is no doubt that the reward will come once conditions are met. Currently, all this is not the case.

Notes

1 European Council. (Thessaloniki: 19 and 20 June 2003). *Thessaloniki Presidency Conclusions*, 11638/03. Available at http://www.consilium.europa.eu/uedocs/cms_data/docs/pressdata/en/ec/76279.pdf.

2 F. Bieber. 2013. "Building Impossible States? State-Building Strategies and EU Membership in the Western Balkans," *Europe-Asia Studies* 63(10): 1783–1802.

3 See S. Grimm, and O. L. Mathis. 2015. "Stability First, Development Second, Democracy Third: The European Union's Policy towards the Post-Conflict Western Balkans, 1991–2010," *Europe-Asia Studies* 67(6): 916–947.

4 *Nations in Transit*. 2015. Freedom House. Available at https://freedomhouse.org/sites/default/files/FH_NIT2015_06.06.15_FINAL.pdf.
5 See in M. Kmezić. 2014. "Overcoming the Crisis of Enlargement," *Contemporary Southeastern Europe* 1(1): 1–8.
6 Regional Cooperation Council. 2015. *Balkan Barometer 2015 Public Opinion Survey*, Sarajevo.
7 Ibid.
8 See for example International Monetary Fund. 2015. *The Western Balkans: 15 Years of Economic Transition. Regional Economic Issues*, Special Report. Available at https://www.imf.org/external/pubs/ft/reo/2015/eur/eng/pdf/erei_sr_030915.pdf.
9 M. Kmezić. 2015. *The Western Balkans and EU Enlargement: Lessons Learned, Ways Forward and Prospects Ahead*, European Parliament, Directorate-General for External Policies. Available at http://www.europarl.europa.eu/thinktank/en/document.html?reference=EXPO_IDA(2015)534999.
10 R. Panagiotou. 2013. "The Greek Crisis as a Crisis of EU Enlargement: How Will the Western Balkans be Affected?," *Southeast European and Black Sea Studies* 13(1): 89–104.
11 *Standard Eurobarometer*. 2013. "Tables of Results: Public Opinion in the European Union," No. 79, Spring 2013, T84. Available at http://ec.europa.eu/public_opinion/archives/eb/eb79/eb79_anx_en.pdf.
12 N. Negriz. 2015. "The Role of the Mass Media on Shaping the Public Opinion about the Enlargement of the European Union," in N. O. Taskiran, and R. Yilmaz. *Handbook of Research on Effective Advertising Strategies in the Social Media Age* (IGI: Hershey).
13 C. Gordon, M. Kmezić and J. Opardija (eds.). 2013. *Stagnation and Drift in the Western Balkans: The Challenges of Political, Economic and Social Change* (Bern: Peter Lang AG) at 22.
14 European Council. (Copenhagen, 21–22 June 1993). *Copenhagen Presidency Conclusions*, SN 180/93.
15 M. Kmezić. 2014. "Overcoming the Crisis of Enlargement," cit.
16 A. Magen. 2007. "Transformative Engagement Through Law. The *Acquis Communautaire* as Instrument of EU External Influence," *European Journal of Law Reform* 9(3): 361–393: 363.
17 European Commission. (Brussels, 12 October 2011). *Communication from the Commission to the European Parliament and the Council, Enlargement Strategy and Main Challenges 2011–2012*, COM(2011) 666 final.
18 See M. Kmezić. 2015. *The Western Balkans and EU Enlargement*, cit.
19 In a 26 February 2007 decision in the case of the Application of the Convention on the Prevention and Punishment of the Crime of Genocide, the International Court of Justice determined that genocide had in fact occurred in the municipality of Srebrenica. See ICJ, *Bosnia and Herzegovina v. Serbia and Montenegro, Case 91*, Judgment of 26 February 2007.
20 *The General Framework Agreement for Peace in Bosnia and Herzegovina*, initialed Dayton, Ohio: 21 November 1995, signed Paris: 14 December 1995, agreed to by Bosnia and Herzegovina, Croatia and Federal Republic of Yugoslavia, 35 (1996) ILM 75.
21 Ibid. Articles 1, 4 and 5, and Paragraphs 1 and 3 of Annex 4 to the Agreement.
22 Ibid. Articles 4, 5.
23 Ibid. Articles 3, 8.
24 Ibid. Articles 2, 3, 6, 12, Annexes 5, 6, 7, 8, 10.
25 Although the status of Brčko District was not agreed upon in Dayton but in the subsequent arbitration process.
26 Specifically, it was required that Bosnia and Herzegovina "implement law on State Border Service; approve and implement laws on judicial and prosecutorial service

in the Federation and law on court and judicial service in the RS." European Commission (March 2000). *EU Roadmap. Steps to Be Taken by Bosnia and Herzegovina to Prepare for a Launch of a Feasibility Study.* Available at http://www.esiweb.org/pdf/bridges/bosnia/EURoadMap.pdf.

27 European Council. (22 March 2004). *Council Regulation on the Establishment of European Partnerships in the Framework of the Stabilisation and Association Process* (EC) No 533/2004.

28 European Parliament. (23 October 2008). *European Parliament Legislative Resolution of 23 October 2008 on the Proposal for a Council and Commission Decision on the Conclusion of the Stabilisation and Association Agreement between the European Communities and their Member States, of the one part, and Bosnia and Herzegovina, of the other part,* 8225/2008 – COM(2008)0182 – C6–0255/2008–2008/0073(AVC).

29 European Commission. (Brussels: October 2008). *2008 Progress Report of Bosnia and Herzegovina Accompanying the Communication from the Commission to the European Parliament and the Council, Enlargement Strategy and Main Challenges 2008–2009* [COM(2008)674].

30 Bosnia and Herzegovina Ministry of Justice. (Sarajevo: June 2008). *Bosnia and Herzogovina Justice Sector Reform Strategy 2008–2012.* Available at http://issat.dcaf.ch/content/download/2249/19520/file/Bosnia%20and%20Herzegovina%20Justice%20Sector%20Reform%20Strategy.pdf.

31 Delegation of the European Union to Bosnia and Herzegovina and European Union Special Representative in Bosnia and Herzegovina (Sarajavo: June 2011). *10 Facts To Know About the EU-BiH Structured Dialogue On Justice.* Available at http://europa.ba/Download.aspx?id=736&lang=EN.

32 Ibid.: 1.

33 See, for example, Delegation of European Union to Bosnia and Herzegovina. *First Set of Preliminary Recommendations from the European Commission, Inaugural Meeting of the "SAA Structured Dialogue on Justice between the European Union and Bosnia and Herzegovina"* (Banja Luka: 6–7 June 2011). Available at http://www.delbih.ec.europa.eu/Download.aspx?id=734&lang=EN.

34 M. Vachudova. 24 February 2014. "The Thieves of Bosnia: The Complicated Legacy of the Dayton Peace Accords," *Foreign Affairs.* Available at http://www.foreignaffairs.com/articles/140966/milada-vachudova/the-thieves-of-bosnia.

35 As of 23 November 2015.

36 European Commission. (Brussels, 20 March 2005) *Communication from the Commission – A European Future for Kosovo* (COM/2005/0156 final). Available at http://eur-lex.europa.eu/legal-content/EN/TXT/?uri=CELEX:52005DC0156.

37 European Commission. (Brussels: 14 October 2009) *Communication of the European Communities. Communication from the Commission to the European Parliament and the Council. Kosovo* – Fulfilling its European Perspective.* Available at http://ec.europa.eu/enlargement/pdf/key_documents/2009/kosovo_study_en.pdf.

38 F. Bieber. 2014. "Greater Serbia and Greater Albania Do Not Exist: The Myth of Bad Serb-Albanian Relations," *Balkans in Europe Policy Blog.* Available at http://www.suedosteuropa.uni-graz.at/biepag/node/26; A. Pavlović, S. Ćirić. 2014. "Opportunity On-Hold: Edi Rama's Visit to Belgrade in the Light of 'the Drone Incident'," *Balkans in Europe Policy Blog.* Available at http://www.suedosteuropa.uni-graz.at/biepag/node/113.

39 "This designation is without prejudice to positions on status, and is in line with UNSCR 1244 and the ICJ Opinion on the Kosovo Declaration of Independence."

40 Council of the European Union. (Brussels: 5 December 2011). *Council Conclusions on Enlargement and Stabilisation and Association Process* (Brussels). Available at http://www.consilium.europa.eu/uedocs/cms_data/docs/pressdata/EN/genaff/126577.pdf.

41 European Commission. (Brussels: 30 May 2012). *Structured Dialogue on the Rule of Law with Kosovo, Conclusions.* Available at http://ec.europa.eu/archives/commission_2010–2014/fule/docs/news/20120530_rold_conclussions_30_may.pdf.

42 Council of the European Union. (Brussels: 26 March 2001). *Stabilisation and Association Agreement between the European Communities and their Member States, of the one part, and the former Yugoslav Republic of Macedonia, of the other part* (6726/01). Available at http://ec.europa.eu/enlargement/pdf/the_former_yugoslav_republic_of_macedonia/saa03_01_en.pdf.

43 Balkans in Europe Policy Advisory Group. 2015. *Unraveling the Political Crisis in Macedonia: Toward Resolution or Calm Before the Storm?* Available at http://www.suedosteuropa.uni-graz.at/biepag/node/158.

44 European Commission. (Skopje: 15 March 2012). *Start of the High Level Accession Dialogue with the Government of the Former Yugoslav Republic of Macedonia, European Commission – MEMO/12/187.* Available at http://europa.eu/rapid/press-release_MEMO-12–187_en.htm?locale=en.

45 Council of the European Union. 29 March 2012. *Ministerial Meeting Opening the Intergovernmental Conference on the Accession of Montenegro to the European Union – Negotiating Framework.* 8339/12 Limite ELARG31. Available at http://ec.europa.eu/enlargement/pdf/st20002_05_mn_framedoc_en.pdf.

46 Council of the European Union. 2008. *Stabilisation and Association Agreement between the European Communities and their Member States of the one part, and the Republic of Serbia, of the other part.* Available at http://ec.europa.eu/enlargement/pdf/serbia/key_document/saa_en.pdf.

47 European Council. 2012. *Conclusions – 1/2 March 2012.* EUCO 4/3/12 REV 3. Available at http://www.consilium.europa.eu/uedocs/cms_data/docs/pressdata/en/ec/128520.pdf.

48 European External Action Service. 2013. *First Agreement of Principles Governing the Normalisation of Relations.* Available at http://www.rts.rs/upload/storyBoxFileData/2013/04/20/3224318/Originalni%20tekst%20Predloga%20sporazuma.pdf.

49 Council of the European Union. 2014. *First Accession Conference with Serbia.* 5486/14 (OR. en) PRESSE 15. Available at http://www.consilium.europa.eu/uedocs/cms_data/docs/pressdata/EN/genaff/140676.pdf.

50 See for example Human Rights Watch. 2015. "A Difficult Profession: Media Freedom under Attack in the Western Balkans." Available at https://www.hrw.org/node/279063.

51 See M. Kmezić. 2015. *The Western Balkans and EU Enlargement: Lessons Learned, Ways Forward and Prospects Ahead*, cit.

52 *Bosnia-Herzegovina – EU: Deep Disappointment on Sejdić-Finci Implementation*, European Commission MEMO. Sarajevo, 18 February 2014. Available at http://europa.eu/rapid/press-release_MEMO-14–117_de.htm.

7 Judicial reform in the Western Balkans

This Chapter of the book concerns the proposed benchmarks set for the independence, accountability, efficiency and effectiveness of the judiciary in the Western Balkans. It will provide an in-depth normative and empirical analysis of the reforms undertaken to reach these benchmark standards in a five-country case-study. The results of the research presented in this Chapter are based upon a combination of three methodological strands:

I A *normative approach*, which performs a content-analysis of the legal rules and administrative regulations which were adopted and implemented as a basis upon which to raise the standards of the region's judicial sector, to meet with the aforementioned benchmarks. For the need of this book the existing legislative framework will be (critically) understood as a prescriptive set of statements whose internal consistency will be scrutinized against the external demands established for the aspiring member states within the EU accession process.

II Problem-oriented *empirical* approach, which will assess the practical aspects of enforcing the rule of law, analyzing progress, and singling out gaps and possible discrepancies and malfunctions between legislation and implementation of reforms. The results of the above mentioned normative analysis will therefore be combined with empirical data gathered from expert interviews with domestic and foreign legal experts, practitioners, journalist and NGO representatives. Although most attention is dedicated to the institutional dynamics of the core court structures, the political and societal context in which these are working will also be considered.

III Lastly, an *institutional* approach will provide better understanding of the ways in which ideas, values and beliefs affect norms, institutions and behavior. Here I will try to establish whether changing one set of rules has implications for others, and particularly, whether it triggers significant resistance to change on the part of those who are advantaged in the broader context. More precisely, this methodological strand will present a clear picture of the mechanisms of institutional change by analysis of the competencies of, and interrelations between the court system, the executive and legislative powers, as well as the civil society.

Independence of the judiciary

Judicial independence lies at the core of the idea of a modern state, as it is a fundamental principle and integral element of all democracies and all democracy building. It is also an essential precondition for the establishment of an effective system of governance based on the rule of law and of critical value in safeguarding the impartiality of judges from undue external influence(s). Moreover, the principle of judicial independence is crucial for upholding a guarantee of legal certainty and predictability in society. It is embedded in direct and formal guarantees of real independence of individual judges as they exercise their core decision-making function. The issue of independence is also intimately linked with the interdependence of various state bodies, as a consequence of the delicate system of balances within the theory of division of powers. It is therefore important that obvious need for the insistence on the independence of the judiciary does not automatically lead to its isolation from the rest of the state institutional set-up.

The roots of the theory of judicial independence are based in the doctrine of separation of powers. According to the doctrine, the judiciary needs to be separate from the executive and legislative branches of government and is supposed to hold them accountable. Montesquieu, the founding father of the tripartite system of division of powers, argued that independent and unchecked judiciary is generally seen as the most important of the divided state powers.[1] Numerous legal scholars have attempted to capture the essence of the judicial independence by providing extensive check-lists of criteria the judiciary must meet, or alternatively focusing on more narrow aspects of judicial institutions.[2] Nonetheless, most of the scholars agree on two key characteristics of an independent judiciary, namely, impartiality in the decision-making process, and relief from any kind of external interference.

Following the same logic, the international standards for the independence of the judiciary most famously set in the Article 10 of the Universal Declaration of Human Rights read:

> The independence of the judiciary shall be guaranteed by the State and enshrined in the Constitution or the law of the country. It is the duty of all governmental and other institutions to respect and observe the independence of the judiciary.[3]

Bearing in mind its seminal importance, each subsequent regional human rights instrument, including the European Convention for Human Rights and the Charter of Fundamental Rights of the European Union, has codified the same article.[4] The requirement for the right to a fair trial by an independent judge is fundamental both to rule of law and the right to a fair trial. In this sense, judicial independence is an institutional response to specific legal, political, economic, cultural and historical influences, inducements, pressures, threats or interferences. As the concept of judicial independence is a reaction to concrete threats to judge's impartiality, legal academia has developed a number of benchmarks for this issue. These include, among others, substantive, personal, collective, internal, structural, and administrative safeguards of judicial independence.

This creates yet another dilemma, namely how to assess the independence of the judiciary. While part of the problem relates to the difficulties of gathering relevant data on this topic, the fact that the judicial independence is more a continuous rather than a dichotomous variable creates a significant obstacle in measuring its actual output. Furthermore, the independence variable may fluctuate—not only in time, but also in relation to different types of courts, i.e. misdemeanor, criminal, civil, commercial, special etc. For example, during the era of Franco's dictatorship in Spain ordinary courts remained quite independent. However, politically sensitive cases were always delegated to the highly politicized *Tribunal de Orden Publico*, through which the regime has carried out most political oppression.[5] Finally, a particular obstacle in calculating judicial independence refers to the fact that formal guarantees of independence can easily be neglected or even manipulated either by external actors, or the judges themselves.

Hence, in order to be able to measure the level of independence of judiciary in five case study countries, this book will primarily focus on its formal manifestations—such as the main organizational issues of the judiciary, namely the selection, promotion and to a limited extent dismissal, of judges. Economic independence will be tested against the annual proposals for the judiciary's budget and salaries of the judges. Finally, empirical evidence gathered via semi-structured expert interviews conducted with a representative sample of expert public will also be taken into account.

Bosnia and Herzegovina

International legal standards suggest that the independence of the judiciary must be guaranteed in the Constitution.[6] Otherwise, the judiciary would regularly be at risk of interference from all other branches of government, as well as various non-political elites. The situation in Bosnia and Herzegovina is, however, somewhat peculiar. The status and independence of judicial institutions are by and large recognized in the Constitutions of the two Entities, the Federation of Bosnia and Herzegovina and Republika Srpska.

The Constitution of Bosnia and Herzegovina was agreed upon, and is subsequently contained in, Annex IV of the 1995 General Framework Agreement for Peace in Bosnia and Herzegovina. The Constitution *de facto* defines two Entities, the Federation of Bosnia and Herzegovina and the Republika Srpska, as constituent parts of Bosnia and Herzegovina. The division of powers between the institutions of Bosnia and Herzegovina and the Entities is regulated by Article III of the Constitution. The Constitution of Republika Srpska, originally adopted during the armed conflict in 1992, was based on the concept of a unitary state. The Constitution of the Federation of Bosnia and Herzegovina was adopted in 1994 as part of the Washington Agreement, reflecting a wartime compromise between Bosniaks and Bosnian Croats, establishing a highly decentralized federation of ten Cantons, each of which has its own constitution. In addition, the Constitution of Bosnia and Herzegovina recognizes the Brčko District as a unit of local self-government within Bosnia and Herzegovina, but with its own institutions, laws and regulations.

Based upon the complex constitutional design described above, it can be observed that Bosnian society is fragmented on several levels: fragmentation of state powers, fragmentation of legislation and fragmentation of judicial bodies that apply the legislation. The plurality of legal orders in Bosnia and Herzegovina is in turn mirrored in the fragmentation of its judicial system, although, according to the supremacy clause, the Constitutional Court of the State rules on disputes between the State and the Entities.[7] Currently there are four judicial systems in the territory of Bosnia and Herzegovina, namely the judicial systems of the state, of the two Entities, and of the Brčko District. Obviously, this division of state, laws and institutions in Bosnia and Herzegovina has potential to influence legal certainty, which according to the Venice Commission's Report on the Rule of Law is "essential to the confidence in the judicial system and the rule of law [... and] to productive business arrangements so as to generate development and economic progress."[8] According to the Report, legal certainty should include the following requirements: publicity, precision, consistency, stability, non-retroactivity and the binding force of judicial decisions.[9] Bosnian judicial system(s) differ considerably in their internal structure, their inter-relationship is not always clearly defined, and in the combination of these two problems it is not unusual to have different legal interpretations of laws and inter-judicial disputes.

Whilst the approaches to guaranteeing the principle of legal certainty remains vague and the courts' network and structures remain fragmented, there does exist a uniform approach to the guarantees of independence of the judiciary in the legal system of Bosnia and Herzegovina. Although this principle is scattered in different pieces of legislation, the independence of the judiciary in Bosnia and Herzegovina today is guaranteed through the administrative independence of the judiciary, ensuring the necessary resources, financial security, and irrevocability and immunity of judges. It is also guaranteed through the personal independence of each individual judge in making judicial decisions based on facts and in accordance with the law, without any limitations or influence. The individual independence of judges in Bosnia and Herzegovina is manifested through the permanence of judicial functions, their autonomy in particular cases, the methods of election to a judicial function, career advancement, etc.[10]

In accordance to the 2004 Agreement on Transfer of Certain Entities' Responsibilities[11] signed by the Prime Ministers of the Federation and the Republika Srpska and the Minister for Justice of Bosnia and Herzegovina, the High Judicial and Prosecutorial Council (HJPC), a single body for the territory of the whole state has been specifically created in Bosnia and

Herzegovina to consolidate and strengthen the independence of the judiciary.[12] The HJPC was established as an independent and autonomous body, founded in accordance with the law at the state level after the transfer of authorities from the Entities in accordance with their constitutional authorities.

The HJPC has broad powers in relation to the judiciary at all levels of government. The HJPC appoints judges, including Court Presidents, lay judges and reserve judges to all courts at the State, Entity, Cantonal, District, Basic and Municipal levels in Bosnia and Herzegovina, including the Brčko District of Bosnia and Herzegovina. It does not however, appoint Judges to the Constitutional Courts of the State and Entities of Bosnia and Herzegovina. It makes proposals to the relevant authorities in relation to the election of judges to the Constitutional Court of Republika Srpska and the nomination of judges to the Constitutional Court of the Federation of Bosnia and Herzegovina. It also decides upon appeals in disciplinary proceedings, upon suspensions of judges, and supervises the advanced professional training of judges and prosecutors. Further to this, it also decides upon the temporary assignment or transfer of judges and prosecutors to another court or prosecutors office's as well as participating in the drafting process of annual budgets for the courts, advocating for adequate and continuous funding of courts in Bosnia and Herzegovina. Finally, it is also responsible for the coordination of projects related to improving all aspects of the administration of courts and setting criteria for the performance evaluations of judges and prosecutors.[13]

The 15 member HJPC is composed via a very difficult national/ethnic/ professional formula: two members are selected by the House of Representatives of the Parliamentary Assembly of Bosnia and Herzegovina and of the Council of Ministers of Bosnia and Herzegovina; two are selected by the Bar Chambers of the Entities; five or six by prosecutors, and five or six by judges. Throughout this, membership of the Council must generally reflect the ethnic structure of the country,[14] with six Bosniaks, five Serbs, three Croats, and one from the group of others, and with five female members.[15] In order to be elected to the HJPC, the aspiring candidate must demonstrate high moral standing, and have a sound reputation for professional efficiency, competence and integrity. Members of the HJPC enjoy immunity from civil liability for opinions expressed and decisions taken within the scope of official duties.

The *Law on HJPC* sets out strict eligibility criteria for appointment to the bench, including a detailed application process. All members of the judiciary, including judges, prosecutors and expert advisors, are appointed by the HJPC,[16] as the sole competent body for the appointment of judges and prosecutors.[17] In a country with such a fragmented judiciary, this represents the first time that there has existed a single body with the task of ensuring the maintenance of an independent, impartial and professional judiciary, and of ensuring the provision of a professional and efficient court system and prosecutorial service.

The vacant positions are published in the three most circulated daily newspapers and in the *Official Gazette of Bosnia and Herzegovina*. The short-listed candidates who fulfil the formal requirements undergo an interview, after which a ranked list is forwarded to the Council. The decision of the Council is published in the *Official Gazette.* Taking into account the fact that other branches of government appoint only two members of the HJPC, it can be concluded that there is a typical independence from political parties achieved in the selection process.

Concerning the ethnic dimension of the judicial independence, the election of judges in Bosnia and Herzegovina is bounded by the complex interplay of various Constitutional frameworks[18] related to the equal rights and participation of all constituent people and "others." Hence, Article 43(2) stipulates that the Council shall implement relevant Constitutional provisions regulating the equal rights and representation of constituent peoples and others when making its final decision on selection of judges.[19] According to the data available in the Technical Information Document presented in the Structural Dialogue by the Council of Ministers of Bosnia and Herzegovina,

> the proportions from the 1991 census are fully followed at the state level courts, while at the Entities they are generally followed. Women represent over 56.75% of judges and 48.5% of prosecutors, which is in line with the threshold of 40% defined by the Law on Gender Equality in Bosnia and Herzegovina.[20]

Most of the judges interviewed welcomed the establishment of the HJPC and gave positive assessments of its performance during the first ten years of its existence as it has "led to an increase of the institutional and individual independence of the judiciary."[21] Particularly important is the introduction of more transparent selection criteria to judicial posts and the fact that the HJPC applies these criteria itself. Judges in Bosnia and Herzegovina see the establishment of the HJPC as being important in order to meet EU standards in the area of rule of law, as "its establishment is perceived as a case of successful transposition of EU standards."[22] Similarly, the Venice Commission praises the HJPC for its role in strengthening the independence of the judiciary and "furthering contacts and co-operation among judges and prosecutors."[23]

Although the HJPC enjoys institutional independence in its operations, questions can be raised relating to its composition. The Venice Commission has expressed some reservations regarding the fact that the HJPC is designed for the recruitment of judges and public prosecutors alike, stating that "the selection could be vulnerable to inter-institutional and inter-personal rivalries in the judiciary."[24] Contrary to the opinion of the Venice Commission, it seems however that the division of the HJPC would lead to the splitting of magistrates' professions into judicial and prosecutorial. Therefore, not only would the two newly established bodies present greater fiscal burdens to the state budget, but they would also suffer from a lack of mutual coordination, becoming more vulnerable to negative external influences.

Secondly, due to the constitutional provisions regulating the equal rights and representation of constituent peoples and others,[25] the qualifications of judges and prosecutors are not always the key criteria for appointment to the HJPC. In practice, application of this norm means that in the case that members of constituent peoples are not represented on the ranking list for appointment to the HJPC according to the latest census, the HJPC can even opt not to select anyone from the ranking list, let alone the best ranking candidate. This is of course, perceived as being quite frustrating by some interviewees, who said that they never know whether or not to apply to a vacant position "because you never know which constituent people is under-represented."[26]

The budgets of courts are determined at the level of the State, the Republika Srpska, the Federation, the cantons, and the Brčko District. As there are no uniform rules for financing the work of judiciary, judicial bodies remain vulnerable to pressure from the local institutions that decide the budget. Still, the individual salaries of the judges currently remain three times higher than the average salary in Bosnia and Herzegovina.[27] Although this ratio is higher than the ratio between average salaries and judicial salaries in the Council of Europe member states,[28] judges complain that the level of salaries is not adjusted to the level of inflation and that there has been no increase to the salaries since 2006, when it was 4.5 times higher than the national average.[29]

Currently, the *Law on the HJPC* is being revised. The Venice Commission recommends that in due course the HJPC be provided with an explicit constitutional basis and greater budgetary competencies. Due to the internal crisis of government in the country however, it does not seem as if the new law will be adopted soon.

Macedonia

Judicial independence in Macedonia is guaranteed in Article 98 paragraph 2 of the Constitution, which stipulates that "the Courts are autonomous and independent."[30] The Constitution also contains safeguards for the independence of judges, such as an unlimited term in office, protection against transfer without consent, and immunity.[31] Similarly, the autonomy and independence of the courts are again reiterated via secondary legislation, namely in the *Law on Courts* which explicitly states that: "Any form of influence on the independence, impartiality and autonomy of a judge in exercising the judicial function, on any grounds or by any entity is prohibited."[32]

In an effort to secure the institutional independence of the judiciary, Macedonia has followed the model applied by other Southeast European countries, and has established the Judicial Council of the Republic of Macedonia (the Council).[33] The Council is an autonomous and independent judicial body aiming to ensure and guarantee the independence of the judicial branch. According to the *Law on the Judicial Council*, the Council consists of 15 members, of which the President of the Supreme Court of the Republic of Macedonia and the Minister of Justice are *ex officio* members. The judges from amidst their ranks elect eight members of the Council. Additionally, three Council members are elected from amongst minority ethnic communities, respecting the principle of equitable representation of citizens from all communities; three members are elected by Parliament, and a further two members are nominated by the President and subsequently elected by the Parliament.[34] With only eight members of the Council coming from the ranks of judges, the Macedonian Judicial Council can be criticized for leaving the door open for political pressure. Furthermore, the Commission responsible for conducting the elections of members of the Council from the ranks of judges, consists of a president, a deputy president, two members and their deputies, all coming from the ranks of the Council,[35] so in theory, none of the Commission members need come from the judicial branch at all.

The Council's main competences are defined in Article 31 of the *Law on the Judicial Council*. These competences include the election and dismissal of judges, presidents of courts and lay judges, the evaluation of work and disciplinary proceedings against judges and the nomination of two judges to the Constitutional Court of the Republic of Macedonia from the ranks of judges. Finally, they are responsible for giving a bi-annual decision on the number of necessary judicial positions for the courts.

The Council holds the key role in the procedure foreseen by the law for the selection of professional judges. The procedure differs with respect to first instance court judges and judges of higher courts. For the former, the Council establishes bi-annually, a number of new positions. Following this decision, vacancy announcements are published in the *Official Gazette* and in daily newspapers. Candidates for positions in first instance courts are required to have completed the initial training by the Academy for Training of Judges and Prosecutors (the Academy) and have applied for the position in response to the public advertisement. The latter, i.e. the judges of higher courts (Appellate Court, Supreme Court), are not required to complete the initial training at the Academy. They are, however, required to have a minimum of five years of working experience in legal matters obtained after the bar exam, as well as the capability to conduct tasks of a managing nature, a commitment to undertake extra work when performing their judicial duty by participating in procedures to resolve the backlog of cases, etc. The Council decides upon the election of a judge by a two-third majority of the total number of members of the Council.

Courts are funded from the Court Budget and part of the State Budget, which provides funding for the Judicial Council, the Court Budget Council and the Academy. The Court Budget is supposed to ensure "a stable, long-term, equal and adequate financing of the judicial branch, with the aim of ensuring its constitutional and legal independence and autonomy."[36] By 2016, the percentage of financial resources allocated to the courts by the Budget of the Republic of Macedonia is set to amount to at least 0.8% of the Gross Domestic Product, on the basis of the fiscal policy and the main parameters for estimation of the earnings and the costs.

The *Law on Judges' Salaries* governs the remuneration of judges.[37] The salaries are calculated both on the basis of the average net income in the country during the previous fiscal year, and a coefficient that depends on the complexity of a judge's tasks and his workload. The average net salary in August 2014 was 21,483 Macedonian Denar, which is approximately 352 Euros.[38] Since the coefficient for judges' salaries varies between 2.8 and 3.7 depending on the type of court in which the judge works and performance of the judge, it can be concluded that judges are adequately financially independent.

However, despite the institutional, administrative, ethnic and economic guarantees of independence provided for the judiciary in Macedonia, recent events raise serious concern over how independent it actually is. Over the past couple of years the Macedonian judiciary has been involved in several proceedings on cases of corruption, tax evasion and other financial crimes against individuals close to the opposition political parties. One of the opposition leaders, Ljube Boškovski, leader of the political party United for Macedonia, has been sentenced to seven years in prison for illegal campaign financing. These proceedings were marked by long and unwarranted periods of detention, followed by harsh prison sentences. Moreover, court proceedings led to the shutting down of the A1 TV station and three daily newspapers,[39] while several journalists who were known for being critical of the government were imprisoned.[40] A comparative analysis of two field surveys conducted in 2009 and 2012 by the Skopje based Institute for Democracy concluded that Macedonian citizens have not seen a significant improvement in the functioning of the judiciary in the three-year period.[41] Thus, the question is: Does the current system of judicial independence encourage formalistic rather than independent decision-making among Macedonian judges?

The respondents interviewed for this study believe that judicial independence has actually made visible progress, mostly due to the Constitutional and legal amendments that placed the election of judges and prosecutors in the hands of independent bodies rather than the National Parliament. The overall perception however, is that the "judiciary is still politicized and in the hands of the political parties."[42] As one NGO activist answered "the problem is that the Ministry of Finance holds the Judicial Council on a financial 'tight leash.' In this way, independence cannot be provided."[43] Similarly the 2015 EU Progress Report on Macedonia reports "backsliding"[44] in terms of judiciary independence. According to the Report, all achievements of the last decade's reforms are effectively undermined by real and potential political interference in the work of the judiciary.

An OSCE survey, conducted among 421 (out of 650) judges in Macedonia, showed that almost half of all judges face external pressures in their work (43%).[45] Asked about the sources of pressure, 19% of the surveyed judges pointed to the representatives of the executive branch of government, who "to a large extent" attempt to influence the work of judges. Every seventh judge surveyed thinks that judges face pressure from the political parties "to a large extent" (14%), while 5% of respondents said that judges are "to a large extent" pressured by judges of a higher rank. Asked whether the judges are independent while presiding and adjudicating, nearly a quarter of all surveyed judges disagree (23% of the judges). Finally, a large majority of surveyed judges, 66%, disagree that the Judicial Council successfully protects the independence of the judiciary, and an additional 66% disagree that the Judicial Council is an independent body.

The main problem in the Macedonian judicial system is that it has failed to create conditions of personal independence of judges, as the Judicial Council was unsuccessful in building its integrity using the existing legislative framework. As a consequence, indirect political pressure, judgments that are unusually expedited in terms of outcome or speed, as well as the content of judgments, particularly in high profile or politically sensitive cases raise serious concern regarding the independence of the judiciary in Macedonia.

Kosovo

In Kosovo, the independence of the Courts is guaranteed by the Constitution and the *Law on Courts.*[46] Article 102(2) of the Constitution stipulates that "the judicial power is unique, independent, fair, apolitical and impartial" clarifying in Article 102(4) that "judges shall be independent and impartial in exercising their functions."[47] Independence is further regulated and protected by Constitutional and legal provisions related to the recruitment, qualifications and appointments of judges and prosecutors. The *Law on Courts* affirms judicial independence in Article 3 by requiring that, "during the exercising of their function and taking decisions [judges] shall be independent, impartial, uninfluenced in any way by natural or legal persons, including public bodies." Article 34 elaborates the duties of judges in more detail adding that Judges shall act objectively, impartially and independently.

The Constitution and the respective laws allocate a high number of competences to the executive in relation to the judicial branch. Namely, the President of Kosovo is vested with limited competences regarding the appointment and dismissal of the President of the Supreme Court, judges and lay judges as well as Chief Prosecutors, prosecutors and judges of the Constitutional Court based on proposals from the Kosovo Judicial Council (KJC), the Kosovo Prosecutorial Council (KPC) and the Assembly of Kosovo.[48] In addition, the Government guides and oversees the work of administrative bodies in Kosovo, which includes all staff working in the judicial system.[49]

The Constitution contains specific provisions for the representation of minority communities in the judicial system.[50] For the Supreme Court, for example, the Constitution requires at least 15%, but at the same time no fewer than three judges from the communities that are not in the majority in Kosovo. The same requirement applies to any Court in Kosovo with appellate jurisdiction, with a minimum of two judges required from the minority communities. Overall, the Constitution also requires that the composition of the judiciary, both at the central and local levels, reflect the ethnic diversity of

Kosovo and internationally recognized principles of gender equality. Yet, judicial personnel from the Serb community remain continuously under-represented in Kosovo's justice-system. Despite the guaranteed representation of Serbs in judicial bodies, only 5.67% of the judicial positions represent minority communities, and only 2.43% of these are from the Serb community.[51]

The Constitution establishes the Kosovo Judicial Council as a key body to ensure the independence and impartiality of the judicial system. The KJC is responsible for ensuring that the Kosovo courts are independent, professional and impartial and fully reflect the multi-ethnic nature of Kosovo, including the principles of gender equality. The KJC is responsible, among other things, for recruiting, proposing candidates for appointment, reappointment to judicial office, transfer, discipline, judicial administration and for developing and overseeing the budget of the judiciary.

The competences of the KJC are elaborated in more detail by the *Law on Kosovo Judicial Council*.[52] The KJC is composed of 13 members: five members are judges elected by the members of the judiciary; four members are elected by deputies of the Assembly, holding seats allocated during the general distribution of seats, whereas at least two of the four must be judges and one must be a member of the Kosovo Chamber of Advocates; two members are elected by the deputies of the Assembly holding reserved or guaranteed seats for the Kosovo Serb community and at least one of these two must be a judge. Finally, two members are elected by the deputies of the Assembly holding reserved or guaranteed seats for other Communities and again at least one of these two must be a judge. Bearing in mind that only five members of the KJC are elected by the judges themselves, it can be concluded that the overall composition of the KJC falls short of international standards, and leaves the room for influence of the Assembly on the independence of the judiciary.

The KJC is responsible for recruiting and proposing candidates for appointment and reappointment to judicial office. Proposals for the appointment of judges are made via an open process. Selections are made based on the merits of the candidates, whilst also adhering to principles of gender equality and the ethnic composition of the respective court's territorial jurisdiction. In this regard the KJC must give preference in its appointment of judges, to members of Communities that are underrepresented in the judiciary, as required by the law.[53] The candidates that fulfill the criteria for election to the office are submitted by the KJC to the President of the Republic, who in turn, appoints them.[54] The President of Kosovo however, is entitled to refuse the appointment or reappointment of the proposed candidate. In this case the President is obliged to provide a written explanation for the refusal to the KJC within 60 days, to which the KJC may propose another candidate, or may again present the refused candidate to the President together with a written justification, at which point the President must appoint the proposed judge.[55] During the 2008 re-appointment procedure during which all judges in Kosovo had to re-apply for their positions, approximately 18.5% of candidates selected by an internationally led process were rejected by the President of the Republic.[56]

Currently, there is an ongoing legal debate regarding the constitutionality of the aforementioned provision, given that the contesting party claims that the mandate of the President is limited to the formal appointment of judges proposed by the KJC, without the right to refuse appointments.

A separate process has been established for the selection and appointment of the Constitutional Court judges.[57] The selection process is handled by a Special Committee established within the Assembly, which then proposes the candidates for the Constitutional Court Judges to the President of Kosovo for formal appointment.[58]

The KJC is responsible for overseeing the preparation and execution of the annual budget for the entire Kosovo judicial system. The judiciary is continuously allocated around 1% of the Kosovo Budget.[59] The budget allocation is among the weakest aspects of the judiciary's independence. While the KJC is independent in proposing and managing its budget, the budget adoption process, which includes both the government and the Assembly, leaves significant room for influence and even revisions of the initially submitted proposals.[60] Despite improvements following the adoption of relevant legislation, and establishment of the KJC, problems regarding judicial independence, and in particular political interference in judicial matters, continue to have a negative impact upon the rule of law and access to justice in Kosovo. Although the existing legislation itself sets a clear path for such interference, mostly through the prevalent non-judicial composition of the KJC and the excessive veto rights of the President of Kosovo in the process of appointment of judges, the potential for informal interference in judicial independence remains particularly problematic. This interference, "stemming primarily from strong family and community connections"[61] is especially difficult to prove, and though the daily newspapers have continuously raised this issue, they have thus far, provided only anecdotal data.

Particularly troubling are attempts at frequent political interference on rulings regarding war crimes in cases, for example in the cases of Klecka[62] and Drenica[63] group. Additionally worrying has been an attempt by the Assembly to investigate the Kiqina case,[64] despite the fact that it had already been through all the steps of the judicial procedure.

In an attempt to provide an immediate remedy for the deficiencies of the domestic legal order, especially when it comes to the war crimes or anti-corruption cases, the international community in Kosovo insisted on raising the jurisdiction and competences of EULEX judges for both criminal and civil proceedings. The *Law on Jurisdiction, Case Selection and Case Allocation of EULEX Judges and Prosecutors* regulates the jurisdiction and competence of EULEX judges over any case investigated or prosecuted by the Special Prosecution Office of the Republic of Kosovo.[65] The Law further defines the circumstances under which EULEX Judges and Prosecutors can be assigned to any case, at any stage of a criminal proceeding, when it is considered necessary to ensure the proper administration of justice. Nevertheless, as learned in an interview with an NGO representative from Kosovo, EULEX has thus far largely failed to improve the rule of law situation in Kosovo, "despite of a couple of investigations against high-level Government officials."[66]

In a nutshell, Kosovo's judicial system is at an early stage of developing a well-functioning justice system. Judicial structures are still prone to political interference,[67] while disputed appointments procedure undermines the activities of the Kosovo Judicial Council.

Serbia

The concrete institutional design for assuring sufficient guarantees for the division of power in Serbia is determined by the Constitution.[68] The Constitution guarantees the division of power into legislative, executive and judiciary. The Serbian Constitution asserts that the relationships between the three branches of power are based on balance and mutual control, while at the same time the judicial power is independent. Hence, the principle of checks and balances, which in parliamentary systems of government characterizes the mutual relationship of the legislative and the executive power, has in the Serbian Constitution been explicitly associated with all three branches of power.

The independence of judges is guaranteed by the Constitution, which prescribes that judges are subordinated only to the Constitution and the law. Pursuant to the Constitution, courts are independent and autonomous in their work and they adjudicate in accordance with the Constitution, laws and other general acts, when stipulated by Law, as well as generally accepted rules of international law and ratified international treaties. The basic principles of judicial independence proclaimed by the Constitution are also confirmed under the provisions of the *Law on Organization of Courts* and the *Law on Judges*.

The *Law on Organization of Courts* prescribes that judicial power is vested in courts and is independent of the legislative and executive powers, and that judicial decisions are binding on all and may not be subject to extrajudicial examination (Article 3.1 and 3.3). Pursuant to the *Law on Organization of Courts*, use of public office, instruments of public information or any public appearance that may unduly influence the course and outcome of legal proceedings is prohibited, as well as any other form of influence on courts and pressure on parties in the proceedings (Article 6).

The *Law on Judges* further elaborates the basic principles stipulated under the Constitution of the Republic of Serbia, and provides that judges are independent and autonomous in their work, that they adjudicate and render judgments in accordance with the Constitution, Law and other general acts, ratified international treaties, and generally accepted rules of international law (Article 1).

The Constitution of the Republic of Serbia and the *Law on Judges* regulate the election and promotion of judges. The number of judges is established pursuant to the "Decision on the Number of Judges in Courts."[69] According to the established number of judges in courts, the High Judicial Council announces the event of the elections to fill the vacancies in the judge's offices.

The provisions of the *Law on Judges* regulate the procedure for the election of judges and the requirements necessary for election (Articles 43–52). A citizen of the Republic of Serbia may be elected as a judge if he or she meets all conditions necessary for employment with government authorities, holds a Law degree, has passed the Bar Exam, and has expertise, competence and worthiness for the judge's office. The High Judicial Council established the criteria and standards for evaluating whether or not the aforementioned requirements have been fulfilled in accordance with the "Decision on the Establishment of Criteria and Standards for Evaluation of Qualification, Competence and Worthiness for Election of Judges and Presidents of Courts."[70] Competence is described as the possession of specific legal knowledge needed to conduct judicial procedures; expertise includes possession of theoretical and practical knowledge necessary to perform judicial functions, while worthiness implies moral qualities that judges should have, and a record of having previously behaved in accordance with these traits. Specific requirements are set for individual court positions: two years of legal practice for a judge at Magistrate Court; three years for the position of judge at the Basic Court; six years for a judge at Higher, Commercial and Higher Magistrate Court; ten years for a judge at the Court of Appeal, Commercial Court of Appeal, and the Administrative Court; and 12 years for the position of a judge at the Higher Cassation Court. The Law excludes discrimination on any grounds within the process of election, promotion and nomination to the office of judge. During the process of election and nomination to the office of judge, the national composition of the population, appropriate representation of members of national minorities and knowledge of professional legal terminology in the language of the national minorities need to be taken into consideration. The High Judicial Council runs the procedure for election by announcing the election of judges, and upon receiving the applications, it gathers opinions and data on the candidates.

Article 147 of the Constitution provides that the National Assembly of the Republic of Serbia shall, upon the proposal of the High Judicial Council, elect a judge who is being elected to the office of judge for the first time for a period of three years. A judge who was elected for the first time *has* to be elected to the permanent office of judge if he/she is graded by the High Judicial Council with having achieved an "exceptionally successful discharge of the duties of a judge" each year during his/her initial three years mandate. Alternatively, a judge who is elected for the first time *may* be elected to the permanent office of judge if he/she is graded with "successful discharge of the duties of judge" during his/her mandate. The criteria for the grading process are established by the High Judicial Council. In accordance with the law, the High Judicial Council alone elects judges to the permanent tenure of office, in the same or another court.

Processes dealing with the "termination of tenure of office" and the dismissal from office constitute an important part of the political independence of a judge's position, since, in theory, they exist to eliminate the risk of arbitrary procedures against "disloyal" judges. The Constitution provides that a judge's tenure shall be terminated at his/her request, upon fulfilling the legal retirement age, or upon dismissal from office for reasons stipulated by law, as well as if he/she is not elected to the permanent office (Article 148). The decision on termination of a judge's office is passed by the High Judicial Council, and the dismissed judge has the right to an appeal before the Constitutional Court.

The *Law on Judges* provides that judges are dismissed from office upon conviction with imprisonment of no less than six months for a criminal offence or for a punishable offence which makes them unworthy to perform the function of a judge, or in the case of a serious disciplinary infringement (Article 62). Additionally, a judge may be dismissed in the case of unprofessional conduct, which is determined according to the criteria and standards for the evaluation of the performance of judges. The initiative for the removal of a judge may be submitted by any person, while the President of the Court, the president of the higher court, the president of the Supreme Court of Cassation, bodies responsible for evaluation of work of judges, the Disciplinary Commission, and the High Judicial Council are entitled to initiate the dismissal procedure. The High Judicial Council establishes the grounds for dismissal and makes a decision in proceedings which are closed to the public. The judge has the right to be immediately notified of the reasons for initiating proceedings, and to be informed about the case, supporting documentation, and the course and outcome of proceedings. The judge has the right to present his/her statements orally before the High Judicial Council. The High Judicial Council must make a reasoned decision within 45 days of the initiation of the procedure, against which the dismissed judge has the right to appeal before the Constitutional Court. The decision of the Constitutional Court is final.

The independence of the Constitutional Court is guaranteed by the Constitutional provisions (Articles 172–174) that concern the process of electing Constitutional Court justices, their immunity, the incompatibility of the judicial function with other functions, as well as the reasons for the termination of the tenure of a Constitutional Court justice.

After the procedural role of the High Judicial Council in the election, promotion, termination of tenure, and dismissal of judges, as elaborated above, we will pause at this point to highlight the impact this body has on a judge's political independence. The High Judicial Council was established with the *Law on the High Judicial Council* in November 2001. The High Judicial Council is an independent and autonomous body that was established to guarantee the political independence of courts and judges.

According to the Constitution, the High Judicial Council has a number of duties: it appoints and relieves judges; it proposes to both the National Assembly a selection of candidates to be elected for the first time, to the post of judge and the election of the President of the Supreme Court of Cassation as well as presidents of courts. It also participates in the proceedings undertaken to terminate the tenure of the President of the Supreme Court of Cassation as well as the presidents of other courts. Further to all of this, it decides on the termination of a judge's tenure without their consent, and approves the detention or arrest of judges during criminal proceedings (Articles 144–154). Additionally, the *Law on the High Judicial Council* provides that this body will propose to the Assembly the candidates for election of judges to the positions of president of various different courts; it decides on the transfer of and appeals of judges, and the rules on the incompatibility of other services and jobs with the judge's office; it appoints juror judges and performs activities of the judicial-administration within its jurisdiction (Article 13). Nonetheless, certain activities of the judiciary's administration—i.e. court security, proposals of the amount and structure of budgetary funding and its subsequent distribution to courts, coupled with the supervision of its spending—have remained in the exclusive jurisdiction of the Ministry of Justice, or as divided competences between the Ministry of Justice and the Council. Furthermore, the decision about the number of court personnel, contrary to the National Judicial Strategy, has been transferred to the jurisdiction of the Ministry.

The High Judicial Council has 11 members and is composed of the President of the Supreme Court of Cassation, the Minister responsible for justice and the President of the Judicial Committee of the National Assembly as members *ex officio*, and an additional eight members elected by the National Assembly.[71] Elected members include six judges holding the posts of permanent judges, of which one must be from the territory of the autonomous provinces; and two respected and prominent lawyers, of which one must be an attorney, and the other a professor at a law faculty.

The *Law on Judges* guarantees the independence of the judges' function by ensuring their financial independence (Article 4.2). The salary of judges is established according to the *Law on Judges* based on the ratios set in the *Law on the Budget*, which establishes the basis for calculating the amount and payment of salaries for public servants. The net amount of salaries for judges ranges from 658 euros for the judge of a Misdemeanor Court as the lowest, to 1,315 euros for the judge at the supreme court of cassation as the highest. Although there are no available data for the average salaries of other participants in court proceedings (attorneys), we might compare judges' salaries with the Republic average net salaries of public servants, who make only 309.71 euro. From this data it can be assumed that the prerequisites for the economic independence of judges are met.

However, the impression remains that despite the conditions set for the economic independence of judges, and an impressive legislative framework described above, Serbian courts are only independent and autonomous in law, while in practice the courts' functions are restricted by "political influence, inefficiency, nepotism, cronyism and corruption,"[72] as effectively summed by the Bertelsmann Index. This is perhaps best illustrated by the HJC's controversial decision taken on 16 December 2009, when 1531 judges were confirmed to a full time post and another 876 elected for the first time. However, at the same time the HJC dismissed 837 judges—almost one third of judiciary- in a non-transparent and non-contradictory procedure without providing any explanation for its action.[73] The Serbian association of judges claimed such general election of judges unconstitutional, while the underlying intention for this action is described as "politically motivated"[74] and yet "another partisan purge."[75] Finally, the Serbian Ombudsperson claimed in his 2012 opinion that: "HJC [...] has over a longer period of time worked in a manner that has given rise to grave doubts about the lawfulness and regularity i.e. legitimacy of the work of this authority."[76]

The impression about the questionable level of actual independence of judiciary is reiterated in a 2012 Survey conducted by the Fund for Open Society, whereby "only 2% of Serbian citizens and 9% of the political elite"[77] considered the Serbian judiciary to be independent from political influence. The reason for the absence of judicial independence can be found in the "disorganization, lack of knowledge, lack of integrity, and fear"[78] of the sitting judges. It is crucial to analyze the cause of the alleged "fear" among members of the judiciary. According to Vasilić, it is precisely the political elites that exercise the pressure on the judiciary.[79] During the previous government, led by the Democratic Party until 2012, political influence was exercised mostly through the implementation of the "unprepared, unprofessional, politically motivated and premature"[80] judicial reform[81] and concretely via the "politicized process of re-election of judges."

However, even after the 2012 change of government, which occurred mostly due to the prevalent statewide corruption, "shocking cases of clear interference of politicians in the work of courts and prosecutors"[82] are still reported. The Serbian Renewal Party led government has continued the same practice of control over judiciary, although using a different set of soft tools. The current tactics mostly rely on a blunt transfer of instructions directed at the judiciary made by the "political elite, powerful individuals or social groups"[83] through instrumentalized media outlets under the umbrella of a "political will."[84] It has become a common practice for government officials to comment on trials, announce arrests, and set detention without a previous court decision.[85]

Moreover, against the constitutional principle of checks and balances, in practice "the whole power is shifted towards the executive branch of government,"[86] and more precisely, to a handful of high ranking political figures. This effectively brings into question the ability of the judiciary to hold the executive accountable. The ability of courts to hold the elites accountable can best be traced by following the recent stream of court proceedings against high profiled political figures, belonging both to the current opposition and ruling coalition alike. These include the anti-corruption cases against the customs director Mihalj Kertes,[87] minister of agriculture Goran Knežević,[88] minister of defense Prvoslav Davinić,[89] minister of transport Marija Rašeta Vukosavljevic,[90] minister of environment Oliver Dulić,[91] minister of traffic and telecommunications Ratko Marčetić,[92] minister of health Leposava

Milićević,[93] minister of agriculture Živanko Radovančev,[94] minister of justice Dragoljub Janković,[95] minister of tourism Slobodan Čerović,[96] commissionaire for refugees Bratislava Buba Morina,[97] vice-governor of the Central Bank Dejan Simić,[98] two bishops of the Serbian Orthodox Church Pachomius and Hilarion,[99] the entire family of the former President Slobodan Milošević,[100] or the "controversial" businessmen Jezdimir Vasiljević,[101] Predrag Ranković Peconi,[102] Stanko Subotić Cane.[103] All of the aforementioned trials ended either in the acquittal of the indicted persons, or the dismissal of charges against them due to an obsolescence of the case. In effect, no member of the either former or present political or economic elite in Serbia has thus far been held accountable by the judiciary. Finally, the recent comment of Serbian Minister of Justice's assistant, in which he refers to the judges as "a group of 2,000 irresponsible people"[104] clearly illustrates the efforts of the executive to limit the extent of judicial independence.

Montenegro

The rule of law is introduced in Article 1 of the Constitution of Montenegro as the fundamental state value.[105] Article 11 defines the traditional regulation of power, following the principle of the division of powers into the legislative, executive and judicial bodies, whereby the courts exercise judicial power. Article 118 explicitly guarantees the autonomy and independence of courts and states that the court shall rule on the basis of the Constitution, laws, and confirmed and published international agreements.

The independence of judges is guaranteed via Article 121, which stipulates that judicial service shall be permanent and that the duties of a judge shall cease at his/her own request, when s/he fulfills the age requirements for pension or if the judge has been sentenced to an unconditional imprisonment sentence. The transfer of a judge against his or her will is only possible by decision of the Judicial Council, or in the case of court restructuring. Furthermore, pursuant to Article 122, judges enjoy functional immunity and shall not be held responsible for the opinions they express or their vote at the time of a court's decision. Finally, in proceedings initiated because of a criminal offense made in the performance of judicial duty, the judge shall not be detained without the approval of the Judicial Council.

The implementation of the constitutional articles pertaining to the judiciary required adoption of appropriate laws, by-laws, and regulations, as well as the development of new institutional mechanisms, and increased the level of attention dedicated to the training and education of all stakeholders in judicial institutions. The most important laws adopted include the *Law on Courts,*[106] the *Law on the Judicial Council,*[107] the *Law on the State Prosecutor's Office,*[108] and the *Law on Education in Judicial Bodies,*[109] which will all now be scrutinized in more detail.

The *Law on Courts* regulates the establishment, organization and jurisdiction of courts, the conditions for selection of judges and lay judges, judicial administration as well as the courts' structure, and other issues of importance regarding their proper and timely functioning. Article 3 of the Law reiterates the independence of the courts by declaring that the judge shall decide "individually and independently."

The Judicial Council of Montenegro is responsible for ensuring the independence, accountability, responsibility and competence of the judiciary. The Council is composed of ten members of whom five are elected and dismissed from among the judges by the Judges Conference, which is composed of all Montenegrin judges and court presidents. The Minister of Justice sits as a member *ex officio* on the Council, while the Parliament nominates two deputies. In addition, the Council includes outside representation consisting of distinguished lawyers or by law professors. The President of Montenegro prepares a list of at least four eminent jurists for the election of members of the Judicial Council and delivers it for the opinion of the Supreme Court. However, the Law does not provide that the opinion of the Supreme Court is binding, which effectively leaves the door open to the President's influence over the work of the Council.

Article 23 stipulates the various competences of the Judicial Council, in addition to the responsibilities stipulated in the Constitution. These are to:

1) investigate complaints about judges;
2) decide on the disciplinary responsibility of judges;
3) give opinions on draft regulations in the field of justice;
4) provide implementation, sustainability and uniformity of the Judicial Information system;
5) implement educational programs and training related to judicial function in cooperation with the Prosecutorial Council;
6) investigate complaints against judges; and
7) propose the number of judges and other employees in the courts.

Chapter IV of the *Law on the Judicial Council* provides in-depth procedures for the election, promotion and transfer of judges. In addition to the general conditions for eligibility for election stipulated in the *Law on Courts*, the Judicial Council takes into account the following skills of candidates for the first election of a judge: professional knowledge, work experience and performance; capacity, which is judged through academic written works and other professional activities; professional ability based on previous career results, including participation in organized forms of training. Alongside assessing their work capability and capacity to analyze legal problems, the Judicial Council also assesses the candidate's ability to perform impartially, conscientiously, diligently, decisively, and responsibly the duties of the office for which he or she is being considered; their communication abilities; relations with colleagues, conduct out of office, integrity and reputation; and managerial experience and qualifications, in relation to the positions of court president. The decision on appointments is made by the Judicial Council after an interview with the candidate.

The Law differentiates between consensual and nonconsensual re-assignment of judges. Namely, judges may be assigned by the Judicial Council to perform judicial service, with their consent, at another court for a period of up to six months during a calendar year, in the event that regular performance of duties in the court to which the judge is being assigned has been called into question due to the disqualification of a judge or his/her inability to attend to his/her duties or due to other justified reasons (Article 30). A judge may only be the subject of a temporary or permanent assignment without his consent in the case of the reorganization of the court structure. The Judicial Council decides about the cessation of the judge's function based on the reasons stipulated in the Constitution and other legal acts. Finally, the Judicial Council decides concerning the immunity of judges in cases when a competent court finds that there are reasons for the judge to be detained.

It is interesting to note how due to its determination to start accession negotiations, the Government of Montenegro decided in December 2011, to revisit the old Action Plan for the Reform of the Judiciary. Based on the screening of the actual implementation of the 2007 Action Plan, the "Commission for the Implementation of the Action Plan" concluded that only 7.5% of the proposed reforms were not implemented during the five-year cycle. In order to implement the remaining measures, the Government adopted a revised *Action Plan for the Implementation of the Strategy for Reform of the Judiciary.*[110] The revised Action Plan amended a number of measures on the independence and efficiency of the judiciary and changed the relevant deadlines. Additionally, the Constitutional Issues and Legislative Committee of the Parliament of Montenegro, at a meeting held on 28 May 2012, proposed long awaited Amendments to the Constitution of Montenegro.[111] Some of the Constitutional Amendments concerned the need to reduce political influence on the appointment of high-level judicial officials through more transparent and merit-based procedures, and where the parliament is involved, the introduction of substantial qualified majority thresholds. Amendment III specifically changes the competences of Parliament in the procedure of electing and releasing from duty the President of the Supreme Court and the President of the Constitutional Court. According to this Amendment, the election and release from duty of the President of the Supreme Court and the President of the Constitutional Court should fall under the competence of the Parliament, which is not in line with the requirement for de-politicization of the election of judicial and constitutional judicial officials. Amendment IX prescribes that the Judicial Council will have ten members, including the President of the Supreme Court, four judges, two renowned lawyers elected by the Parliament, two renowned lawyers appointed by the President of Montenegro and the minister in charge of judicial affairs. This solution aims to ensure a balance in the number of the members of the Judiciary Council who are judges and those who are not, by fixing their ratio at five of each.

The adoption of these amendments has been praised by the Commission as "a strong signal that Montenegro is able to achieve a large political consensus on key rule of law related reforms, which have been highlighted by the EU as a priority in the accession process,"[112] while the amendments have been addressed as "fundamental to an effective judicial system."[113]

However, while the constitutional amendments introduced in 2013 strengthened the independence of the judiciary by reducing political influence on the appointment of high-level judicial and prosecutorial officials, full implementation of these fundamental principles is still not achieved.

Accountability of the judiciary

Human capacity for failure is inherent, deeply rooted and frequent. In order to deal with individual and systematic failures in a democratic society, judicial independence and accountability need to act as two sides of the same coin. History has taught us repeatedly that even the most lucid and moderate of rulers can transform into autocratic tyrants. Therefore, any sovereign should be held accountable to another authority that can act independently within a system of checks and balances. Given that the judges are provided with real independence in performing their core function, they are primarily accountable to legal norms, but more importantly there is a need for a systematic mechanism for the evaluation of their performance, followed by the implementation of appropriate measures in the case of corruption, or an erroneous decision. Namely, it takes an effective system of checks and balances between judicial independence and judicial accountability to assure citizens of the impartiality of the adjudication process. On a theoretical level, as opposed to the normative, there are two approaches for dealing with judicial accountability: "one in which [judicial accountability] is assumed to be exogenously given and its (economic) consequences are analyzed and another, in which [it] is the endogenous variable to be explained by other factors."[114] Finally, to zoom in on the field of judicial accountability we see it as a condition in which judges are constrained by "external means and by internal norms."[115]

Besides "hard accountability" such as mechanisms of selection, promotion and disciplinary control, Piana argues that judicial actors are also subject to "a wide array of soft accountabilities which are compromised of the obligation of being transparent to the public, responsive to colleagues (in particular senior judges) and morally honest."[116] Although she considers these soft mechanisms of accountability to be more powerful and effective than the hard ones might be, soft accountability is inherent exclusively in mature, firm and consistent legal cultures, which are unfortunately, as yet, still to develop in the Western Balkans.

For this reason, this study borrows and subsequently analyzes five types of judicial accountabilities, following Mark Bovens who proposes the following:

1) legal,
2) administrative,
3) political,

4) social, and
5) professional accountability of judges.[117]

Administrative accountability ensures the principle of judicial efficiency in terms of time and money, and as such this study will deal with it separately. This leaves out three types of accountability which will be scrutinized closely in this section: institutional, which refers to the appointment, selection, promotion and disciplinary control over judiciary, social accountability exercised by the civil society "watchdogs," and finally professional accountability exercised by peer judges.

Bosnia and Herzegovina

Accountability of judges is defined in the *Law on High Judicial and Prosecutorial Council.*[118] Article 17 states the Council's competence to receive complaints against judges and prosecutors; conduct disciplinary proceedings; determine disciplinary liability, and impose disciplinary measures on, or suspensions of judges, lay judges and reserve judges; decide upon appeals in disciplinary proceedings; and decide upon issues of incompatibility of other functions performed by judges. It is also competent to decide upon the temporary assignment or transfer of judges to another court; to set criteria for the performance evaluations of judges and prosecutors and finally, to issue codes of ethics for judges. Bearing in mind already mentioned fragmentation of state and institutions in Bosnia and Herzegovina it is of particular importance to mention that the wording of Article 19 creates an obligation for all courts, governmental bodies, as well as all judges and employees of courts to comply with requests by the Council for information, documents, and other materials related to the realization of the competencies of the Council.

The disciplinary liability of a judge is regulated in Chapter VI of the Law wherein an exhaustive list of disciplinary offenses for judges is envisaged.[119] The list includes *inter alia*: violations of the duty of impartiality; acting with bias or prejudice due to a party's race, colour, sex, religion, ethnic background, national origin, sexual orientation or social and economic status. Other offences include: the violation of the obligation to exhibit proper behaviour towards parties in a proceeding; disclosure of confidential information arising in the judicial function; corruption; exploiting his or her position as a judge in order to obtain unjustified advantages; the neglect of, or careless exercise of official duties; issuing decisions in patent violation of the law or persistent and unjustified violation of procedural rules. Further sanctioned are: unjustified delays in issuing decisions or any other act related to the exercise of judicial functions, or any other repeated disregard of the duties of the judicial function; being sentenced to imprisonment for a crime; and failure to fulfil any mandatory training obligations or any other obligations imposed by law. Accountability for any of the abovementioned disciplinary offences is decided regardless of the intent or negligence of the liable judge, but bearing in mind the principle of proportionality. The Council may enact one or more of the following disciplinary measures: a written warning which shall not be made public, public reprimand, reduction in salary, temporary or permanent reassignment to another court, demotion of a judge, or removal from office. As a separate measure the Council may order that a judge participate in rehabilitation programs, counselling, or professional training.[120]

The Council regulates the formation and operation of the disciplinary bodies. Disciplinary proceedings are conducted by the First Disciplinary Panel, and the Second Instance Disciplinary Panel serves as the Panel of Appeal. Members of the First and Second Instance Disciplinary Panels are appointed for a two-year term by the President of the Council. Both panels are independently able to adjudicate on disciplinary liability and the imposition of disciplinary measures. In the first instance the Panel is composed of three members, at least two of whom are members of the Council. Appeals on the decisions of the First Instance Disciplinary Panel are decided by the Second Instance Disciplinary Panel, which is composed of three members of the Council. It may confirm, reject or alter the decision of disciplinary measures imposed by the First Instance Disciplinary Panel. Once initiated, disciplinary proceedings can last up to a year, depending on the complexity and the total number of disciplinary cases under consideration by the Committee in that period. In a third instance, a judge who has been removed by decision of the Council may appeal to the Court of Bosnia and Herzegovina solely on the grounds of material violation of the procedures and/or erroneous application of the law during the disciplinary proceedings.

Furthermore, within the Council, the Office of the Disciplinary Counsel performs prosecutorial functions for allegations concerning the misconduct of judges in accordance with the Rules of Procedure of the Council.[121] The Office of the Disciplinary Counsel acts upon the receipt of a complaint or its own initiative. It investigates allegations of misconduct against judges and initiates cases for disciplinary violations before the disciplinary panels of the Council. The Office of the Disciplinary Counsel is led by the Chief Counsel, an individual of high moral standing who either is a judge or prosecutor. The Chief Counsel of the Disciplinary Counsel is elected by the Council. Disciplinary procedures led by the Counsel guarantee fairness, transparency,[122] and confidentiality.[123]

During the disciplinary proceedings, the Counsel may request that the judge be suspended from active duty. Suspension is required in any case where the judge or prosecutor is in custody. The request is decided upon by the First Instance Disciplinary Council, while the appeals of decisions relating to suspensions are made to the Second Instance Disciplinary Panel of the Council. Approximately 1,200 complaints are received on a yearly basis by the Counsel.[124] Most of them were dismissed and a total of 80 disciplinary measures were issued during the previous period. A total of 6 judges were dismissed as a measure of disciplinary sanction.

Additionally, the codes of ethics[125] for judges and prosecutors deal with the fundamental standards of ethical conduct in Bosnia and Herzegovina. The purpose of these codes is to assist judges and prosecutors when faced with ethical and professional dilemmas, and to help the executive and legislative authorities, as well as the public better understand and support the judiciary.

Kosovo

The Kosovo Judicial Council (KJC) is the institution, which evaluates and disciplines both the sitting and lay judges. Pursuant to article 43 of the *Law on the Kosovo Judicial Council* "[t]he Office of Disciplinary Counsel shall be established as a separate and independent body that serves both the Kosovo Judicial Council and the Kosovo Prosecutorial Council. With respect to the judicial system, the Counsel shall be responsible for investigating alleged misconduct of judges and lay judges and presenting the evidence and the case supporting disciplinary action for misconduct to the Disciplinary Committee."[126] The Office of Disciplinary Counsel is guaranteed independence in administrating its functions. It is responsible for investigating judges or lay judges when there is a reasonable basis to believe that misconduct may have occurred, and for making recommendations and presenting the evidence supporting disciplinary action to the Disciplinary Committee. Any natural or legal person may file a complaint to initiate investigation against a judge. Alternatively, the Office of Disciplinary Counsel may initiate the investigation on its own initiative, when there is a reasonable basis to believe that a judge or lay judge may have engaged in misconduct. A charge of misconduct against either a judge or lay judge can be for any of the following: negligence in performing, a failure to perform, or abuse of judicial functions; failure to perform judicial functions independently and impartially; and violation of the applicable code of ethics.

In a preliminary proceeding the Office of Disciplinary Counsel investigates all matters referred to it, and determines whether recommendations of disciplinary action should be presented to the standing committee of the KJC, namely the Disciplinary Committee. The Office of Disciplinary Counsel shall recommend to the Disciplinary Committee of the Council the initiation of disciplinary proceedings against a judge or lay judge on the basis of a conducted investigation. The Disciplinary Committee may suspend a judge or lay-judge with pay during any period of investigation or during the disciplinary proceedings.[127]

Pursuant to article 37 of the *Law on the Kosovo Judicial Council*, the Disciplinary Committee may: impose either a reprimand or a reprimand coupled with a directive to take corrective actions; a temporary reduction of salary by up to 50%, and finally, propose the removal of a judge or lay judge from office. The appellate body that oversees the disciplinary proceedings is the KJC. In 2014 the Disciplinary Committee of the Kosovo Judicial Council received a total of 19 final reports by the Office of the Disciplinary Counsel, and initiated and subsequently conducted *ex officio* two disciplinary procedures by the KJC. During the review of these reports the Disciplinary

Committee imposed 7 reprimands, 1 reprimand with instruction for corrective action, 2 decisions for temporary salary reduction to 50% of monthly pay, and 11 decisions for release from responsibility.[128]

In addition, the KJC established the Regulation on the Evaluation of Performance of Judges,[129] and appointed members of the Committee for the evaluation of the performance of judges. The Committee consists of 11 members and three deputy members. The Committee regularly evaluates all permanently appointed judges every three years, while in addition it evaluates the performance of the first time elected judges, six months prior to the decision on their permanent appointment is made. The Committee assesses the personal integrity and general professional abilities of a judge, their legal and technical abilities, and their professional commitment.[130] Court presidents and judges in leading positions are additionally evaluated for their organizational, managerial and leadership skills.[131]

According to the latest available data the Evaluation Committee evaluated the performance of 88 judges. This evaluation process led to the recommendations proposing the reappointment of 87 judges, each with a three-year mandate, except for one judge "who was not recommended from the President's Office due to his low performance."[132]

It is important to reiterate that one of the main competences of the earlier described EULEX Mission in Kosovo is to assist Kosovo authorities in further developing and strengthening an independent judiciary, police and customs service in line with the Europe's best practices. During this process the Mission plays an important role in mentoring and monitoring in the area of rule of law, thus strengthening the judicial accountability benchmark. According to the latest extension of the Mission's mandate in June 2014, it would not take on new court cases and would gradually hand over competencies to the Kosovo judicial system, with aim to end it's mandate in June 2016.

Macedonia

Accountability of judges in Macedonia is established through the *Law on the Judicial Council*, the *Law on Judges*, and a number of relevant pieces of secondary legislation, including the Code of Judicial Ethics, the Rulebook regarding the Procedure for Disciplinary Responsibility of the Judges, the Rulebook on procedure and the manner of establishing unprofessional and conduct in bad faith of the Judicial Function, Rulebook on Disciplinary Responsibility, Court Book of Rules, and Rulebook on Evaluation and Audit of the Work of the Judges.

The Council is the key actor in maintaining judges' accountability due to its broad competences which range from: the monitoring and evaluation of the work of the judges; deciding on the disciplinary accountability of the judges; decisions to revoke the immunity of a judge; to deciding upon requests for approving detention for a judge; and acting upon complaints by citizens and legal Entities on the work of the judges and the courts.[133] From its own ranks the Council nominates a Disciplinary Commission consisting of five members which conducts disciplinary procedures against judges, upon the receipt of a request to institute a disciplinary procedure by a member of the Council, the President of the court, the President of a higher court or by the general session of the Supreme Court of the Republic of Macedonia.

Disciplinary liability of a judge may be triggered in any of the following circumstances: failure to respect the specified schedule for acting upon cases; obstruction of the supervision of the judicial proceedings by a higher instance court; for indecent and undignified behavior in public; failure to wear the judicial robe; the reception of gifts and other benefits related to the exercise of judicial office and taking part in partisan or political activities. Liability can also be triggered if the judge exercises another public office or function that creates a conflict of interest with their judicial role; causes severe disruption to court relations, or finally; fails to fulfill their mentor obligations towards assistants.

Judges can also be sanctioned for poor time management if during one calendar year they conduct court procedures inefficiently and are unpunctual, or when they fail to meet procedural deadlines in more than five cases. They can also be punished if in the course of one calendar year more than 20% of the total number of his/her resolved cases are revoked, or more than 30% of the total number of his/her resolved cases are modified. Additionally, the court president is dismissed from the presidential function in the case of misuse of office and exceeding official authorizations; illegal and unintended disposal of the funds of the court; failure to exercise, or untimely exercising of the works of the judicial administration; influencing the independence of other judges; violation of the rules governing case assignment; and failure to implement the work program.[134]

In a preliminary proceeding, the Disciplinary Commission submits a report which contains a proposal, stating the grounds for the request to the Council, which in turn decides to institute or to suspend a disciplinary procedure. It consists of a hearing in front of a Commission, which then forwards its opinion to the Council. Based on the opinion and the discussion at the session of the Council, it may terminate the disciplinary procedure, issue a disciplinary measure adequate to the committed violation, or dismiss the judge due to violation of procedure. A judge is dismissed from office for exercising their position and power either in bad faith, or unprofessionally.[135] Once a judge's responsibility has been determined the Council can issue a written warning, a public reprimand, and a salary deduction that ranges from 15% up to 30% from the monthly salary. Judges can appeal against their dismissal orders, or the disciplinary measures, to the Council for Decisions on Appeals of the Judicial Council, established by the Supreme Court of the Republic of Macedonia.

The existing legislative framework raises two fundamental concerns. First is the dilemma of implementation, namely how the existing laws are being implemented in practice. In its 2013 Progress Report for example, the European Commission has expressed concern regarding the proportionality of the application of disciplinary proceedings by the Judicial Council.[136] Namely, in 2012 only three judges were dismissed by the Council and consequently their dismissal was upheld on appeal, while the number remains similar in previous years—six dismissed judges in 2011, only two in 2010, etc. In contrast, the Council considered 879 complaints filed against judges and courts during 2012, which shows a surprisingly low ratio of disciplinary proceedings ending in the dismissal of judges. The second concern relates to the "predictability" and "precision"[137] of the current legislation governing the disciplining and dismissal of judges, which requires further attention by the lawmakers.

Montenegro

Efforts to ensure the accountability of judges in Montenegro fall within the competence of the Judicial Council of Montenegro. It plays a key role in dismissal of judges and other disciplinary proceedings.[138] The apparent deficiency of the existing legislative framework governing the accountability of the Montenegrin judiciary lies in the fact that it does not establish a mandatory evaluation procedure for judges' performance.

The Law on the Judicial Council prescribes the disciplinary measures applicable to judges in cases of neglectful performance of judicial function or harming the reputation of the judicial function in cases prescribed by law.[139] The *Law on Courts*[140] specifies in more detail what constitutes undue performance, harm to the reputation of judicial function, negligent and unprofessional execution of office of judges and court presidents.[141] The wording of Article 33 of the *Law on Courts* suggests that grounds for disciplinary proceedings can be found in undue performance of the judicial function "for a longer time or in a greater number of cases," and violation of deadlines without "reasonable justification."[142] Closer scrutiny of the aforementioned Article however, uncovers the vagueness of the entire disciplinary proceeding. Namely, it leaves room for arbitrary interpretation of the terms such as the "longer term," or a "greater number of cases," and thus leads towards the uneven implementation of disciplinary measures.

Every natural and legal person is entitled to file a complaint about the work and conduct of a judge. The Judicial Council verifies the allegations with the President of the court where the judge against whom the complaint was filed is working.[143] If the inquiry finds that there are grounds for disciplinary proceedings, the President of the Court forwards the complaint to the Disciplinary Commission of the Judicial Council. The Disciplinary Commission is appointed by the Judicial Council for a period of two years.[144] One thing that harms the independence of this body however is that neither the law nor the Rules of Procedure of the Judicial Council specify the procedure of appointment of the Disciplinary Commission members.[145] After the conclusion of the disciplinary procedure the Disciplinary Commission announces the decision to reject the proposal as unfounded, or to accept the proposal and impose a disciplinary measure, or to terminate the proceedings and refer the case to the Judicial Council. An appeal against the decision of the Disciplinary Committee may be submitted to the Judicial Council by the person who submitted the Proposal or by the person against whom the Proposal was submitted.

The Constitution of Montenegro stipulates that a judge shall be dismissed from office: when convicted for an offense that makes him/her unsuitable to hold judicial office; for incompetent or negligent performance of a judicial function; or, finally, permanent loss of capacity to perform judicial function.[146] Similarly as in the case of disciplinary responsibility, the procedure for dismissal is prone to arbitrariness due to legislative vagueness. This can best be illustrated by two examples of dismissal of judges based on their negligent performance and unprofessional conduct. In the first case, a judge of the Basic Court in Podgorica was dismissed after it had been established that the judge had failed to take any action in a total of 121 cases.[147] And, only three months later, in the decision on a dismissal of a judge of the Basic Court in Pljevlja due to an unprofessional conduct, it was explained that the judge had failed to act in total of 11 cases.[148] First of all, in these two cases it is not clear on what basis the actions against judges are differentiated in regards to the benchmarks of negligence and unprofessionalism. Second, it is easy to observe significant differences in the number of cases based on which the work of these judges has been assessed as negligent, or unprofessional. Hence, these two terms need to be clearly defined by the lawmakers in the future, in order to avoid arbitrary acts of the disciplinary bodies. An initiative for removal of judges may be submitted by either the President of the Court in which the judge works, the President of an immediately higher court, the Minister of Justice, President of the Supreme Court, or least three members of the Judicial Council. Upon receiving the initiative, the Judicial Council nominates a Commission for Examination of the Conditions for Dismissal (Commission) composed of a Chairperson and two members from amongst its members. The Commission renders a decision on removal of the judge in the first instance. The Judicial Council decides upon the appeal in the first instance, while its decision may be challenged at the Administrative Court which makes the final and executive decision.

As indicated above, Montenegro lacks a system of individual and periodical evaluation of judges. This weakens the control of their accountability and also prevents a fair and transparent system of promotions. According to the Screening Report on Chapters 23 and 24, "[d]isciplinary procedures can only lead to very mild disciplinary sanctions and therefore fail to produce a deterrent effect."[149] Furthermore, the procedural rules for dismissal of judges are vaguely defined, and could even "jeopardise the full right to defence."[150]

Since 2008, when the Disciplinary Commission was instituted, five judges were dismissed, while ten received disciplinary sanctions.[151] Upon closer inspection of the work of the Judicial Council and the Disciplinary Commission in the previous period, we see that these two institutions "interpret differently violations of the rules of procedure—the Commission as an act that is not a disciplinary offense and for which one cannot be held responsible, and the Council as an act that can be qualified as unprofessional performance, and for which a judge can be dismissed."[152] Different scopes of application for provisions and the procedures related to accountability of judges have led to arbitrariness in decision-making and to an unequal treatment of judges. This is why the disciplinary system needs to be reviewed, disciplinary offenses and procedures need to be better specified, while further action to strengthen the principle of proportionality in regards to sanctions is still missing. Moreover, regular evaluation of judges' performance needs to be introduced in order to reinforce the principle of accountability of judiciary.

Serbia

The *Law on Judges* stipulates that the work of all judges and presidents of courts is subject to regular evaluation (Article 32). Evaluation of the performance of judges is enacted on in a procedure that ensures the participation of the judge or the president of the court whose work is being evaluated. Evaluation covers all aspects of the judge's job, namely quantity, quality and commitment to judicial work. Based on the performance ratings—which are "performs judge's office with extreme success"; "successfully performs a judicial function"; and "fails to meet requirements"—the evaluation may result in an election, promotion, mandatory training for the judge or removal from office. The quality of performance of a judge is evaluated on the assessment of their decision-making, the efficiency of case-processing (expressed through the percentage of repealed decisions under legal remedy) and professionalism of their conduct. The quantity is evaluated on the basis of the number of cases that a judge resolves during a year. By taking into account a qualitative evaluation of the work of judges, the evaluation procedures have managed to avoid the trap of over-quantification, but still it remains unclear if they take into consideration criteria such as the complexity of cases and other specific circumstances, such as court location and human resources. The evaluation of judges of lower courts is conducted by Councils established in courts of a directly higher instance. The High Judicial Council evaluates the work of presidents of the courts and decides on complaints. Evaluation of permanent judges is conducted once every three years, while the performance of judges elected for the first time is conducted each year.

The *Law on Judges* introduces the concept of accountability for judges as well as the usage of disciplinary measures, regulates what constitutes an infringement and what sanctions can be applied. It also regulates the conduct of disciplinary proceedings and the bodies for conducting disciplinary proceedings. The High Judicial Council plays an important role in the disciplinary procedures against judges via the *Rulebook on Disciplinary Proceedings and Disciplinary Accountability of Judges* (Article 93.3). It elects the members of the Disciplinary Commission, a working standing-body of the High Judicial Council. Members of the Disciplinary Commission are appointed from among judges. The prescribed disciplinary sanctions that may be imposed by the Disciplinary Commission are public reprimand, salary reduction of up to 50% for a period not exceeding one year, and prohibition of advancement in service for a period of up to three years. The judge against whom the disciplinary proceedings are conducted has the right to an appeal before the High Judicial Council, which makes the final decision.

Last but not least, external complaint mechanisms to channel public mistrust of the work of the judiciary are important. Besides the competent judicial authority, litigants and other participants in legal proceedings have the right to file a complaint to the High Personnel Council on the performance of judges if they think that there is any kind of unauthorized influence on the course and outcome of the proceedings. Although internal rules and norms establish efficient mechanisms for holding judicial officers accountable in Serbia, a number of NGO "watchdogs" scrutinize and monitor daily the work of the judiciary, thus enhancing the standards in the field of accountability of judges. Some of these include the Belgrade Centre for Human Rights, the Youth Initiative for Human Rights, the Yugoslav Committee of Lawyers, etc. One further recommendation is that the Ombudsman institutions should also be made competent to receive external complaints against the judiciary made by the civil society.

Accountability is further guaranteed by issues of criminal and civil liability and the professional discipline of judges. Restrictions related to the accountability of judges are provided in the Constitution regarding the protection of judges in the exercise of their office. Namely, a judge may not be held accountable for his/her expressed opinion in the process of judicial decision making, except in cases of criminal offence or violation of a law by a judge (Article 151), more, broader, rights regarding judges' immunity are provided for under the *Law on Judges* (Article 5). On the other hand, a judge may not hold office in legislative or executive bodies, may not be a member of a political party, engage in any paid public or private work, or offer paid legal services or advice.

Judges' accountability is further fostered through guarantees of their non-transferability.[153] The *Law on Judges* elaborates non-transferability in more detail by stipulating that a judge can be transferred to another court, another state agency, institution or international organization in the field of justice only upon his/her written consent (Article 19). Exceptionally, the judge may be moved for a period not longer than one year to another court without consent in the event of termination or suspension of the court for which he/she was elected based on the decision of the High Judicial Council (Article 20).

The promotion of a judge implies the election of the judge to a court of a higher rank, regardless of the type of court. Apart from the prescribed general requirements and necessary experience in the legal profession, the basic criterion for election to the office of a higher-ranking judge is their performance, which is evaluated. During the evaluation of candidates, additional standards are considered: membership in a selected or arbitration court, published professional papers, presentations at national or international expert meetings, participation in the training of judges, academic qualifications, as well as computer literacy and knowledge of foreign languages.

Since 2012 only two judges have been dismissed from office, while one judge was sanctioned following disciplinary procedures in 2013 and punished with a salary reduction of 40% for a period of one year.[154] Bearing in mind the ongoing "allegations of corruption in the judiciary,"[155] noted also in the European Commission Progress Report, it is striking to observe the low number of disciplinary procedures against judges in Serbia. Therefore, the key, outstanding issue remaining in order to secure the accountability of judges is the more systematic application of the existing disciplinary rules.

Efficiency of the judiciary

Despite the fact that independence and accountability are often viewed as the founding values of the modern judiciary, recent trends point towards the necessity for the addition of efficiency of judicial administration as another pillar of the functional justice system. Traditional judicial bureaucracy which relied on complex formal procedures neglected the practical needs of the citizens for efficient and effective justice. In response, over the past three decades, the role of the modern liberal democratic state has been influenced by the increasing demands of taxpayers and voters for a more efficient and less expensive public administration.[156] Inevitably, the development of more responsive, modernized, and efficient public bodies influenced the organizational structure of judicial administration. Apart from the growing public dissatisfaction and increased media exposure, equally important for the establishment of a more efficient judiciary has been the technological progress and computerization at the end of the 1980s, which introduced new possibilities for case management and transparency of the work of courts. Old proverbs such as *est mola tarda dei, verum molit illa minutim* [the mills of the gods are late to grind, but they grind small], or *pravda je spora ali dostižna* [justice is slow but attainable], were thus, no longer true. Rather, justice delayed became justice denied.

In practical terms, liberal democratic governments became increasingly aware of the need for more efficient judicial proceedings, and established independent committees with the goal to assess the "reasonable time" trial expectations. The 1996 Woolf Report in England highlighted the "organisational barriers to justice and the inequalities faced by many parties who had no recourse to justice because of the costs of lengthy and inefficient litigation."[157] The Leemhuis Committee report in the Netherlands addressed the problem of "organisational barriers through failures of the judicial organisation to limit backlogs growing in the courts and inefficient organization."[158]

The legal foundation for the efficiency of judicial administration in international law is famously set in the Article 6(1) of the European Convention on Human Rights. It reads that "[i]n the determination of his civil rights and obligations or of any criminal charge against him, everyone is entitled to a fair and public hearing within a reasonable time [...]."[159] Achieving "reasonable time," as stipulated in the Article 6(1), produced, during the past three decades a growing caseload for the European Court of Human Rights, against the Council of Europe member states, for extensive delays in court proceedings against their citizens. If not for other reasons, European states were forced at least to reconsider the matter of the efficiency of the domestic courts because of the judgments of the European Court of Human Rights.

As a consequence, nowadays, national legislation is more concerned with the efficiency of justice, in particular by including requirements of organizational quality and efficiency to meet the demands of the Article 6 European Convention on Human Rights. However, according to the key findings of the 2014 EU Justice Scoreboard, even the EU member states are facing challenges with regard to the efficiency of their justice systems. These are particularly relating to the "[l]engthy first instance proceedings together with low clearance rates or a large number of pending cases [...]."[160]

In order to establish how well the Western Balkans judiciaries perform against the benchmark of efficiency of the judiciary, this section of the study provides both a normative and empirical analysis of the indicators of efficiency including the court structure with particular focus on specialized institutions of justice, length of court proceedings, the clearance rate, the number of pending cases, and the availability of information and communication technology (ICT) tools for courts.

Bosnia and Herzegovina

The judiciary in Bosnia and Herzegovina suffers from an unusually high number of backlogged cases. This backlog is caused by many unresolved cases from previous years, the merging of the courts after the 2003 judicial reforms, a large influx of new cases and an insufficient number of judges and court administrative staff. According to the High Judicial and Prosecutorial Council Annual Report, the backlog throughout the country accounted for 2,112,622 unresolved cases in all of the courts in Bosnia and Herzegovina. Statistically this means that each second citizen of Bosnia and Herzegovina is currently awaiting the outcome of an ongoing judicial trial. The bulk of these cases, more precisely 1,664,328, fall into the category of the "utility cases,"[161] while 448,294 are "other" types of unresolved cases.

The evident disproportion of the total number of unresolved cases between "utilities" and "other" cases clearly requires an innovative approach, as the current solution, which foresees courts and judges as the primary means for the collection of indisputable debt, has basically brought the judiciary to a grinding halt. More precisely, these cases should be transferred from the courts to non-judicial parts of law administration—private or public enforcement agencies, or public notaries.

The High Judicial and Prosecutorial Council of Bosnia and Herzegovina is currently implementing two projects within the framework of the Instrument for Pre-Accession Assistance of the European Union (IPA) aiming to reduce the backlog of cases, namely via the "Consolidation and Further Development of the Judicial Communication and Information System," and "Judicial Efficiency," which is financed additionally by the Kingdoms of Norway and Sweden. The working group in charge of the implementation of these projects has identified the following mechanisms necessary for reduction of the backlog, focusing mainly on utility cases: electronic submission of proposals for the execution and processing of "utility" cases; improvement of the service provided by judicial executorial officers; improving methods of delivery of judicial documents. Moreover, 44 courts were required to draft plans for the resolution of old cases in line with the adopted judicial quotas. In 2011 the Council established the Judicial Efficiency Unit. The Judicial Efficiency Unit is responsible for the monitoring of implementation of backlog reduction plans, as well as for the provision of support to courts to improve their efficiency. Finally, in 2012 the HJPC adopted rules on measures for the performance of judges, legal associates and other employees in the courts in Bosnia and Herzegovina.[162] Pertinent application of this document is expected to provide in turn the rules for the common application of rules for performance-evaluation, aimed at improving the efficiency of judges' performance.

As with regards to the lack of the judges and court administrative staff, already in 2008, the Council suggested an increase of 55 new judges and 160 additional posts to be included in the systematization process as well as the budgets for courts. Nevertheless, due to budgetary restrictions, only 22 new judges, or 10.2% of the proposed number were employed.[163]

Efforts of the Bosnian authorities to decrease the backlog of cases resulted in 73,992 resolved old cases in 2012, 29,373 of those being non-utilities cases. Still, "the average time necessary to complete a criminal case is 135 days; for administrative cases it is 401 days, and for civil cases up to 489 days."[164] Notwithstanding the positive results, courts should continue to invest more efforts into resolving the backlog of cases, particularly regarding the specific backlog of war crimes,[165] and de-burdening the judiciary of their responsibility for cases for unpaid utility bills.

By comparison to the problem of the backlog, the judicial ICT is fully functional. This is as a result of the activities undertaken by the Council within the framework of the IPA 2009 program for support to the judiciary of Bosnia and Herzegovina, which was interwoven with the IPA project for support to the police reform. Namely, the EU led projects on the technical implementation of the system for the electronic exchange of data between law enforcement and prosecutors' office records, and the optimization and consolidation of ICT resources in the judiciary[166] are widely recognized as the most successful projects related to the judiciary reform in Bosnia and Herzegovina.[167]

Finally, within the IPA 2009, the activities undertaken to create the Case Management System (CMS) began, while in 2011 they continued with the digitalization of all incoming documents to the courts, the system of automatic assigning of the cases to judges, and establishment of the Judicial Documentation Center. By now the CMS in courts and prosecutors' offices includes over 3.4 million registered cases and produces automated reports on judicial performances, which contribute to strategic planning decisions.

Kosovo

The Kosovo Judicial Council is the body responsible for the management of court administration and the specification of rules for determining the proper functioning of the courts. Guarantees for an efficient justice system are included in the Kosovo's *Law on Courts.* It requires the courts to function in an efficient manner to ensure the prompt resolution of cases. In addition, it guarantees the right to a fair trial "within a reasonable timeframe."[168] The implementation of judicial efficiency remains nevertheless, challenged by a lack of resources, proper management, capacity and infrastructure.

A backlog of cases is the most critical issue facing Kosovo's judiciary. It is constantly criticized in the European Commission Progress Reports.[169] During 2013, Kosovo courts had in total, 466,255 cases pending (including cases received during 2013) A total of 363,506 of these pending cases are more than two years old, and can therefore be considered "old cases." Out of this number 134,276 cases relate to minor offences cases, a further 108,657 cases are pending for judicial enforcement, while 102,743 require full attention of the judges.[170] According to the estimates by the Kosovo Judicial Council "the rate of clearing cases on Republic's level is 80.3%."[171]

The main factors contributing to the backlog of cases include, but are not limited to, legislative obstacles that lead to lengthy delays and procedural shortcomings in the execution of civil and criminal judgments,[172] along with a lack of sufficient human and financial resources in Kosovo's courts, and poor management.

The Kosovo Judicial Council has thus far adopted two strategic documents which aim to reduce the existing backlog. Following the success of the "National Backlog Reduction Strategy," which led to the conclusion of approximately 75% of cases older than 31 December 2008, in 2013 the Council established the Committee for Reconsideration of the National Backlog Reduction Strategy.[173] The Committee, which consisted of five local members and three international members,[174] evaluated the results of the ongoing efforts to decrease the backlog, and produced a new National Backlog Reduction Strategy. According to the new strategy, the Council has provided action framework for reduction of backlog, while in the years to come it remains for the courts to prepare and implement tangible measures.

The Kosovo judiciary is composed of only 321 judges, roughly 17 judges per 100,000 inhabitants.[175] Despite the understanding that the deficit in the number of judges influences overall underperformance of judicial efficiency, at this point I need to reiterate that the number of judges in Kosovo's legal system must observe constitutional provisions related to reserved positions for minorities. Consequently, in the case that the vacant positions falling outside of the reserved ethnic quota system remain unfulfilled, the Council is not able to hire more Albanian judges.

Legislative efforts for increasing the efficiency of the judiciary include the adoption of Laws on Arbitration and Mediation.[176] In addition, in 2008, the Assembly adopted a *Law on the Notary* that regulates the functioning of the notary as a public activity in Kosovo.[177] In 2009, the government started another amendment process for the law governing case execution procedures, with the purpose of improving the system for the enforcement of judgments, in particular in terms of the length of procedures and efficiency of proceedings. This amendment will also establish a bailiff system, which will become operational in 2014. Furthermore, the creation of the Special Chamber of the Supreme Court which has exclusive power over all cases and procedures relating to the privatization process is expected to facilitate the work of judges in ordinary courts.

The management of the overall judicial system also has room for significant improvement. The Presidents of the courts and the court administrators lack sufficient experience in management. In addition, judges in general lack sufficient human resource support to fulfill their duties. The court infrastructure is overcrowded and substandard at best. Since most courts only have one courtroom, trials are held in under-sized judges' offices, which constitute a serious breach to the right to a public hearing. Lately, the Kosovo Judicial Council has implemented several projects for the construction and renovation of courts, such as the construction of the buildings of the Basic Court in Gjilan, the Basic Court in Ferizaj–Shterpce, the Basic Court in Ferizaj and the Basic Court of the Mitrovica–Vushtri branch. Together with the completion of a new Palace of Justice, which was supported by the European Commission, it is expected that the problem of infrastructure will be resolved in the near future.

Due to the low level of computerization in Kosovo's courts, court cases are generally tracked manually. Furthermore, in courts where the Case Management Information System has been previously introduced, its effects were limited due to outdated computer hardware and lack of IT expertise among judges. Aiming to increase judicial efficiency, the Kosovo Judicial Council supported by the Norwegian Government, in 2013 started the Case Management Information System Project. The overall objective of this project is to create a legal basis for a more efficient judiciary in Kosovo through the introduction of Information and Communication Technology in all courts. By the end of the project, in 2017, it is foreseen that Kosovo's courts will transform into e-courts, particularly as a result of proactive court management, and work from reports and data in real time. We will also see the introduction of on-line services for citizens through a court web portal. It is significant also, that during the second phase of project implementation it is envisaged that all judges and court staff will receive basic ICT training and typing skills.

Finally, the problem posed by the attempted extension of Kosovo's rule of law structures to the northern part of the country, inhabited by a majority Serbian population, affects the efficiency of the overall judicial system. Namely, while the Court in the North is currently administered by the EULEX judges, prosecutors and international and local administrative staff, it is almost not accessible for Kosovo's judges and prosecutors. The fact that the Mitrovica Minor Offences Court, Municipal Court and District Court operate from the premises of the Vushtrri Municipal Court located in the southern part of Mitrovica municipality seriously challenges the functioning of Kosovo's justice system. The first Agreement on the principles governing the normalization of relations between Pristina and Belgrade, brokered on 19 April 2013 within the EU-Facilitated High Level Political Dialogue between Serbia and Kosovo, addresses this issue. The Agreement clearly reads that all judicial authorities need to be integrated and operate within the Kosovo legal framework. More importantly, it stipulates that the Appellate Court in Pristina should establish a Panel composed of majority Serbian judges. Nevertheless, as noted earlier in this study, at the time of writing of this book the implementation of the aforementioned Agreement remains all but certain.

Macedonia

One of the goals of the National Judicial Reform Strategy initiated in Macedonia in 2004 was the improvement of the efficiency of the judiciary. In practice, this meant re-organizing, in an efficient manner, the work of the courts, which were overburdened with a serious backlog of pending cases. From over a million pending cases in 2005, the backlog of the total number of unresolved cases was reduced to 174,538 at the end of 2012.[178] The greatest effort in this regard was made by the Basic Courts and the Courts of Appeal, while the newly formed Administrative Court, and the Supreme Court have increased the backlog of pending cases in the same period. In 2012, the last year of the High Judicial Council's reporting period, the majority of courts at all levels were able to process as many cases as they received. There are now no courts with significant backlogs. Finally, in its 2013 Progress Report, the European Commission concluded that "[t]he key long-term reforms in [the area of efficiency of judiciary] have already been completed over the course of the last decade, in line with European standards."[179] It is interesting to observe, however, that there is still no reliable information on the average overall duration of court proceedings.

Government strategies to reduce the backlog included the following measures: the aforementioned establishment of an Administrative Court and High Administrative Court; the introduction of legal aid and non-judicial mediation; the establishment of an automated case management system and e-justice; the strengthening of court administrative and management capabilities at all court levels; and the increase of the number of judges and the Judge Councils at all court levels. This has taken place alongside the introduction of new enforcement procedures in which professional bailiffs and public notaries took over the responsibilities of the courts, as well as the complete re-drafting of the criminal procedure legislation, and reform of the police.

The EU has considerably influenced the establishment of an efficient judiciary in Macedonia, mainly by providing advice and expertise, but also by dedicating significant financial means to support the ongoing reforms. The EU's expertise and financial assistance has been especially conspicuous regarding the creation of new institutions, most notably the Administrative Court.[180] Nevertheless, a range of actors, among them USAid, the Council of Europe, the Organization for Security and Cooperation in Europe (OSCE) and the World Bank, have also played a pro-active role during the reform process in the judiciary. These organizations have contributed jointly to the modernization of court infrastructure, the improvement of the spatial capacity of courts, creation of the Automatic Budget Management System and the Automated Court Case Management Information System, etc.

Despite the evident progress in judicial efficiency, there are side effects to the efforts invested so far, which are worth mentioning. They raise questions relating to the cost–benefit aspect of the efficiency of justice versus the quality of justice. First, the reforms undertaken have been costly, particularly since the introduction of new institutions and IT systems. Covering the expenses generated by these reforms has driven up the cost of accessing justice for the public, who often cannot now afford to avail themselves of legal remedies, which in turn, has seen a reduction of cases. Bearing in mind that most of the costs were covered by international donors, it remains to be seen whether the judiciary will be able to maintain the same level of efficiency once it relies mostly on domestic resources. Second, since the adoption of the strategy on reducing the backlog of pending cases, courts have drastically increased the number of processed cases. The main concern related to this purely quantitative improvement is whether it will result in a general lowering in the quality of justice, or even the violation of a human right to a fair trial.

Although Macedonia is the frontrunner among the Western Balkans countries in terms of efficiency of judicial institutions, as described above, its current normative system is not without room for further improvement. Particular efforts are needed in order to ensure the monthly targets imposed on judges concerning the number of cases to be processed do not affect the quality of justice along the way. In a nutshell, to paraphrase the words of a respondent in the questionnaire prepared within this study, Macedonia should discuss rather the needs, not weaknesses of the efficiency of judiciary in order to further improve it.

Montenegro

Bearing in mind the creation of prerequisites for further improvements to the efficiency of the judicial system, the Montenegrin Government adopted in 2007 the "Strategy for the Reform of the Judiciary 2007–2012" accompanied by an "Action Plan" for its implementation. During this period, numerous positive steps have been made in the area of the efficiency of judiciary. There has been a reduction in the number of backlogged cases: a review of the substantive law and procedural law; promotion of alternative dispute resolution, and establishment of the Judicial Information System. In addition, the *Law on Protecting the Right to Trial within a Reasonable Time* was adopted in 2011. A significant number of the envisaged reforms, however, are still facing shortcomings, as major problems which reduce the efficiency of the judiciary still include the burden of the backlog of cases, lengthy judicial proceedings, and an inadequate ICT and judicial infrastructure. Based on these findings, the Government of Montenegro adopted the Strategy for the Reform of the Judiciary for the 2014–2018 period. Measures to be implemented in the upcoming years include: streamlining the judicial network and the misdemeanor system, enhancing criminal and civil law, reducing the number of cases in the backlog, enhancing judicial management and administration system, enhancing alternative dispute resolution, and developing a Judicial Information System (JIS).

Montenegro has a three-tier court system comprising 15 basic courts, two high courts, an Appellate Court and a Supreme Court. It also includes two commercial courts, an administrative court, and the Constitutional Court. It is interesting to observe that misdemeanor courts are still not part of the court network. Judicial power is exercised by 262 judges supported by 49 bailiffs and 1,084 administrative staff. Although initial steps have been taken to rationalize the court network, Montenegro remains one of the countries with the highest number of basic courts, judges, prosecutors and administrative staff per capita in Europe.[181]

The abovementioned backlog consisted of 36,024 pending cases in 2013. From this figure, Montenegrin courts are still working on 4,251 cases that are older than three years. Similarly to the other case studies described in this study, a large number of the pending cases fall into the category of unenforced court decisions. In a bid to eliminate this problem, the Framework Program, aimed at resolving the backlog of cases has been adopted in all the courts. It introduces immediate solutions such as case-delegation, overtime, temporary rearrangement of working hours, reassignment of judges who are less burdened to a court dealing with the backlog of cases, and the monthly and quarterly submission of reports to the president of the court by judges adjudicating cases. Furthermore, in accordance with the *Law on Courts*, it was made obligatory for presidents of the courts to adopt specific annual programs for resolving the backlog of cases if the number of pending cases in the court or in a specific division is higher than the influx of cases over a three month period.

Additionally, the *Law on Protecting the Right to Trial within a Reasonable Time* was adopted, introducing two legal remedies, namely a request for review and an action for fair redress. In 2011 the new Criminal Procedure Code was adopted, envisaging the concept of prosecutorial investigation, mediation in criminal proceedings, and the introduction of plea-bargaining, which is expected to contribute to shortening case proceedings. Moreover, novelties introduced by the Civil Procedure Law include the introduction of court settlement, mediation procedures and arbitration procedures. These alternative methods of dispute resolution envisage the establishment of new non-judicial institutions, such as the Centre for Mediation, and the Permanent Arbitration Court. Despite the existence of a proper legal framework for alternative dispute resolution, it can be observed that the "public is not sufficiently aware of the advantages of this mechanism."[182] Furthermore, pursuant to the *Law on Notaries*,[183] 44 notaries took office as part of the public service in the legal system in July 2011. As for the problems involving resolution of the enforcement cases, Montenegro adopted the *Law on Public Enforcement Officers*,[184] as a new profession in judiciary. Although 32 positions of public enforcement officers have been envisaged, thus far only 12 public enforcement officers have been appointed, due to the "lack of motivation for this profession."[185]

A basic infrastructure for the Judicial Information System was developed in 2010 enabling electronic work on cases in all the judicial institutions, in order to accelerate the delivery of the cases. Nevertheless, the proper functioning of the JIS is prevented due to insufficient human resources, whilst insufficient amounts of funding are allocated for the maintenance and upgrade of the system. Lack of finances leads to fundamental problems such as slow internet connections, or reliance on outdated equipment. Regarding the judicial infrastructure, lack of finances contributed to the fact that there were no significant investments in court facilities in the recent period. Courtrooms are often inadequate and in poor shape, while the fact that trials often take place in judge's offices negatively influence the right to a public trial. Judicial management still falls within the competence of the president of the court.

Serbia

A problem endemic to the Serbian judiciary is, precisely, a lack of human and technical resources, as well as an inadequate court structure, which has led to a huge backlog of cases and unduly lengthy procedures. In an effort to deal with this problem, the Ministry of Justice of the Republic of Serbia initiated a reform of court structure, in which the fifth pillar is entirely dedicated to the efficiency of judiciary.[186] Still, despite the normative changes achieved, a large backlog of pending cases remains a matter of concern, in particular as the recent decrease in the number of permanent judges has impacted negatively on the overall efficiency of the judicial system. Furthermore, the EU in its Progress Report stated that the reduction of the number of judges and prosecutors was not based on a proper needs assessment.[187]

According to the Decision on the Number of Judges[188] there are 3,095 judges envisaged for the territory of the Republic. In addition there are 11,040 non-judicial court staff. Serbia has 1.8 courts per 100,000 inhabitants.[189] The clearance rate in Serbian courts is 85.4% for non-litigious and 91.6% for civil litigious cases.[190] According to the most recent statistics, the number of cases pending before Serbian courts is higher than three million, together with the backlog of enforcement cases.[191] This figure includes over 190,000 cases that have been pending for more than ten years in basic courts, and over 540,000 cases that have been pending for five to ten years. Although the main concern is that the existing backlogs violate the principle of a right to trial within a reasonable time, efficiency of the judiciary in Serbia must also be introduced in order to bring the country into line with the European standards.

Since 2010 the new court system has been operationalized with the aim of redistributing the workload and in order to "alleviate the previous disparity between overburdened urban courts and underused rural courts."[192] Even in the early stages of the implementation of the new working-practices of the new court structure, it became evident that not only did it *not* result in the balanced distribution of the workload between courts, but it has also negatively influenced the access to justice since the number of court seats was significantly reduced. The new Serbian Government prepared a new Action Plan for the implementation of the National Judicial Reform Strategy for the period 2013–2018, with one of the goals being to critically assess the new court structure.

On an institutional level, the new court network has introduced a number of new court institutions in order to reduce the existing backlog. These include the following courts of special jurisdiction: the Administrative Court, Commercial Courts, Commercial Court of Appeal, 45 Misdemeanor Courts and the High Misdemeanor Court. A commercial court is established for the territory of one or several towns, that is, several municipalities. An appellate court is established for the territory of several higher courts. A misdemeanor court is established for the territory of a town, that is, one or more municipalities. The Commercial Appellate Court, the Higher Misdemeanor Court, and the Administrative Court are established for the territory of the Republic of Serbia, with seats in Belgrade. These courts have departments outside their seats where they adjudicate permanently and undertake other court activities.

Furthermore, since 2003, special departments within the Serbian court system have existed for handling war crimes and organized crime. Both departments are fully operational, with special prosecutorial offices. Since the reform of the court structure in 2010, these departments have been part of the Belgrade Higher Court. Pursuant to the *Law on the Organization and Competencies of Government Authorities in Prosecuting Perpetrators of War Crimes*[193] of July 2003, special departments for war crimes and organized crime have jurisdiction over alleged violations of the Basic Criminal Code, in addition to crimes against humanity, violations of international law, and criminal acts as defined by Article 5 of the Statute of the International Criminal Tribunal for the former Yugoslavia (ICTY). The Belgrade Higher Court's war crimes department, comprised of six judges and one assistant, exercises first instance jurisdiction over all cases of war crimes tried in the Republic of Serbia. The special department on organized crime exercises first instance jurisdiction over offenses involving criminal conspiracies, such as money laundering, human trafficking, and extortion, as well as illicit trade in arms, ammunition, and explosive substances. It is comprised of 13 judges, working with 2 assistants. Decisions of these Specialized Departments may be appealed to the Belgrade Appellate Court. Finally, in 2009, Special Divisions for combating major technological crime were established within the Higher Public Prosecution Office and the Higher Court in Belgrade, with jurisdiction over the entire territory of the Republic of Serbia.[194] Judges allocated to the Criminal Division of the relevant court participate in the work of the court division.

To reduce the number of cases before the courts, the lawmakers have envisaged the creation of the roles of bailiffs, court managers, notaries public, and independent enforcement agents. While the number of bailiffs is still insufficient, and most of them remain concentrated mainly in Belgrade and other major cities, the introduction of notaries public was postponed for late 2014 because too few candidates passed the public notaries' examination. The *Law on Court Organization* states that every republic-level court and court providing material, financial, and technical support for more than 30 judges must have a court manager.[195] The backlog of enforcement cases is a particularly pressing concern. Enforcement was organized within first instance courts with judges who were not adequately recognized in the court system. To eliminate this problem, independent enforcement agents were introduced, to have a key role in every phase of the enforcement process. Nevertheless, they are also facing the same type of obstacle as judges, namely the existing culture of not paying bills to creditors.[196]

Elsewhere, some procedural laws were changed in order to speed up the processes in front of the courts. Most notably the Criminal Procedure Code introduced the public prosecutor as the lead for criminal investigations both in the pre-investigative and investigative phases. Additional measures have been introduced through the stipulation in the *Law on Judges*, which urges a judge to notify the President of the Court about the reasons that caused him or her to extend the proceedings in first instance for over six months (Article 28).

It is interesting to mention the impressive results from a pilot project conducted by the East-West Management Institute with six Serbian partner courts[197] that led the reduction of their "old-case" backlogs by 49%, from 23,000 down to 12,000.[198] The tactics that have been implemented to overcome the backlog problem in the six pilot courts consisted of increased cooperation, communication, organization within the courts and other constituents, and better procedural measures. Following the success of the pilot phase, in July 2013, the East-West Management Institute presented a National Plan for Backlog Reduction that would reduce the number of backlogged cases by 80% over the next five years. In the meantime, courts remain overburdened by cases in an absence of "incentives for alternative dispute settling procedures that would decrease the workload of sitting judges, namely conciliation procedures and arbitration."[199]

Effectiveness of the judiciary

Effectiveness of the judiciary is the fourth and last benchmark to be considered within this book, in order to establish the influence of the EU integration on the reform of the judiciary in the five selected case-study countries. This book understands the phrase "effectiveness of judicial servants," as meaning the ability of a judge to make sound judgments, to be equipped with professional erudition, and to have the skill to prosecute or render judgments effectively in accordance with the law.

As it is commonly said, although last to be analyzed, the effectiveness of the judiciary is far from being the least important benchmark. In the hypothetical case that all the other benchmarks—independence, accountability and effectiveness—are implemented in accordance with the best standards, they would still mean little if the judiciary is incompetent and unprofessional. Another reason for leaving the effectiveness benchmark for the end is due to the fact that it is particularly interlinked with the efficiency of the judiciary, and cannot be analyzed from an isolated perspective. Namely, focusing on effectiveness alone, in the long run, threatens the access to justice and public trust in the judiciary, because of the ever-increasing costs of and delays in court proceedings. This is why it is unusually important that the professional competence and productivity of the judiciary are balanced.

The Western Balkans judiciary has embraced the notion of judicial independence and accountability as a means of preserving and perpetuating the exclusive role of judges in the judicial sector, thus, indirectly entrenching "traditional ways"[200] of conducting judicial processes. Despite the setting up of a fresh legislative and institutional framework, professional competence still remains one of the most widespread problems facing the judiciary of the Western Balkans.[201] The extent of the degradation of judges' competence is at a level where even the quality of the written judicial decisions is criticized as reflecting poor analytical, research, and writing skills.[202] With the exception of the constitutional courts, a majority of judges continue in their formalist reading of the law, rather than performing their assumed transitional roles. Improperly supported by their education, "judges often look for a way out of more difficult legal cases, by disposing them based on purely formalistic grounds."[203] In this way, the simplified version of textual positivism and the ideology of bound judicial decision-making are able to survive the process of far-reaching judicial reforms. Legacies of communist and socialist legal culture,[204] although without the connection to the former political systems remain alive and well, and continue to influence contemporary legal thought. Political eruptions in the process of democratic transformation, particularly the institutional usurpation of higher education in Serbia[205] and Kosovo,[206] have additionally affected the professional competence of the judiciary.

The problem becomes even more worrisome knowing that the aspiring EU members have, through the Stabilisation and Association Agreement, taken over the commitment to gradually harmonize domestic legal norms with EU law. This means that in the foreseeable future, in order to account the *Acquis Communautaire* in its full meaning, judges will not only need to consider the mere "limited law"[207] of the texts of harmonizing legislation, where the judges try to follow only the letter of the law, however problematic and absurd the results this course produces, but also texts of European directives, their reasoning and rationale, European Court of Justice Jurisprudence, as well as the case law of the EU member states.

On the other hand, as said in the previous section, problems relating to the efficiency benchmark pertain to the lack of technical resources, an inadequate court structure, a huge backlog of cases, unduly lengthy procedures, and also the lack of court management training for sitting judges. Very often IT employees, in the courts and prosecutors' offices, do not have the required level of qualifications and education. They are frequently promoted from the ranks of administrative staff without special IT training and experience.[208] Furthermore, Court Presidents are not trained in court management and only a few courts are equipped with administrative and managerial staff members. Besides providing training to judges on court administration issues, an improvement would also be possible by employing trained junior legal and professional administrative staff for specific quasi-judicial tasks, such as maintaining records and case management. Clear delineation of different officials, such as the court secretary, court manager in charge of organizing tasks in the court, court clerk and recording clerk would relieve judges of administrative tasks and divert their focus to their adjudicative functions.

The Western Balkans nurtures continental legal traditions, with civil service, or career models, that give preference to new law graduates and young professionals who are then gradually promoted throughout their legal careers.[209] At the same time, education in law schools often lacks any practical orientation. Even judicial and bar examinations only test the applicants' technical legal knowledge. In combination with the already mentioned factors, such as low judicial capacities, budgetary constraints and the influence of cultural predispositions, it is precisely the lack of effective and efficient judges that cripples the Western Balkans' judicial reform, as part of the EU pre-accession condition. In an attempt to address this shortcoming, all of the case study countries have established special centers for training judges.

Bosnia and Herzegovina

As mentioned several times already, the judiciary in Bosnia and Herzegovina is marked by fragmentation along the entity lines. Hence, it comes as little surprise that there are two institutions for the education of judges and prosecutors in Bosnia and Herzegovina—the Judicial and Prosecutorial Training Centre in the Federation of Bosnia and Herzegovina, and the Judicial and Prosecutorial Training Centre in Republika Srpska (the Centers). In addition, the Judicial Commission of Brčko District provides expert training for the judges and the public prosecutor of Brčko District.[210] The *Law on the Judicial and*

Prosecutorial Training Centre in the Federation of Bosnia and Herzegovina[211] and the *Law on Judicial and Prosecutorial Training Centre in Republika Srpska*,[212] passed in 2002 by the Office of the High Representative, regulates issues of the establishment, status and activities of these institutions, as well as other issues of importance to the work of the Centers.

The fact that there are two judicial training centers opens up the question of quality of judiciary and the standardization of judicial practice. In an attempt to prevent the development of two different training programs, the lawmakers had envisaged a strong supervisory role for the High Judicial and Prosecutorial Council, which, as seen earlier, remains one of the rare state-wide judicial bodies. Hence, the main task of the Centers is to ensure, under the monitoring of the High Judicial and Prosecutorial Council, that training programs for judges and prosecutors are designed and implemented in accordance with the criteria of competence and impartiality, and uniformity. The Council is additionally involved in some of the competencies of the both Centers. It supervises the establishment of the introductory training programs for those intending to pursue the career of judge or prosecutor; consults the Steering Boards on the establishment of the programs of advanced professional training for judges and prosecutors, including minor offence court judges; it consults the Steering Boards on the establishment of specialized training programs in consultation with the Council, and finally it participates in the appointment and dismissal of the Directors of the Centers and judges and prosecutors to serve as trainers. Furthermore, based on the 2005 Agreement on Cooperation, all Bosnian and Herzegovinian judicial training centers regularly communicate and exchange information on educational activities for judges and prosecutors, have joint sessions of the Governing Boards, and coordinate operational programs and training plans.

The Centers organize advanced professional training for previously appointed judges and prosecutors, as well as initial training for persons wishing to engage in the profession of judge or prosecutor. According to the Initial and Continuous Judicial and Prosecutorial Training Mid-Term Strategic Plan for 2012–2015,[213] which has been approved by the HJPC, the overall goal of both Judicial and Prosecutorial Training Centers (JPTCs) in Bosnia and Herzegovina is to provide training that contributes to a more professional judiciary, capable of responding to the challenges of a rapidly developing legal environment and possessing the ability to adjust to evolving European requirements in the legal/judicial field.

Since 2007, the Centres conduct a three-year initial training cycle for judges. In 2011, the first generation of new judges completed the first cycle of three years' professional training, and commenced the second cycle of training for professional staff. Finally, in 2013, the Centers began with the implementation of training programs for newly appointed judges and prosecutors as a special form of initial training. As part of this training, there were in 2013, a total of four seminars, three on the implementation of the European Convention on Human Rights, organized in cooperation with the Council of Europe and one on court management, specifically, using a CMS system.

Advanced professional training is compulsory for all judges in Bosnia and Herzegovina. The Centers deliver custom training for the judiciary in Bosnia and Herzegovina, covering all areas of law and other, non-legal disciplines relevant to the practice of judges and prosecutors. Judges and prosecutors are provided with classes in interpreting and applying substantive and procedural laws, ethical-standards for judges and prosecutors, the latest scientific and professional achievements in the field of law, judicial and prosecutorial practice in other countries, and other areas determined by the Governing Board. Part of the continuous training consists of vocational training wherein judges maintain and expand their knowledge in the fields of court management, culture and social relations, necessary to performing their functions. The Council determines the minimum requirements for the advanced professional training that each judge and prosecutor must receive annually to satisfy this professional obligation. In 2013, the Center for Training of Judges and Prosecutors of the Republika Srpska organized a total of 107 seminars, and achieved a total of 2,375 days of education—103.3% of judges fulfilled the required number of days in training.[214]

Kosovo

The effectiveness of Kosovo's judiciary has been significantly challenged by the lack of competence and professionalism of many of the sitting judges and prosecutors, due to the poor quality of legal education as well as by the ten-year interruption in formal schooling and legal training during the 1990s.[215] These shortcomings are gradually being addressed through various efforts to improve the quality of legal education in Kosovo, as well as by continuous efforts to strengthen and increase the capacity-building efforts for the training of judges, prosecutors and judicial personnel.

The main institution responsible for the training of judges and prosecutors is the Kosovo Judicial Institute (KJI), established in 2008 under UNMIK's administration.[216] Apart from training, the KJI is responsible for the organization of the preparatory exam and the professional preparation of the candidates for careers as future judges and prosecutors, as well as for the training of other professionals working in the judicial and prosecutorial system of Kosovo. The Law prescribes that the KJI should be composed of a Managing Board and the Director. The Managing Board has 13 members, with the President of the Kosovo Judicial and Prosecutorial Council and the Director of Department of Judicial Administration serving as ex officio members of the Board. The other nine members are appointed by the Assembly of Kosovo, bearing in mind that two members must be appointed by UNMIK and the OSCE respectively, and at least two members of the overall membership of the Managing Board must be from amongst the minority communities. Additionally, the Statute of the KJI envisages the establishment of the

Program Council to serve as a complimentary body to the Managing Board. The Program Council participates in preparing and updating the training programs and the selection process of KJI trainers, and advises the KJI managing bodies.

The KJI conducts a series of Continuous Training Programs: the training program for promotion; the initial training program and preparatory exam; the training of other professionals of the judicial field; and a "training of trainers" program. From the 2013 Report of the KJI it is easy to observe that most of its attention is dedicated to carrying out continuous training, with 112 dedicated training days, 31 days of training for promotions, 11 days of initial training, and only five days dedicated to training of administrative staff.[217]

The Kosovo Judicial and Prosecutorial Council proposes the organization of the Continuous Training Program as the basic training course for lay judges. According to the KJI 2013 Report, this "continuous training" aims at developing the following: the best professional practices, advancing professional writing and legal reasoning, development of interdisciplinary and personal skills, knowledge about the international and European legislation, and finally, developing management and ICT skills. Continuous Training courses are organized in the form of seminars, discussion, roundtables, workshops, trial simulation and conferences. During 2013, 1,136 judges participated in continuous trainings.

The KJI is responsible for the organization of special training courses for newly promoted judges, or the promotion of judges who have been or will be promoted from a lower instance within the judicial system. Recently appointed judges are obliged to attend the special training courses for promotion without any secession from employment. The training program for promotion is conducted through training modules that last from one to five days and are tailored to meet the needs of the institutes of criminal law, civil law, and administrative law. In addition, various skill acquiring modules are offered including on legal writing and reasoning, media and public relations, ICT, etc.

The Initial Training Program is intended for the candidates who wish to become future judges once they successfully pass the Preparatory Exam. The selection of the candidates for the initial training is done on the basis of work experience, the results of the bar exam and of the preparatory exam for judges. Based on the *Law on Establishment of the Kosovo Judicial Institute*, the KJI publicly announces the organization of the preparatory exam, consisting of both written and oral exams, and the admission of 22 candidates for judges and 12 candidates for prosecutors.[218] The purpose of the preparatory exam is to determine if the level of professional knowledge required for attending the initial training program has been acquired, and if the level of competence for the performance of judicial and prosecutorial office is present. Successful candidates are admitted to the 16 month long initial training program, which is divided into three stages. The first five months of training are conducted on general legal topics, while during the subsequent three months candidates attend training according to their profile as judges or prosecutors. Finally, the last eight months of the initial training program are conducted in the courts and taking part in prosecutions under supervision of a mentor. During training, candidates receive an honorarium from the Kosovo Consolidated Budget. Thus far, four generations of candidates have completed the initial training program, and out of 141 candidates for judges or prosecutors, 127 have been appointed and are already practicing their profession as judges or prosecutors.[219] It is curious to observe that in the current, fifth generation of candidates for the initial training program, there were no members of minority communities represented.

Finally, the KJI is responsible for the provision of special training to professionals in the judicial branch, namely professional associates of courts, and enforcement officers of the Basic Courts. This special training aims to enhance the professional skills of these professionals. in 2014, three training activities were conducted for professional associates, and two for enforcement officers of Basic Courts treating various topics of criminal and civil law, and enforcement actions, respectively.

Under Article 6 of the *Law on Establishing the Kosovo Judicial Institute*, the Kosovo Consolidated Budget as the main source of financial support covers the financial costs of the KJI, but in addition, the KJI is allowed to receive donor's grants also. For 2013 the budget of the KJI was 526,089 euros, while an additional 138,169 euros were collected through donations, mostly from USAid, UNDP, EU, OSCE, Embassy of Great Britain, the Council of Europe, the Turkish International Development Agency and the Turkish Academy of Justice as well as the International Red Cross and the European Institute for Public Administration.

Macedonia

The *Law on the Academy for the Training of Judges and Prosecutors*[220] established the Academy with the aim of providing competent and efficient conducting of the activities by the professional services in the judiciary.[221] The Academy began its work in 2007 as a public institution responsible for the admission and professional training of candidates for positions as judges and public prosecutors, as well as the provision of continuous training and professional improvement for judges and public prosecutors, continuous training of the professional services in the judiciary and the public prosecution, and training of the judicial staff.

The Academy conducts the initial training for future judges with the aim of helping them acquire practical and theoretical knowledge and skills in order to create "highly trained, competent and efficient candidates for judges in the Basic Courts."[222] In order to qualify for the initial training program, potential candidates are required to take the entry exam. The academy is obliged to organize and conduct preparatory classes for all persons with timely and complete applications for the initial training program. Within these preparatory classes, participants prepare for the entry exam. The entry exam is comprised of a qualification test, a psychological test, integrity test, and an exam. Questions in the qualification test cover the areas of substantive and procedure criminal and civil law, trade law, constitutional and administrative law, international law, and EU law. The psychological test determines the capability of the candidates for executing their judicial function, while the integrity test is based on the existent domestic and international ethical and professional codes for performing their function as judges. Finally, the exam is supposed to verify the level of overall legal knowledge and capabilities of the candidate, ensuring they are suitable for admission to the initial training program, which is done by means of a practical problem oriented written test, and an oral exam designed to verify the candidate's knowledge and ability of expression.

The number of participants in the initial training program is decided annually by the Judicial Council of the Republic of Macedonia, bearing in mind the total number of vacant positions for judges in the Basic Courts, as well as the projected number of vacancies that should be filled following the end of the Initial Training. By acquiring the status of a participant in the initial training of the Academy, the participant is employed on a part-time basis in the Academy for the duration of the initial training, and has the right to a salary amounting to of 50% of the salary of a higher judicial advisor in a basic court. The initial training encompasses the implementation of the substantive and procedural laws, judicial practice and ethics, international legal standards, as well as the skills required for the judicial and the prosecutorial function. The initial training lasts 24 months and is conducted in two phases, a nine month long theoretical training period at the Academy, and 15 months of practical training in the courts. Following the completion of both phases of the initial training, and upon passing the exam, the participants in the initial training program acquire the status of candidates for judges and public prosecutors. The *Law on Courts* requires all newly appointed first-instance judges to have completed the initial training program, nevertheless, the Judicial Council continues to ignore the legislative requirements, appointing 39 first instance judges in 2012, only four of whom were Academy graduates, and 13 in 2013, only one of whom was an Academy graduate.[223] At the same time, nine of the 80 candidate judges and prosecutors who have completed the initial training at the Academy since 2009 are still waiting to be appointed to their first post.[224] The irregularity of the implementation of the legally guaranteed principle of merit-based recruitment, signals a clear message to the potential future candidates for the initial training program at the Academy. Hence, it is no surprise that despite the repeated calls for applications and even an increase in the stipend of accepted candidates, there were not sufficient applicants for the 2014 initial training program.

Continuous training is compulsory for judges and presidents of courts, while in addition the Academy conducts continuous training for court administrative staff, which is undertaken on a voluntary basis. The *Law on the Academy* distinguishes between newly appointed judges, and judges with three or more years' judicial experience, so that the former are obliged to attend the specialized continuous training immediately following their appointment as judges, while the latter are obliged to attend at least 20 training days during one year. The number of training days decreases progressively with the work experience, so that at the end, the duration of the continuous training for the judges with more than 15 years of judicial experience is only three training days per year.

The newly appointed judges are obliged, immediately following their appointment, to attend an intensive, continuous ten days of training on topics deemed necessary to deepen the participants' knowledge in various legal disciplines, and to develop the complementary skills necessary for the professional execution of their judicial function. The general program is created to ensure the continuous professional development and the development of skills regarding the need to constantly bear in mind the frequent changes and amendments in the current national legislation, as well as the latest developments in the European and international legislation. The program includes training in criminal law, civil law, trade law, constitutional law, administrative law, and EU law. Apart from legal training, this continuous training focuses on the acquisition of complementary skills for the judges in the fields of psychology, court ethics, communication skills, case management, public relations, and ICT. Presidents of courts are in addition, trained in court and budget management and public relations with the media. In 2014 the Academy had 280 training events, attended by 7,560 participants, of whom 3,844 participants were judges and 961 expert staff from courts.[225]

The funds for the operation of the Academy are provided from the Budget of the Republic of Macedonia, international donations, and independent income from publishing, and conducting training for non-judicial public servants. Moreover, the Academy was highly dependent on EU assistance which has provided for the creation of regional training centers, an e-training module and the strengthening of its IT infrastructure.[226] In addition to financial assistance, the Academy was supported with expertise in developing adequate models that would function in the domestic context. For 2013, 445,601 euros were dedicated for the Academy from the state budget. This amount signals a decrease in the annual budget awarded by the state to the Academy, which in addition lacks professional staff and adequate premises given the scope of its activities. Hence, it can be concluded that greater efforts are needed to support and make sustainable the work of the Academy.

Montenegro

Professional development for holders of judicial office commenced in 2000, with the establishment of the Center for the Training of Judges of the Republic of Montenegro. The initial founders of the Center were the Ministry of Justice of Montenegro, the Association of Judges of Montenegro, the Foundation Open Society Institute, and the American Bar Association/

Central and East-European Legal Initiative (ABA/Ceeli) During the first seven years of its work, the Center has organized seminars, roundtables, workshops, courses, regional conferences, and study visits in which approximately 90% of Montenegrin judges, associates, trainees and other court staff have participated.[227] Nevertheless, the Center operated as a non-profitable organization, without appropriate legal background, and most importantly without the ability to provide initial training for future judges.

In order to remove these deficiencies, the *Law on Judiciary Training*[228] was adopted in 2006, establishing the Judicial Training Centre of Montenegro as the only national institution for the training and professional education of judges. The main objective of the Centre is the acquisition, maintenance and improvement of the knowledge, capacities and skills of judiciary officials, with the goal of providing for the "autonomous, independent, unbiased, professional and efficient"[229] performance of the judiciary. The Law specifies in detail the manner and forms of initial and in-service training of judiciary officials. The Center is organized as a special organizational unit of the Supreme Court of the Republic of Montenegro, hence funding for the training is mainly provided within the budget of the Supreme Court, as well as from the donations and grants. It is managed by the executive director, who is appointed by the president of the Supreme Court, and composed of the special bodies formed for the organization and conduct of training: Coordination Board, Program Committee for in-service training, Program Committee for initial training, and an Examination Board.

The initial training is organized for the judicial assistants in courts and graduate lawyers who have passed the bar examination, and aims to prepare them for the performance of judicial office. The number of attendants of the initial training course is determined according to the decision of the Coordination Board, bearing in mind annual needs and vacancies among holders of judiciary office. The selection of the attendees of this initial education course is decided by the Examination Commission based on the results achieved in the initial training entrance examination, which has both written and oral components. In the last year the Center received 49 applications for the entrance exam, and according to the results of the written test and evaluation of the Examination Board, accepted 21 candidates into the initial training program.[230] The program consists of modules in criminal, civil, and European law, and acquisition of judicial skills. After completing the initial training program, implemented through 18 two-day seminars, participants are eligible to take final exams before the Examination Commission. The candidates who pass the final examination receive a certificate for passing the examination, while the Center submits a list of these candidates, ranked according to the results achieved, to the Judicial Council. According to the *Law on Judiciary Training*, the list of the graduates from the initial training must be given consideration when proposing candidates for the election or appointment of judiciary officials.[231]

In-service training is defined as further professional training and professional development of judiciary officials through special programs.[232] Judiciary officials have both the "right and obligation"[233] to undergo further professional training. Obligatory training is organized for judges in the cases of promotion, change of specialization, or introduction of new procedures. In-service training distinguishes between the judges who have been in office for less than three years, senior judges, and presidents of courts. It is comprised of training in the organization and functioning of the judiciary system, codes of ethics, application of laws and other regulations, introduction to most significant areas of international law, international standards and recommendations, including the European Union law and the issue of human rights, as well as the enhancement of professional skills. Judges who are in office for more than three years receive additional training on new legislation, alternative ways of case resolution, and increased efficiency in case resolution. The training for courts' presidents is composed of acquisition of knowledge in the fields of organization and internal operation of judiciary bodies; the efficient management of cases; case backlog management; alternative methods of case resolution; codes of ethics, and public relations. According to the annual report of the Center, in 2014 it held 72 activities related to the continuous training of Montenegrin judges.[234] Due to the lack of human and financial resources, continuing training programs are conducted with the cooperation and support of domestic and international strategic partners, namely the OSCE—Mission to Montenegro, the US Embassy in Podgorica, UNDP—Office Montenegro, EIPA from Luxembourg, the German Foundation for International Legal Cooperation, the AIRE Centre from London (Advice on Individual Rights in Europe), GIZ (Regional Fund for South East Europe), and others.

The existing solution leaves the matter of administrative and financial self-sustainability of the Judicial Training Centre unresolved. In addition, the European Commission has called upon the Center to strengthen the training on public procurement issues, and the use of mediation, particularly through awareness-raising campaigns. The most problematic aspect of the Center's work however, remains the lack of a transparent and merit based recruitment process, following the successful completion of the initial training program. It would be appropriate to establish a recruitment system founded on compulsory initial training, the completion of which is necessary before being appointed to the position of judge.

Serbia

Legal education in Serbia is almost entirely based on theoretical legal positivism, and it therefore fails to overcome the problem of "mechanical jurisprudence"[235] whereby in a simplified intellectual world of "limited law,"[236] everything is either legally binding or legally irrelevant. Moreover, law is usually taught by professors who have never practiced it. Consequently, Serbian law students have little knowledge of the realities of practicing law. Harmonization with the *Acquis* and, more importantly, the application of the EU law, creates therefore an unprecedented challenge for the Serbian judiciary.

In an attempt to provide an answer to these challenges, the Judicial Centre for Training and Professional Development (the Center) was established in 2001 as a *sui generis* and *ad hoc* semi-public institution under the patronage of the Supreme Court. Over the next eight years, via this institution, Serbian judges were able to gain access to institutional resources for continual professional development, according to modern educational methods. By the end of 2008, the Centre held a total of 916 training sessions, reaching 25,577 beneficiaries—15,305 judges, 4,800 prosecutors, 4,506 lawyers and 966 others. Despite the impressive numbers, however, it had very limited success in raising the quality of the judiciary. The main deficiency of the Center has proved to be the lack of an adequate legal framework, which has left this institution outside of the scope of the judiciary system. As a result, the Center has not yet been able to establish the initial training for judges, or the compulsory continuous training of sitting judges, but only permanent training programs for judges and prosecutors.

Under the *Law on the Judicial Academy*,[237] adopted in December 2009, the Judicial Centre for Training and Professional Development was transformed into the Judicial Academy. The main purpose of the Judicial Academy is to provide training for the competent, professional, independent, impartial and efficient performances of judges and public prosecutors. Above all, its mission is to change the existing legal culture among the members of judiciary.

The management of the Judicial Academy comprises of the Steering Committee, the Director of the Academy and the Program Council. The Steering Committee of the Serbian Judicial Academy is made up of nine members: three representatives appointed by the High Judicial Council, one of whom, by the Association of Judges; three representatives appointed by the State Prosecutorial Council, one of whom is proposed by the Association of Prosecutors; and three members appointed by the Government, one of whom is the state secretary in the Ministry of Justice responsible for judiciary, and one employee of the Judicial Academy. The Program Council is the professional body of the Academy responsible for establishing the initial and continuous training programs. It is composed of 11 members, appointed by the Steering Committee, from the ranks of judges and prosecutors, other legal experts and judicial and prosecutorial staff. At least five members of the Program Council are magistrates, three of those being prosecutors, of whom the Judges' Association or Prosecutors' Association proposes one member, while one member is nominated from the ranks of the judicial and prosecutorial staff members. The law does not elaborate on the formal criteria and process of their selection however, which, again, leaves open the possibility for manipulation.

The training of judges and prosecutors at the Judicial Academy implies the organized acquisition of and the advancement of practical and theoretical knowledge and skills required for the independent, professional and efficient performance while in office. The Judicial Academy provides initial and continuous training.

The establishment of the initial training at the Judicial Academy is deemed crucial for the process of the election of magistrates. Candidates are admitted to the initial training program based on the results of an entrance examination, which includes a written exam, personality test and oral exam. Apart from the applicable substantive and procedural law in the field of civil, criminal and misdemeanor law, candidates are tested in the written exam for their knowledge of general culture and a foreign language. The personality test has been designed to evaluate the ability to work under pressure, communicate with other people, work to meet tight deadlines as well as the other personal characteristics of each candidate. It is precisely through this entrance exam that the Academy fulfills its primary function, to provide an open and transparent method of selection for entrance into the judiciary branch.

The admitted candidates take part in the initial training program, which consists of the application of substantive and procedural laws, judicial and prosecutorial practice, and ethical standards for judges and prosecutors. They are also educated on international legal standards, the internal organization of the operations of the courts and prosecutor's offices, and the latest scientific and professional papers in the fields of national and international law, as well as being helped to develop the skills required for the performance of judicial and prosecutorial duties. The practical part of the initial training is conducted in a court of law, or the public prosecutor's office as well as in other state bodies, bar chambers and other organizations, all under the supervision of a mentor. Initial training lasts for 24 months, at 40 hours per week. The number of participants in the initial training is defined each year by the High Judicial Council and by the State Prosecutorial Council, based on the number of vacancies for judicial institutions, in the year following the completion of the initial training. Participants in the initial training course establish an employment relationship in the Academy during the program, so that they are compensated with 70% of the average salary of the basic court judge.

After completing the initial training, participants are obliged to apply to the post of misdemeanor judge, basic court judge, or a deputy basic public prosecutor. Only if there are no candidates who have completed the initial training, can other candidates who fulfill the general requirements for election to the office of judge or public prosecutor, be nominated for election to the offices of judge.

The continuous training is for judges who have already been elected, and public prosecutors. Continuous training is voluntary unless it is, exceptionally, envisaged as mandatory by a decision of the High Judicial Council. This usually occurs in cases of: changes in specialization; significant changes in regulations; the introduction of new methods of work; the need to eradicate shortcomings in the work of a judge or deputy public prosecutor observed in the course of their work. Finally, it is also intended for judges who are elected to office for the first time and have not yet completed the initial training program. The *Law on Judges* states that participation in the continuous training program will impact the career advancement of judges and deputy public prosecutors.

In this regard, the Judicial Academy is obliged to keep records on participants in the continuous training, and submit the relevant information to the High Judicial Council upon request. Nevertheless, the existing legal framework does not create sufficient incentive for judges to participate in voluntary training.

The continuous education program is organized in accordance with the key areas identified by the Program Council: criminal law, civil law, commercial law, administrative law, human rights, EU legislation, misdemeanor law, delinquency of minors and special programs. The special program of the continuous training, which is offered by the Judicial Academy, is dedicated to the education of judges and prosecutors on more complex legal issues, such as court ethics, disciplinary responsibility of judges, and includes a special training program for the Presidents and Secretaries of the courts on court management, and programs for the public relations services of the courts and prosecution. In 2012, 332 training courses were conducted. So far, a total number of 9,500 participants completed the training courses conducted by the Judicial Academy.

Finally, the third type of training conducted at the Judicial Academy is the training in judicial administration. Bearing in mind the existing problem of a lack of efficiency in the Serbian Courts, the Academy provides training and the organized acquisition of knowledge and skills for judicial staff. This type of training consists, mainly, of the acquisition of knowledge and skills necessary for the professional and efficient performance of duties, i.e. training in court management systems, filing of cases, information technology, public relations, and annual operational planning. In collaboration with USAid, the Judicial Academy provides a five-day seminar for training court managers, secretaries and other administrative staff in courts and public prosecutors' offices. In cooperation with the Ministry of Justice, the Academy provides training for administrative staff, judges and public prosecutors on the implementation of information-communication technology. Up until today, approximately 32% of staff members in the courts' and prosecutors' offices have attended administrative training programs.

Basic funding for the Judicial Academy is provided by the budget of the Republic of Serbia, and, in the current fiscal year (2015), is set at 1,590,000 euros. Commitment to the financing of the Judicial Academy from the budget is established by the *Law on Judges* as an obligation of the Republic of Serbia.[238] From this fund, the Academy is able to service its main tasks, such as funding for the initial training program which includes salaries for the participants of the initial training program, and the annually set priorities for continuous training program.[239] Other parts of the program, however, remain financed through international donations, gifts and the revenues of published materials and project realization. Thus far, the EU, the USAid program, the Council of Europe, United Nations, the OSCE Mission to Serbia, the Kingdom of Norway's Government, and the Kingdom of Netherlands' Government, have supported the programs of the Judicial Academy.

At the moment of the completion of this study, the first generation of judges trained at the academy began their professional careers as judges in the first instance and misdemeanour courts. Despite the successful track records, consisting of a number of delivered cases and performance efficiencies, it is still premature to assume the impact of this institution on the change of the legal culture. However, the mere fact that judges are responding, in such a high number, to the call to participate in these non-compulsory, in-service trainings, gives hope for the improvement that is already visible. Until recently it has been unthinkable for a judge to make a reference to the European Court for Human Rights in his or her judgment. Today, not only is this practice common, but the decisions made by the European Court for Human Rights are even considered by the Supreme Court for the creation of legal practices.[240]

The National Judicial Academy of the Republic of Serbia is not a part of the regular educational system, but rather, an integral part of the judicial system. However, despite the comprehensive legislative framework, as described in this study, it seems that the legislation has failed to define the place of the Judicial Academy within the Serbian judicial system. Namely, the 2006 Constitution of the Republic of Serbia abolished the compact High Judicial Council as the institution designated for recruitment of judges and public prosecutors alike, and instead, set up the High Judicial Council and High Prosecutorial Council as two, separate, public bodies. This solution has led to the breaking of magistrates' professions into judicial and prosecutorial. Hence, the two newly established bodies are, not only, greater fiscal burdens to the state budget, but also suffer from a lack of mutual coordination. This argument is also expressed in the Monitoring Report prepared by the European Commission that reads that "further legislative and institutional changes are needed for the Academy."[241]

Although the Judicial Academy continues to enjoy support from political elites and international donors,[242] this support is not unequivocal. A part of the judicial and prosecutorial assistants, concerned with their unprivileged status in comparison to the students of the Academy filed a complaint to the Constitutional Court arguing that the *Law on the Judicial Academy* is unconstitutional, particularly in regard to the first election of judges.

Finally, the outcome of the mission of the Judicial Academy depends on other non-legal conditions, falling within the scope of sociology and politics. Namely, successful attainment of the rule of law is also a social outcome, not a merely legal one.[243] Similarly, judges interpret legal norms, not only as a linguistic exercise, but as a teleological process. In this regard, teaching at the Judicial Academy should not simply remain on the normative and theoretical level, but rather, must be, or become, socially normative.[244] Additionally, it is important to improve the cooperation between law schools and the Judicial Academy in order to ensure compliance and alignment of academic and training curricula, to enhance the exchange of lecturers, and to introduce the internship of students in courts and public prosecutors' offices.

Notes

1 See A. M. Cohler, B. C. Miller and H. S. Stone (eds.). 1989. *The Spirit of the Laws by Charles de Secondat baron de Montesquieu* (Cambridge University Press: Cambridge).

2 See W. M. Landes and R. A. Posner. 1975. "The Independent Judiciary in an Interest-Group Perspective," *Journal of Law and Economics* 18: 875–901; M. C. Larkins. 1996. "Judicial Independence and Democratization: A Theoretical and Conceptual Analysis," *American Journal of Comparative Law* 44: 605–626; J. Ramseyer. 1998. "Judicial Independence," in P. Newman, *The New Palgrave Dictionary of Economics and the Law* (New York: Stockton Press): 383–387; M. Ramseyer. 1994. "The Puzzling (In)dependence of Courts: A Comparative Approach," *Journal of Legal Studies* 23(2): 721–747; M. Schapiro. 1981. *Courts: A Comparative and Political Analysis* (University of Chicago Press: Chicago); S. Shetreet. 1985. "Judicial Independence: New Conceptual Dimensions and Contemporary Challenges," in S. Shetreet and J. Deschenes. (eds.) *Judicial Independence: The Contemporary Debate* (Martinus Nijhoff: Dordrecht): 590–681.

3 United Nations Basic Principles on the Independence of the Judiciary, adopted by the Seventh United Nations Congress on the Prevention of Crime and the Treatment of Offenders held at Milan from 26 August to 6 September 1985 and endorsed by General Assembly resolutions 40/32 of 29 November 1985 and 40/146 of 13 December 1985.

4 See Council of Europe. Strasbourg: 1950. *European Convention for the Protection of Human Rights and Fundamental Freedoms*, Article 6. Opened for signature on 4 November 1950, entered into force 3 September 1953; European Parliament. Brussels: 2000. *Charter of Fundamental Rights of the European Union*, Article 47, *Official Journal of the European Communities* C364/1; See also Inter-American Specialized Conference on Human Rights. San Jose: 1969. *American Convention on Human Rights*, Articles 8–10. OAS Treaty Series No. 36, entered into force 18 July 1978; and Organization of African Unity. Banjul: 1981. *African Charter on Human and Peoples' Rights*, Article 7, OAU Doc. CAB/LEG/67/3 rev. 5, 21 I.L.M. 58, entered into force 21 October 1986.

5 See J. Toharia. 1975. "Judicial Independence in an Authoritarian Regime: The Case of Contemporary Spain," *Law and Society Review* 9(3): 475–496.

6 See for example; United Nations. New York: 1985. *United Nations Basic Principles on the Independence of the Judiciary*, United Nations General Assembly Resolutions 40/32 of 29 November 1985 and 40/146 of 13 December 1985. It reads that "the independence of the judiciary shall be guaranteed by the State and enshrined in the Constitution or the laws. It is the duty of public institutions to respect and observe the independence of the judiciary."

7 A supremacy clause guarantees the legal integration of Bosnia and Herzegovina by establishing the supremacy of the State Constitution over all other sources of law including the Entity Constitutions.

8 European Commission for Democracy through Law (Venice Commission). Strasbourg: 4 April 2011. *Report on the Rule of Law Adopted by the Venice Commission at its 86th Plenary Session* (Venice, 25–26 March 2011), paragraph 44.

9 Ibid., paragraphs 44–51.

10 See A. Kadribašić. 2014. "Democratic Transition, Rule of Law and Europeanization: Limited Progress in Bosnia and Herzegovina, in M. Kmezić (ed.), *Europeanization by Rule of Law Implementation in the Western Balkans*, Institute for Democracy, Skopje: 63–90.

11 The Agreement states that

> [t]he parties desire to consolidate the authority over the Entities' judiciaries in order to strengthen the independence of the judiciary through the establishment of a single High Judicial and Prosecutorial Council of Bosnia and Herzegovina. (…) The council shall bear primary responsibility, as defined by the agreement, for the judiciary at all levels throughout Bosnia and Herzegovina and shall oversee judges and prosecutors in a manner that instills public confidence and trust in the judiciary.

See in the Republika Srpska government's, the Federation of Bosnia and Herzegovina government's and the Council of Ministers of Bosnia and Herzegovina's *Agreement on the Transfer of Certain Entity Responsibilities through the Establishment of the High Judicial and Prosecutorial Council of Bosnia and Herzegovina* (Sarajevo: 11 March 2004).

12 Parliamentary Assembly of Bosnia and Herzegovina. Sarajevo: 2005. *Law on High Judicial and Prosecutorial Council of Bosnia and Herzegovina*, Article 17. *Official Gazette of Bosnia and Herzegovina* 25/04 and 93/05. The Council has competency over the complete judiciary in Bosnia and Herzegovina, which includes the following courts and prosecutor's offices: the Court of Bosnia and Herzegovina; the Prosecutor's Office of Bosnia and Herzegovina; the Constitutional Courts of Republika Srpska and the Federation of Bosnia and Herzegovina; the Supreme Courts of Republika Srpska and the Federation of Bosnia and Herzegovina; the District and Basic Courts of Republika Srpska; the Cantonal and Municipal Courts of the Federation of Bosnia and Herzegovina; the Republic Prosecutor's Office of the Republika Srpska and the Federation's Prosecutors of the Federation of Bosnia and Herzegovina; the District Prosecutors' Offices in Republika Srpska and the Cantonal Prosecutors' Offices in the Federation of Bosnia and Herzegovina; The Appellate Court of Brčko District of Bosnia and Herzegovina, the Basic Court of Brčko District of Bosnia and Herzegovina and the Prosecutor's Office of the Brčko District of Bosnia and Herzegovina.

13 *Law on High Judicial and Prosecutorial Council of Bosnia and Herzegovina*, Article 17, cit.

14 According to the Preamble of the Constitution of Bosnia and Herzegovina "Bosniacs, Croats, and Serbs, as constituent peoples (along with Others)" constitute the ethnic structure of Bosnia and Herzegovina.

15 The quota for all ethnic and gender representation is regulated in Article 4.4. of the *Law on High Judicial and Prosecutorial Council of Bosnia and Herzegovina*, cit.

16 Chapter V, *Law on High Judicial and Prosecutorial Council of Bosnia and Herzegovina*, cit.

17 Before the HJPC was established, the appointment of judges and prosecutors was contained in the mandate of the legislative and executive bodies, which could then influence the independence of judges and prosecutors.

18 Here reference is made to the constitutions of the two Bosnia and Herzegovina Entities. Both the Constitution of the Federation of Bosnia and Herzegovina (Article 17a) and the Constitution of Republika Srpska (Amendment LXXVII) stipulate that "Constituent peoples and Others shall be proportionately represented in all courts according to the 1991 census until Annex 7 (Agreement on Refugees and Displaced Persons) is fully implemented." See in Parliament of the Federation of Bosnia and Herzegovina. Sarajevo: 1994. *Constitution of the Federation of Bosnia and Herzegovina, Official Gazette of the Federation of Bosnia and Herzegovina*, 1/94, 13/97, 16/02, 22/02, 52/02, 60/02, 18/03, 63/03; and National Assembly of the Republic of Srpska. Pale: 1992. *Constitution of the*

Republic of Srpska, Official Gazette of the Republic of Srpska 3/92, 6/92, 8/92, 15/92 and 19/92, and Amendments I–CXXII.

19 National Assembly of Bosnia and Herzegovina. Sarajevo: 2004. *Law on High Judicial and Prosecutorial Council of Bosnia and Herzegovina.* Article 43.2. *Official Gazette of the Federation of Bosnia and Herzegovina* 25/04 and 93/05.

20 A. Kadribašić. 2014. "Democratic Transition, Rule of Law and Europeanization: Limited Progress in Bosnia and Herzegovina," at 76.

21 Interview with Judge, Sarajevo, Bosnia and Herzegovina, 2013.

22 Ibid.

23 European Commission for Democracy through Law (Venice Commission). Venice: 2012. *Opinion on Legal Certainty and Independence of Judiciary in Bosnia and Herzegovina*, para. 85. Opinion No. 648/2011.

24 *Opinion on Legal Certainty and Independence of Judiciary in Bosnia and Herzegovina*, para. 88, cit.

25 *Law on the High Judicial and Prosecutorial Council of Bosnia and Herzegovina.* Article 43.2. cit.

26 Interview with Judge, Sarajevo, BiH, 2013.

27 See A. Kadribašić. 2014. "Democratic Transition, Rule of Law and Europeanization: Limited Progress in Bosnia and Herzegovina," cit.

28 In the Council of Europe Member States the ratio between average salaries and judges salaries is 2.5 according to the latest report of the European Commission for the Efficiency of Justice. See also Evaluation of Judicial Systems, The European Commission for the Efficiency of Justice, CoE, 2012. Available at http://www.coe.int/t/dghl/cooperation/cepej/evaluation/2012/Rapport_en.pdf.

29 Interview with a judge, Sarajevo, 2013.

30 National Assembly of the Republic of Macedonia. Skopje: 1991. *The Constitution of the Republic of Macedonia* Article 98 para.2, *Official Gazette of Republic of Macedonia* 52/91, 31/98, 91/01.

31 Article 98 and 99, *The Constitution of the Republic of Macedonia*, cit.

32 National Assembly of the Republic of Macedonia. Skopje: 2006. *Law on Courts, Article 11 para 2, Official Gazette of the Republic of Macedonia* 58/2006.

33 National Assembly of the Republic of Macedonia. Skopje: 2006. *The Law on the Judicial Council, Official Gazette of the Republic of Macedonia* 60/2006.

34 Article 6, *The Law on the Judicial Council*, cit.

35 Article 14, *The Law on the Judicial Council*, cit.

36 National Assembly of the Republic of Macedonia. Skopje: 2003. *Law on Court Budget, Official Gazette of the Republic of Macedonia* 60/03, 37/06, 103/08, 145/2010.

37 National Assembly of the Republic of Macedonia. Skopje: 2007. *Law on Judges' Salaries, Official Gazette of the Republic of Macedonia* 110/2007

38 State Statistical Office of the Republic of Macedonia. Skopje: 2014 "Average Monthly Net Wage Paid per Employee."

39 S. Dimovski, S.J. Marušić. 27 July 2011. "Macedonia's A1 TV Bankrupt, Facing Closure," Balkansinsight, Skopje. Available at http://www.balkaninsight.com/en/article/bankruptcy-for-macedonia-s-most-prominent-tv.

40 Balkans Investigative Network. 21 October 2013. "Macedonia Jails Journalist Tomislav Kezarovski," Skopje. Available at http://www.balkaninsight.com/en/article/macedonia-jails-journalist-tomislav-kezarovski.

41 Institute for Democracy and Institute for Political Research. 2012. *Istrazhuvanje sprovedeno na sudiite, sudskata administracija i javnosta za evaluacija na sudskiot system i reformate vo sudstvoto vo Republika Makedonija (Komparativna analiza 2009–2012)* (Skopje).

42 V. Misev. 2014 "Europeanization by Rule of Law Implementation in the Western Balkans: Republic of Macedonia. The EU's Effect in Promoting an Efficient and

Independent Macedonian Judiciary" in M. Kmezić (ed.), *Europeanization by Rule of Law Implementation in the Western Balkans*, Institute for Democracy, Skopje: at 154.

43 Interview with a member of an NGO, Skopje 2012.

44 European Commission. *The Former Yugoslav Republic of Macedonia 2015 Progress Report*, SWD(2015) 211 final (Brussels: 12 December 2015). Available at http://ec.europa.eu/enlargement/pdf/key_documents/2015/20151110_report_the_former_yugoslav_republic_of_macedonia.pdf.

45 Organization for Security and Co-operation in Europe. Spillover Mission in Skopje. *Legal Analysis. Independence of the Judiciary* (Skopje: December 2009).

46 Assembly of the Republic of Kosovo. *Law on Courts. No. 03/L-199*, Article 3 (Pristina: 2010).

47 Assembly of the Republic of Kosovo. *Constitution of the Republic of Kosovo.* Article 102. *Official Gazette of Republic of Kosovo* 25 (Pristina: 2008). Available at http://www.kuvendikosoves.org/common/docs/Constitution1%20of%20the%20Republic%20of%20Kosovo.pdf.

48 Ibid. Article 84 para. 15 to para. 19.

49 Ibid.

50 Ibid. Article 104, 108, 109, 110.

51 Kosovo Judicial Council. *Kosovo Judicial Council Annual Report 2011.* (Pristina: 2012).

52 Assembly of the Republic of Kosovo. *Law on Kosovo Judicial Council* 03/L-233. Article 3. (Pristina: 2010). Available at http://www.kuvendikosoves.org/common/docs/ligjet/2010–223-alb.pdf.

53 *Law on Kosovo Judicial Council* 03/L-233. cit.; Assembly of the Republic of Kosovo. *Law on Kosovo Prosecutorial Council* 03/L-224 (Pristina: 2010), Article 17 and Article 18.

54 *Constitution of the Republic of Kosovo*, cit. Article 104; *Kosovo Judicial Council* 03/L-233. Article 18 and Article 19; *Law on Kosovo Prosecutorial Council* 03/L-224, cit.; furthermore, the criteria to qualify for appointment as a Judge are outlined in Articles 26, 27 and 28 of the *Law on Courts*, while the criteria to qualify for appointment as a Prosecutor are outlined in Articles 19 and 20 of the *Law on the State Prosecutor.*

55 *Kosovo Judicial Council* 03/L-233, cit. Article 18.2 and Article 19.2; *Law on Kosovo Prosecutorial Council* 03/L-224, cit.

56 T. Baland and K. N. Wood. 2010. *Report on the Work of Kosovo's Independent Judicial and Prosecutorial Commission*, Independent Judicial and Prosecutorial Commission (Pristina) p. 15.

57 The criteria for appointment as a constitutional court judge are outlined in Article 113 of the Constitution of Kosovo and Article 4 of the *Law on the Constitutional Court.*

58 *Constitution of the Republic of Kosovo*, cit. Article 114.2.

59 Kosovo Judicial Council. *Kosovo Judicial Council 2013 Statistical Report* (Pristina: 2014).

60 *Kosovo Judicial Council* 03/L-233, cit. Article 15; *Law on Kosovo Prosecutorial Council* 03/L-224, cit. and Article 13.

61 Interview with an International Community representative in Kosovo, Skopje, 2013.

62 The so-called "Klecka" case involving former Kosovo's minister Fatmir Limaj and nine other defendants is the most high-profile war crimes prosecution before the Kosovo's courts. After the Basic Court of Pristina had acquitted ten defendants of the War Crimes charges on 17 September 2013, the case was brought up with the Court of Appeals by a Special Prosecutor. See E. Peci. 2013. "Ex-Kosovo Liberation Army Fighters' Custody Extended," *Balkan Transitional Justice.*

Available at http://www.balkaninsight.com/en/article/kosovo-parliament-to-probe-kiqina-case.

63 The EU rule-of-law mission to Kosovo is currently prosecuting 15 former Kosovo Liberation Army fighters, members of the so called Drenica group, for alleged war crimes against civilian detainees during the 1999 armed conflicts in Kosovo. A few of the suspects in the Drenica Group case have high-profile political positions. See A. Gray. 2014. "The Criminal Consequences of Kosovo's Post-War Disorder," *Balkan Transitional Justice.* Available at http://www.balkaninsight.com/en/article/the-criminal-consequences-of-kosovo-s-post-war-disorder.

64 E. Peci. 2013. "Kosovo Parliament Rejects Family 'Revenge' Murders Probe," *Balkan Transitional Justice.* Available at http://www.balkaninsight.com/en/article/kosovo-parliament-to-probe-kiqina-case.

65 The Special Prosecution Office of the Republic of Kosovo (SPRK) was established as a specialized prosecutorial office operating within the Office of the State Prosecutor of Kosovo. Assembly of the Republic of Kosovo. *Law on the Special Prosecution Office of the Republic of Kosovo* 03/L-052 (Pristina: 2010), Article 1. Available at http://www.assembly-kosova.org/?cid=2,191,259.

66 Interview with a NGO representative, Pristina, 2013.

67 See also European Commission. *Kosovo* 2015 Report*, SWD(2015) 2015 final (Brussels: 12 November 2015). Available at http://ec.europa.eu/enlargement/pdf/key_documents/2015/20151110_report_kosovo.pdf.

68 National Assembly of the Republic of Serbia. Constitution of the Republic of Serbia. *Official Gazette of the Republic of Serbia* 83/2006 (Belgrade: 2006).

69 National Assembly of the Republic of Serbia. Decision on the Number of Judges in Courts. *Official Gazette of the Republic of Serbia* 43/2009, 91/2009 and 35/2010 (Belgrade: 2009).

70 National Assembly of the Republic of Serbia. Decision on the Establishment of Criteria and Standards for Evaluation of Qualification, Competence and Worthiness for Election of Judges and Presidents of Courts, High Judicial Council. *Official Gazette of the Republic of Serbia* 49/09 (Belgrade: 2009).

71 National Assembly of the Republic of Serbia. *Constitution of the Republic of Serbia, Official Gazette of the Republic of Serbia* 83/2006 (Belgrade: 2006). Article 153.

72 Bertelsmann Stiftung. 2014. *BTI 2014 – Serbia Country Report*. (Gütersloh: Bertelsmann Stiftung): 9.

73 See Judge's Association of Serbia. "Short Overview of Judicial Developments in Serbia" (Belgrade: 2013). Available at http://www.sudije.rs/files/file/pdf/Short%20Review%20of%20Judicial%20Developments%20in%20Serbia.pdf.

74 Interview with a judge, Begrade, January 2014.

75 D. Dolenec. 2013. *Democratic Institutions and Authoritarian Rule in Southeast Europe*, cit.:187.

76 Ombudsperson. Opinion of the Ombudsperson in relation to the revision of the procedure for general re-election of judges (Belgrade: 12 January 2012). Available in Serbian at http://www.ombudsman.rs/index.php/lang-sr/2011-12-11-11-34-45/2104-2012-01-12-10-56-39.

77 Taken from the Business Anti-Corruption Portal. 2012. *Serbian Judicial System.*

78 Interview with a judge, Belgrade, June 2014.

79 J. Vasilić. 2014. "The Judiciary is not Independent due to Government," NIN 3336 (4 December 2014).

80 Interview with a judge, Belgrade, March 2014.

81 The reform included: (1) reduction and partial replacement of judges and prosecutors by staging a general election, which was actually the re-election of those who already had a permanent function; (2) changing the courts network; changes in the network of courts was carried out without any clear criteria and preparation; (3) change in procedural laws, which was carried out to achieve the

acceleration of judicial proceedings via administrative measures, rather than substantive dispute resolution. The opinion of authoritative bodies of the Council of Europe, European Union and other specialized international organizations was that this "reform" did not succeed in any element.

82 T. Spaić. 2014. "Judiciary Reform or how to Make the Serbian Judiciary Worthy?," *The New Century* No 07: 24.

83 Interview with a Law Professor, Belgrade, January 2014.

84 Ibid.

85 The case of the businessman Miroslav Mišković is perhaps the best known, but not the only example of such practice. See "Miskovic Continued Detention was Unconstitutional," *Vreme* (10 October 2013). Available in Serbian at http://www.vreme.com/cms/view.php?id=1143163.

86 Interview with a Law Professor, Belgrade, January 2014.

87 "1990s-era Customs Chief Acquitted in Corruption Case," *BETA, TANJUG* (14 February 2014). Available at http://www.b92.net/eng/news/crimes.php?yyyy=2014&mm=02&dd=10&nav_id=89275.

88 "Special Court Acquits Agriculture Minister," *BETA* (12 November 2012). Available at http://www.b92.net/eng/news/crimes.php?yyyy=2012&mm=11&dd=01&nav_id=82948.

89 "Davinic Acquitted in Army Procurement Scandal," *TANJUG* (5 July 2012).

90 "Ex-minister Acquitted of Corruption Charges," *B92, TANJUG* (12 July 2012). Available at http://www.b92.net/eng/news/crimes.php?yyyy=2012&mm=07&dd=18&nav_id=81334.

91 "Appelate Court Annuls the Indictment against Dulic," *TANJUG, BETA* (28 June 2013). Available in Serbian at http://www.blic.rs/Vesti/Hronika/390529/Apelacioni-sud-ukinuo-optuznicu-protiv-Dulica.

92 "An Alarming Number of Obsolete Cases," BETA (21 July 2014). Available in Serbian at http://www.b92.net/info/vesti/index.php?yyyy=2014&mm=07&dd=21&nav_id=879205.

93 Ibid.

94 V. Rakić-Vodinelić. "Corrupt Obsolescence 'Reformed' Judiciary," *Peščanik* (14 February 2014). Available at http://pescanik.net/koruptivna-zastarelost-reformisanog-pravosuda-ii/.

95 Ibid.

96 Ibid.

97 T. Spaić, V. Cvijić, M. Ilić and N. Latković. 2014. "Crimes in Serbia Barred by the Authorities," *Blic* (23 March 2014).

98 "Suitcase Affair Defendants Acquitted," *TANJUG* (21 May 2010). Available at http://www.b92.net/eng/news/crimes.php?yyyy=2010&mm=05&dd=21&nav_id=67292.

99 "The Judges in the Cases of Pachomius and Hilarion Judged Against Justice," *Blic* (23 November 2007). Available in Serbian at http://www.blic.rs/Vesti/Hronika/20751/Sudije-u-slucajevima-Ilariona-i-Pahomija-sudile-protiv-pravde.

100 "'Serbia Shows Crime Pays' Ex Official Says after EU Decision," *B92* (29 October 2014). Available at http://www.b92.net/eng/news/politics.php?yyyy=2014&mm=10&dd=29&nav_id=92061.

101 "Jezdimir Vasiljevic is Acquitted" *Beta, TANJUG* (21 February 2014). Available at http://www.b92.net/info/vesti/index.php?yyyy=2013&mm=02&dd=20&nav_id=688375.

102 "Peconi Acquitted from Prosecution," *Novosti* (30 November 2012). Available in Serbian at http://www.novosti.rs/vesti/naslovna/hronika/aktuelNo.291.html:408433-Peconi-oslobodjen-zbog-zastarelosti.

103 T. Spaić, V. Cvijić, M. Ilić and N. Latković. 2014. "Crimes in Serbia Barred by the Authorities," cit.

104 T. Spaić. 2014. "Judiciary Reform or How to Make the Serbian Judiciary Worthy?," cit. 26.

105 The Parliament of the Republic of Montenegro. *Constitution of the Republic of Montenegro, Official Gazette of the Republic of Montenegro* 1/2007. (Podgorica: 2006). Article 1 (2).

106 The Parliament of the Republic of Montenegro. *Law on Courts. Official Gazette of the Republic of Montenegro* 5/2002, 49/2004; *Official Gazette of the Republic of Montenegro* 22/2008 and 39/2011 (Podgorica: 2002).

107 The Parliament of the Republic of Montenegro. *Law on the Judicial Council. Official Gazette of the Republic of Montenegro* 13/2008 and 39/2011 (Podgorica: 2008).

108 The Parliament of the Republic of Montenegro. *Law on State Prosecutor's Office. Official Gazette of the Republic of Montenegro* 69/2003; *Official Gazette of the Republic of Montenegro* 40/2008 and 38/11 (Podgorica: 2003).

109 The Parliament of the Republic of Montenegro. *Law on Education in Judicial Bodies. Official Gazette of the Republic of Montenegro* 27/2006 (Podgorica: 2006).

110 Government of Montenegro. December 2011. *Action Plan for the Implementation of the Strategy for Reform of the Judiciary 2007–2012*. Podgorica. Available in Montenegrin at http://www.pravda.gov.me/biblioteka/strategije.

111 European Commission for Democracy through Law. 6.07.2012. *Draft Amendments to the Constitutional Provisions Relating to the Judiciary of Montenegro.* Opinion No. 677/2012 Strasbourg.

112 European Commission. 1 August 2013. *Statement on the Adoption of Constitutional Amendments in Montenegro.* MEMO/13/735. Brussels.

113 Ibid.

114 S. Voigt. 2005. "The Economic Effects of Judicial Accountability: Some Preliminary Insights," *International Centre for Economic Research Working Paper* No. 19: 10.

115 J. G. S. Koppell. 2005. "Pathologies of Accountability: ICANN and the Challenge of 'Multiple Accountabilities Disorder'," *Public Administration Review* 65(1): 94–108 at 94.

116 D. Piana. 2010. *Judicial Accountabilities in New Europe* (London: Ashgate): 300.

117 M. Bovens. 2007. "Analysing and Assessing Accountability: A Conceptual Framework," *European Law Journal* 13(4): 447–468.

118 *Law on the High Judicial and Prosecutorial Council of Bosnia and Herzegovina.* cit.

119 Ibid. Article 56

120 Ibid. Article 58.

121 High Judicial and Prosecutorial Council of Bosnia and Herzegovina. *Rules of Procedure of the High Judicial and Prosecutorial Council of Bosnia and Herzegovina, Official Gazette of Bosnia and Herzegovina* 59/04 (Sarajevo: 2004).

122 *Law on the High Judicial and Prosecutorial Council of Bosnia and Herzegovina.* Article 68, cit.

123 Ibid. Article 70.

124 European Commission. *Technical Information Requested by the European Commission.* European Union–Bosnia and Herzegovina SAP Structured Dialogue on Justice (Brussels: July 2011).

125 High Judicial and Prosecutorial Council of Bosnia and Herzegovina. *Code of Judicial Ethics and the Code of Prosecutorial Ethics, Official Gazette of Bosnia and Herzegovina* 13/06 (Sarajevo: 2006).

126 *Law on Kosovo Judicial Council* 03/L-233. Article 43, cit.

127 Ibid. Article 35.

128 These data pertain to disciplinary proceedings against both judges and public prosecutors. Kosovo Judicial Council. *Annual Report of Kosovo Judicial Council* (Pristina: 14 July 2014).

129 Kosovo Judicial Council. *Regulation on the Evaluation of Performance of Judges*, Decision No: KJC 50/1–2012, dated 2 April 2012, and KJC No. 85/2013, dated 6 September 2013. Adopted on 24 April 2012, amended on 2 May 2013 and 10 June 2013.
130 Ibid. Article 2(1).
131 Ibid. Article 2(2).
132 *Annual Report of Kosovo Judicial Council*, 2013, at 15, cit.
133 *The Law on the Judicial Council*, Article 31, cit.
134 *Law on Courts*, Article 79, cit.
135 Ibid. Article 74.
136 The Former Yugoslav Republic of Macedonia 2013 Progress Report, cit.
137 European Commission. *EU Commission HLAD Spring Report* (Strasbourg: 16 April 2013). Available at http://ec.europa.eu/enlargement/pdf/key_documents/2013/mk_spring_report_2013_en.pdf.
138 *Constitution of the Republic of Montenegro*, Articles 125 (1), 126 and 128, cit.
139 *Law on the Judicial Council*, Article 50, cit.
140 *The Law on Courts*, cit.
141 Ibid. Article 33.
142 Ibid. Article 33a.
143 Judicial Council of Montenegro. *Rules of Procedure of the Judicial Council, Official Gazette of the Republic of Montenegro* 11/2007 (Podgorica: 2007). Articles 54–69.
144 *Law on the Judicial Council*. Article 51, cit.
145 See V. Radulović, T. Gorjanc Prelević, A. Šoć. 2013. *Judicial Council of Montenegro: Operation Analysis 2008–2013* (Golbiprint: Podgorica).
146 *Constitution of the Republic of Montenegro*. Article 121, cit.
147 Disciplinary Commission of the Judicial Council (Podgorica: 1 October 2008) *Decission Su.R.* No. 367/08.
148 Disciplinary Commission of the Judicial Council (Podgorica: 26 December 2008) *Decission Su.R. No. 636/08*.
149 European Commission. (Brussels: 12 November 2012) *Screening Report Montenegro*, Chapter 23 – *Judiciary and Fundamental Rights*, MD 281/12. Available at http://ec.europa.eu/enlargement/pdf/montenegro/screening_reports/20130218_screening_report_montenegro_ch23.pdf.
150 Ibid.
151 Interview with an NGO representative, Podgorica, 2013.
152 Judicial Council of Montenegro: *Operation Analysis 2008–2013* (Podgorica: 2014). P. 122.
153 *Constitution of the Republic of Serbia*. Article 150, cit.
154 *Operation Analysis 2008–2013*, cit.
155 European Commission. *Serbia 2013 Progress Report*, SWD(2013) 412 final (Brussels, 16 October 2013): 39.
156 See in H. R. v. Gunsteren. 1986. "The Ethical Context of Bureaucracy and Performance Analysis," in F.-X. Kaufmann, G. Majone, V. Ostrom and W. Wirth (eds.), *Guidance, Control, and Evaluation in the Public Sector: The Bielefeld Interdisciplinary Project* (De Gruyter: Berlin): 267.
157 G. Yein Ng, M. Velicogna and C. Dallara. (2007). *Monitoring and Evaluation of Court System: A Comparative Study* (European Commission for Efficiency of Justice: 2007): 5. Available at http://www.coe.int/t/dghl/cooperation/cepej/series/Etudes6Suivi_en.pdf.
158 Ibid.
159 Council of Europe. Rome: 1950. *Convention for the Protection of Human Rights and Fundamental Freedoms* (*European Convention on Human Rights*, as amended by the provisions of Protocol No. 14 (CETS No. 194) from its entry into force on 1 June 2010). Article 6(1).

160 Communication from the Commission to the European Parliament, the Council, the European Central Bank, the European Economic and Social Committee and the Committee of the Regions. Brussels: 2014. *2014 EU Justice Scoreboard*, COM(2014) 155 final: 8.

161 The common name for the bulk of pending cases stemming from unpaid water, refuse, heating and TV subscription fees in Bosnia and Herzegovina.

162 High Judicial and Prosecutorial Council of Bosnia and Herzegovina. Sarajevo: 2012. *Rules on Measures for the Performance of Judges, Legal Associates and Other Employees in the Courts in Bosnia and Herzegovina, Official Gazette of Bosnia and Herzegovina* No. 43/12.

163 See A. Kadribašić. 2014. "Democratic Transition, Rule of Law and Europeanization: Limited Progress in Bosnia and Herzegovina," cit.

164 Ibid., 85.

165 The Conclusions of the 3287th Council meeting on General Affairs, held in Brussels on 17 December 2013 state that the "proper handling of war crimes cases is a crucial endeavor. Justice needs to be guaranteed for the victims and their families and to support the broader efforts towards reconciling societies within Bosnia and Herzegovina, as well as in the whole region. All individuals suspected of war crimes must be brought to justice."

166 Approximately 6,000 computers, 2,500 printers and 350 servers were donated by various donors to the Bosnian judicial institutions according to the latest HJPC Report.

167 Interview with a judge, Sarajevo, 2013.

168 *Law on Courts* 03/L-199, cit. Article 7(2).

169 See European Commission. *Kosovo* 2010, 2011, 2012, 2013 Progress Reports* (Brussels: 2010, 2011, 2012, 2013). Available at http://ec.europa.eu/enlargement/countries/detailed-country-information/kosovo/index_en.htm.

170 Kosovo Judicial Council 2013 Report, cit.: 18.

171 Ibid.

172 See also in Organization for Security and Co-operation in Europe. January 2012. *Execution of Judgments.* Available at http://www.osce.org/kosovo/87004.

173 Kosovo Judicial Council (Pristina: 2013). Decision No. 52/2013.

174 Representatives of USAID, EULEX, and EU Office Project in Kosovo.

175 Kosovo Judicial Council 2013 Report, cit.

176 Assembly of the Republic of Kosovo. *Law on Arbitration* 02/L-75 (Pristina: 2006); Assembly of the Republic of Kosovo. *Law on Mediation* 03/L-057 (Pristina: 2006).

177 Assembly of the Republic of Kosovo. *Law on the Notary* 04/L-002 (Pristina: 2008).

178 See V. Misev. "Europeanization by Rule of Law Implementation in the Western Balkans: Republic of Macedonia. The EU's Effect in Promoting an Efficient and Independent Macedonian Judiciary," cit.

179 The Former Yugoslav Republic of Macedonia 2013 Progress Report, cit. 11.

180 In 2007, 1.1 million euros were allocated to help strengthen the capacities of the Administrative Court and to support the reform of the administrative procedure, and in 2008, 0.7 million euros were allocated to support the capacities of the Academy for the training of judges and prosecutors (for the establishment of e-learning and decentralized training).

181 See more in A. Bibežić, M. Kmezić. 2014. "Approximation of Membership as an Impetus for Rule of Law," in M. Kmezić (ed.), *Europeanization by Rule of Law Implementation in the Western Balkans*, Institute for Democracy, Skopje: 159–182.

182 Interview with a judge, Podgorica, 2013.

183 The Parliament of the Republic of Montenegro. *Law on Notaries, Official Gazette of the Republic of Montenegro* 68/05 and 49/08 (Podgorica: 2008).

184 The Parliament of the Republic of Montenegro. *Law on Public Enforcement Officers, Official Gazette of the Republic of Montenegro* 61/2011 (Podgorica: 2011).
185 Interview with a NGO expert, Podgorica, 2014.
186 National Assembly of the Republic of Serbia. National Judicial Reform Strategy. *Official Gazette of the Republic of Serbia* 44/2006 (Belgrade: 26 May 2006).
187 Progress Report, Serbia 2013.
188 National Assembly of the Republic of Serbia. *Decision on Number of Judges, Official Gazette* 106/13,115/13 and 5/14. (Belgrade: 2014).
189 The European Commission for the Efficiency of Justice. *European Judicial Systems. Edition 2012 (2010 data), Efficiency and Quality of Justice.* (Strasbourg: 2012). Available at http://www.coe.int/t/dghl/cooperation/cepej/evaluation/2012/Rapport_en.pdf.
190 Ibid.
191 Data taken over from The National Assembly of the Republic of Serbia. *National Judicial Reform Strategy for the Period 2013–2018, Official Gazette of the Republic of Serbia* 57/2013 (Belgrade: 1 July 2013).
192 Organization for Security and Co-Operation in Europe. Mission to Serbia. 2011. *Judicial System in Serbia:* 3. Available at http://www.osce.org/serbia/82759.
193 National Assembly of the Republic of Serbia. *Law on the Organization and Competencies of Government Authorities in Prosecuting Perpetrators of War Crimes, Official Gazette of the Republic of Serbia* 67/03 (Belgrade: 1 July 2003) as amended, see *Official Gazette of the Republic of Serbia* 135/04 (Belgrade); *Official Gazette of the Republic of Serbia* 61/05.
194 National Assembly of the Republic of Serbia. *Law on Organisation and Jurisdiction of Government Authorities in Suppression of High Technological Crime. Official Gazette of the Republic of Serbia* 61/2005 and 104/2009 (Belgrade: 2009).
195 Court managers are working in the Higher Court in Belgrade, the Higher Court in Niš, the Appellate Court in Novi Sad, the Higher Misdemeanor Court in Belgrade, Misdemeanor Court in Belgrade, Commercial Court in Niš and Basic Court in Novi Sad.
196 For example, at the Belgrade First Basic Court alone, *Infostan*, the largest utility company in Serbia, has around 600,000 debtors' cases in the system.
197 These are the Basic Court in Subotica, the Basic Court in Vranje, the Basic Court in Vrsac, the Higher Court in Novi Pazar, the Basic Court in Niš, and the Higher Court in Belgrade.
198 East-West Management Institute. Belgrade: 2014. *Newsletter July 2014*. Separation of Powers Program – Best Practices Guide for Backlog Reduction and Prevention.
199 Interview with a judge, Belgrade, March 2013.
200 Interview with a Law Professor, Belgrade, January 2014.
201 Interview with a Law Professor, Belgrade, January 2014. Interview with a NGO representative, Skopje December 2013, and Interview with an international community representative, Pristina, October 2013.
202 Interview with a NGO representative, Pristina, October 2013.
203 Interview with a Law Professor, Belgrade, January 2014.
204 See Chapter 4 of this book.
205 Interview with a Law Professor, Belgrade, January 2014.
206 Interview with a judge, Pristina, August 2013.
207 Z. Kuhn. 2011. *The Judiciary in Central and Eastern Europe*, cit. The term "limited law" is used in general jurisprudence in order to observe the lack of interest in theories of interpretation of legal acts and scepticism towards teleological reasoning.
208 Interview with a Director of a Judicial Academy, Belgrade, January 2014.

209 There is no single European model for initial and in-service training of judges. Three models existing throughout Europe relate to particular features of the different judicial systems. While a number of countries offer lengthy formal training in specialized establishments, followed by intensive didactic training (South European model), others provide a sort of apprenticeship under the supervision of an experienced judge, who imparts knowledge and professional advice on the basis of concrete examples (French model). Furthermore, common law countries rely purely on gathering of professional experience.

210 The Brčko District Assembly. *Law on Judicial Commission of Brčko District of BiH, Official Gazette of the Brčko District of BiH* 7.19 (Brčko: 2007).

211 Parliament of the Federation of Bosnia and Herzegovina. *The Law on the Judicial and Prosecutorial Training Centre in Federation of BiH, Official Gazette of Federation of BiH* 24/02, 40/02, 52/02 and 21/03 (Sarajevo: 2002).

212 National Assembly of the Republika Srpska. *The Law on the Judicial and Prosecutorial Training Centre in Republika Srpska, Official Gazette of Republika Srpska* 49/02 and 77/02 (Banja Luka: 2002).

213 High Judicial and Prosecutorial Council of Bosnia and Herzegovina. *Mid-Term Strategic Plan for 2012–2015, Initial and Continuous Judicial and Prosecutorial Training* (Sarajevo: 2011).

214 Some judges participated in two or more seminars.

215 ABA/ROLI, August 2007. *Judicial Reform Index for Kosovo.* Volume III. Available at http://www.americanbar.org/advocacy/rule_of_law/where_we_work/europe_eurasia/kosovo.html.

216 The Assembly of Kosovo. *Law on Establishing the Kosovo Judicial Institute, Official Gazette* 02/L-25 O (Pristina: 2008).

217 Kosovo Judicial Institute. *Annual Report 2013* (Pristina: 2014).

218 As already explained in the section on the independence of the judiciary, it is within the competence of the Kosovo Judicial Council and Kosovo Prosecutorial Council to determine the exact number of candidates for the initial training program.

219 *Judicial Training: A Perspective from Kosovo.* 2015. Kosovo Judicial Institute. Available at https://igjk.rks-gov.net/Uploads/Documents/Nje_Perspektive_nga_KosovaEN_.pdf.

220 National Assembly of the Republic of Macedonia. *Law on the Academy for the Training of Judges and Prosecutors, Official Gazette of the Republic of Macedonia* 13/2006, 88/2010, 166/2012 and 26/2013 (Skopje: 2006).

221 Ibid. Article 2.

222 Ibid. Article 42.

223 See the Former Yugoslav Republic of Macedonia 2013 Progress Report, cit.: 40.

224 Academy for Judges and Public Prosecutors. *Report on the Work of the Academy for Judges and Public Prosecutors for 2013* (Skopje: 2014): 11.

225 Academy for Judges and Public Prosecutors. *Report on the Work of the Academy for Judges and Public Prosecutors for 2014* (Skopje: 2015).

226 Interview with an employee at the Academy for Training of Judges and Prosecutors, Skopje 2012.

227 See more detail in Supreme Court of Montenegro. Centre for Judicial Training. 2012. *Annual Report on Work of the Judicial Training Centre for 2011.* Podgorica.

228 The Parliament of the Republic of Montenegro. *The Law on Judiciary Training, Official Gazette of the Republic of Montenegro* 27/2006 (Podgorica: 2006).

229 Ibid. Article 3.

230 Judicial Training Centre. *Annual Activity Report Judicial Training Centre of Montenegro for the Year 2013* (Podgorica: 2014).

231 *The Law on Judiciary Training*, cit. Article 34.

232 Ibid. Article 35.
233 Ibid. Article 4.
234 Judicial Training Centre. *Annual Activity Report Judicial Training Centre of Montenegro for the Year 2014* (Podgorica: 2015).
235 R. Pound. 1908. "Mechanical Jurisprudence," *Columbia Law Review* 8, 605–623 at 605.
236 Z. Kuhn. 2011. *The Judiciary in Central and Eastern Europe*, cit.: 210.
237 National Assembly of the Republic of Serbia. *The Law on the Judicial Academy, Official Gazette of the Republic of Serbia* 104/2009 (Belgrade: 2009).
238 *Law on Judges*, Article 43. cit.
239 Annual priorities for the continuous training programme are set according to the practical need. Since in 2013 new *Law on Criminal Proceedings* entered the power, it has been set as a priority for the programme. Throughout the year 107 educational events were held in this area for approximately 1,400 beneficiaries coming from the ranks of judges, public prosecutors and police.
240 See for example *Lepojević v. Serbia, application No. 13909/05*, European Court for Human Rights, Strasbourg, 6 November 2007. The Court held that domestic courts in the case Lepojić violated the right to freedom of expression guaranteed in the Art. 10 of the European Convention on Human Rights because of criminal conviction and subsequent civil judgment rendered against Lepojević.
241 *Serbia: 2013 Progress Report*, European Commission: Brussels (2013).
242 Interview with the Director of the Judicial Academy, Belgrade, January 2014.
243 See J. Shklar. 1987. "Political Theory and the Rule of Law," in A. C. Hutchinson and P. Monahan (eds.), *The Rule of Law: Ideal or Ideology?* (Carswell Legal Publications).
244 M. Kmezić. 2015. "The Judicial Academy as *conditio sine qua non* for the Effectiveness and Efficiency of the Serbian Judiciary," *European Public Law* (21)3: 509–525.

Part III

8 Comparative analysis

Introduction

Just over two decades ago, after the fall of the Berlin Wall, it seemed that the Western ideals of democracy, rule of law and individual rights would be spread undisturbed throughout the world, thus leading to "the end of history,"[1] as famously suggested by Fukuyama. Instead, an array of nationalistic, ethnic, and religious conflicts, global economic crisis, and terrorist acts, as well as the war on terror, soon dissolved the "triumphalist confidence of the 1990s."[2]

In an answer to the new lines of global conflict caused by the differences between the liberal West and non-liberal East, the developed North and undeveloped South, Islamic and Christian religious communities, between global corporations and third world countries, etc.—a widespread agreement was created on the point that the "rule of law is good for everyone."[3] This acknowledgment has led to the multiple efforts to export democracy and the rule of law.[4] Over the past 20 years the "rule of law revival"[5] has with more or less success influenced political and economic liberalization in Asia, Latin America, the former Soviet Union, sub-Saharan Africa, the Middle East, Eastern Europe, and the Western Balkans.

The EU is a relative latecomer to the arena of democracy and rule of law promotion. The Union is engaged in the process of rule of law export as part of its enlargement policy towards the Western Balkans and Turkey, its neighborhood policy towards Russia, the so-called Newly Independent States and the Southern Mediterranean countries, and finally its external policies towards a number of countries from Asia, Latin America and Africa. Notwithstanding the evident success of the EU's influence on democratic transformation of the so-called third countries, the focus of this book has been on the analysis of the rule of law promotion taking place within the current process of EU enlargement.

The EU's comprehensive strategy to promote effective rule of law exercised through the SAP in the Western Balkans consists of the progressive development of contractual relations and institutional ties based on an enhanced political dialogue and monitoring process, supported by financial assistance and technical aid, and complemented by the demand to comply with a clear set of political conditions. All of these processes are intimately interwoven within the famous Copenhagen conditions, which were originally established at the 1993 European Council for the ten countries taking part in the 2004 enlargement. After 2000, the EU sought to account for the Western Balkans particularities with the SAP, which requires *inter alia* that the candidate country has achieved stability of institutions guaranteeing democracy, the rule of law, human rights and respect for and protection of minorities.

In practice, the EU enlargement is understood not only as a foreign policy approach in the context of international relations, but also as a form of "governance export"[6] and "norm diffusion."[7] Hence, democratic consolidation, including the establishment of an effective system of rule of law, is part of the more general top-down process of Europeanization that regards the influence of EU institutions, rules and policy-making processes and their impact on the laws, institutions and identities of candidate countries. Hence, the main research question this book attempts to answer is whether the EU institutions have had an influence, and if so of what kind, on implementation of the rule of law in Bosnia-Herzegovina, Kosovo, Macedonia, Montenegro and Serbia. For clarity's sake, let us recall other research questions, since precisely these will provide the structure for the comparative conclusions of this study addressed in this chapter. What are EU requirements developed in the monitoring process? Which organizational-institutional reforms have been made? Which gate-keeper elites resisted these reforms? Who (critical civil society actors) supported these reforms? What have been the effects and how have they changed over the last decade with regard to independence, responsibility, efficiency, and effectiveness benchmarks? Does the possible success of judicial reform actually corresponds with countries' current stage of EU integration? Finally, does the current EU approach to the rule of law reform in candidate countries work beyond the critical phase of norm adoption?

As explained in Chapter 1, rule of law is a vaguely defined concept, the substance of which is often elusive. Another conceptual problem arises from the fact that the effects of judicial sector reform are not easily captured, due to the lack of a coherent theory of judicial governance, and the difficulty of measuring the actual performance of the judicial system, as has been observed in regard to monitoring activities during the 2004 and 2007 Eastern enlargement processes.[8] Bearing this in mind, this study has developed an integrated set of benchmarks in order to apply and test the empirical findings elaborated in the course of this research. Hence, to address the question of the EU's influence on judiciary reform in the Western Balkan accession countries, this book has sought to trace evidence of such influence along the lines of judicial independence, accountability, efficiency and effectiveness. Since 2012, the author of this study has investigated the institutional reform carried out in the judicial sector by a content analysis of legal rules and administrative regulations and empirically tested their implementation. Based on the elaborated integrative operationalization of the research hypothesis, this study was able to critically assess not only the endogenous factors favoring or preventing the reform of the judicial sector, but also the dynamic rule setting in the EU rule of law monitoring process and to conclude whether incomprehensiveness, vagueness and establishment of *ad hoc* new requirements is part of the problem rather than the solution.

Analytically, this study has approached the problem armed with a number of key notions. First, this study intended to overcome the separation of research by EU legal scholars, lawyers, and political scientists and to re-integrate the different aspects of legal and political analyses through the logic of "functional interdependence."[9] Second, the study has tried to identify with more precision the independent variables for the rule of law implementation during the EU pre-accession process by purposefully selecting countries that are involved in different stages of the EU integrations. Finally, the comparative method also helped to identify and specify the independent variables both in the normative and empirical analyses.

It is hoped that this book will not merely plug the existing research gaps in comparative politics, international relations, political science, international legal studies, and studies on European integrations, but also will provide assistance to myriad policy-makers and practitioners in the SEE countries, EU institutions, other multilateral institutions at the regional and global level, as well as non-state organizations and networks who are dealing with the rule of law promotion, judiciary reform, norm-socialization and Europeanization issues. This book has sought to contend with this conundrum by conceptualizing key components of the puzzle and then testing them against the normative and empirical analysis within a comparative analytical framework, with the main goal of capturing the dynamics and potential success or failure of Europeanization influence on the rule of law implementation in the SEE.

Measuring the results

Immediately after 2000, the main weaknesses of the judiciary systems common to all the WB countries were identified as: (1) an inadequate constitutional and legal framework, resulting in a lack of judicial independence and accountability, (2) an overly complex and extended system of courts, (3) huge backlogs of cases, excessive delays in court proceedings, and difficult enforcement of court judgments, (4), unclear selection, dismissal, performance, and promotion standards for judges, (5) corruption of the judicial bodies, (6) a lack of integrated performance measurement capacities for the judiciary, (7) outdated administration practices, hampering judicial effectiveness and efficiency, (8) lack of initial and continuous training for judges and inadequate curriculum of law faculties, hindering the development of professional staff competent to implement the *Acquis* in domestic legal system, and (9) poorly equipped judicial facilities and underutilization of information technology, restricting access to justice. The following section will present the outcome of the ongoing efforts to improve the performance of the courts in the Western Balkan accession countries along the lines of previously set benchmarks of judicial independence, accountability, efficiency and effectiveness.

Independence

A comprehensive comparative study of judicial institutions in the WB confirms that an insufficient culture of judicial independence and separation of powers and functions is still persistent across the region. This is mainly the consequence of a lack of the political preconditions for judicial independence and the presence of legacies of the old political and/or legal culture. In order to achieve the independence and self-government of the judiciary, all analyzed countries have established a Judicial Council—an autonomous body dealing with the main organizational issues of the judiciary, namely selection, promotion and to a limited extent dismissal of judges, and in some cases proposals for the budget (see Table 8.1).

The Judicial Councils in the WB for the most part follow the Southern European model,[10] as their main responsibility is the appointment and disciplining of personnel. In some cases the role of Judicial Councils in appointment and promotion is effective (e.g. in Bosnia-Herzegovina, Macedonia and Montenegro), in some others it is slightly limited (Serbia, where the Judicial Council makes binding recommendations), while in Kosovo it remains rather limited due to the *de facto*, although not *de jure*, veto power exercised by the country's President. Removal of judges is in the exclusive competence of the Judicial Council in all five countries, although in Kosovo and Serbia the right to a Supreme Court and Constitutional Court appeal, respectively, is permitted. In Kosovo and Bosnia-Herzegovina, the role of the Judicial Council is extended to oversee the initial and continuous training of judges, as well as to administer the work of courts. Such legal solutions should be interpreted in light of the increased international community presence in the two countries, particularly in terms of the direct influence of this presence on institution building, as well as its indirect influence epitomized in the dominant role of foreign financial aid in the process of state-building.

The salaries of judges are a significant element of their social and economic status, intimately linked to their independent position. In this regard, the economic independence of judges provides an additional guarantee for preventing forbidden influence on judges. The salaries of the judicial branch are regulated by special laws that take into consideration the salaries of all public officials. In comparison to the average of these salaries, it can be observed that the prescribed salaries of judges meet satisfying standards, except in Kosovo. However, general economic malaise has made it a fairly common temptation for judicial servants to engage in bribe taking.

A general problem regarding the independence benchmark remains evident in the lack of appropriate procedures to make the role of the Judicial Councils more binding, as well as the need for greater inclusiveness of these institutions in the process of drafting the legislative reforms. A possible threat to judicial independence is the lack of clearly established criteria for career advancement, as well as in the rules for appointing the courts' presidents, which leave room for political influence on the process. Most importantly, and particularly worrisome is the

Table 8.1 Judicial Councils

Judicial Council	*BiH*	*Kosovo*	*Macedonia*	*Montenegro*	*Serbia*
Appoints judges	Yes	Makes non-binding recommendation to the President of the Republic	Yes	Yes	Makes binding recommendation to the National Assembly
Removes judges from position	Yes	Yes (although appeal to supreme court is permitted)	Yes	Makes recommendation to the Parliament	Yes (although appeal to constitutional court is permitted)
Oversees judicial training	Yes	Yes	No	No	No
Prepares budget	No	Yes	No	Proposes the budget to the Parliament	No
Administers the work of courts	Yes	Yes	No	No	No

observed trend of political (formal and more often informal) influence over the judiciary, to which the current EU strategy does not have an appropriate response.

Accountability

The accountability and independence of judiciaries are two sides of the same coin in a democratic society. Namely, despite their constitutionally guaranteed independence, judges must be held accountable for their actions and decisions. Judges are constrained by existing laws, procedures and practices to prevent them from ruling perversely or corruptly. Hence, judges are placed under judicial and/or administrative control resulting in evaluation of their performance and the carrying out of disciplinary proceedings.

Performance evaluation in the countries of interest is conducted by the higher courts in accordance with standardized criteria established by the Judicial Council. Evaluation covers mainly quantitative criteria, namely the percentage of repealed decisions under legal remedy and the number of resolved cases per year, except in Serbia where evaluation requires accounting for all aspects of the judge's job—namely quantity, quality and commitment to judicial work. Quality is evaluated by an analysis of decision-making, the efficiency of case processing, and professionalism in conduct. Qualitative evaluation escapes the trap of over-quantification, but it remains unclear if it takes into consideration more compound criteria, such as the complexity of cases and other specific circumstances, such as court location and human resources. Evaluation may result in election, promotion or removal from office. In Serbia, evaluation may additionally result in mandatory training.

Disciplinary proceedings are conducted by the Judicial Councils—or Disciplinary Commission in Serbia—in accordance with the Code of Ethics and/or Rulebook on Disciplinary Proceedings. Available disciplinary sanctions include public reprimand, salary reduction of up to 50% for a limited period of time, and prohibition of advancement in service for a period of up to three years. Besides the competent authority, litigants and other participants in legal proceedings have the right to file a complaint concerning the performance of judges in cases of perceived unauthorized influence on the course and outcome of court proceedings.

However, major problems can still be observed in the implementation of judicial accountability in all five case study countries. While in Macedonia, for example, there have been only a few dismissals of judges, in Serbia 800 of a total of 3,000 judges lost their jobs in a process that lacked transparency and was criticized several times by EU officials. However, the review procedure was again neither transparent nor fair, which was also repeatedly highlighted by international and independent observers.

Poor enforcement of the judicial accountability calls for the inclusion of the public—both general and expert—as "watchdogs" over the performance of the judiciary in all five case study countries. Namely, according to the law, unless decided otherwise, hearings, trials and rulings should be open to the public, which creates a possibility for citizens and the media to discuss and criticize the work of the courts. A number of NGOs are already taking part in this process, as they daily scrutinize and monitor the work of the judiciary, thus enhancing standards in the field of the accountability of judges.

Effectiveness

The efficiency and effectiveness of the judiciary are interlinked and cannot be analyzed in an isolated perspective. That is, by focusing merely on effectiveness, in the long run, access to justice and the public trust in the judiciary are threatened because of ever increasing costs and delays. This is why the professional competence and productivity of the judiciary need to be in balance. Problems faced by Western Balkans judiciaries in relation to the efficiency benchmark are a lack of human and technical resources, an inadequate court structure, huge backlogs of cases and unduly lengthy procedures.

In an effort to eliminate the problem of lengthy case resolution, all five countries have undergone restructuring of their respective court networks. A three-tier court structure has been established in all of the countries, but significant problems were observed in Kosovo, Bosnia-Herzegovina and Serbia. Namely, Kosovo faces the problem of implementation of the Brussels Agreement on Normalization of Relations between Serbia and Kosovo, which envisages the integration of judicial authorities from the Serb-inhabited northern part of the country within the Kosovo legal framework. Additionally, the Appellate Court in Pristina is supposed to establish a panel composed of a majority of Serb judges to deal with all Kosovo Serb-majority municipalities. In Bosnia-Herzegovina, the complex defragmentation of the country has an influence on the functioning of the whole justice system.

Additionally, specialization of institutions has contributed to the relaxation of work of regular courts, as well as to an improvement of the quality of judgments and the competence of judges who are specially skilled and trained for resolving specific and complex cases. In all WB countries, commercial and administrative courts have been established, while in Serbia special departments for organized crimes and war crimes and the Division for combating high technological crime have been set up.

Improvements in infrastructure and administration directly contribute to more efficient case resolution by allowing judges to concentrate more on adjudication. Most of the WB courts are hopelessly overbooked, and there are even courts with a single courtroom. Although guaranteed by law, the right to public hearing is often breached as a result of such shortcomings. State funding of the strategic investment in the judicial sector is rather limited and therefore international financial assistance still plays a pivotal role in funding for equipment and related costs that enhance the institutions' capacity to deliver quality services. Nevertheless, in all countries, the administrative capacity of the courts needs to be further developed. Namely, basic administrative issues such as case registration, technical systems connecting all courts and court units, statistics, reporting systems and monitoring units are still not fully operational. Furthermore, Court Presidents are not trained in court management, while only a few Courts are equipped with administrative and managerial staff members. Besides providing training to judges on court administration issues, improvement also seems possible by employing trained junior legal and professional administrative staff for specific quasi-judicial tasks, such as maintaining records or case management. This would relieve judges of administrative tasks and divert their focus to their adjudicative functions.

Despite all the undertaken reforms, huge backlogs of pending cases, especially in civil and enforcement proceedings, remain a matter of grave concern and regular criticism on the part of the EU in all five countries of concern. Furthermore, it is not uncommon for judicial proceedings to take years or even decades to resolve cases brought before the courts or to enforce decisions. Additional efforts in legal reform should thus not only focus on proceedings, but also on the enforcement procedures as well as on the de-criminalization of certain offences, the simplification of procedural rules and alternative methods of dispute resolution, namely conciliation procedures and arbitration.

Efficiency

Independence and accountability benchmarks make little sense if law enforcement bodies remain incompetent. By competence of judicial servants, it can be understood that they must have sound judgment, professional erudition, and the skill to prosecute or render judgments effectively in accordance with the law. Current judicial elites in the WB have accepted the concept of judicial independence and accountability as a means of "preserving and perpetuating the exclusive role of judges in the judicial sector,"[11] thus indirectly entrenching traditional values and ways of conducting judicial processes. Despite the establishment of modern legislative and institutional frameworks, the professional competence of the judiciary still remains one of the most widespread problems in the WB. Political eruptions in the process of transformation severely affected the professional competence of the judiciary in the WB countries, and continue to undermine the competence of the judiciary, particularly in Bosnia and Herzegovina and Kosovo. In Kosovo, for example, even the quality of written judicial decisions is widely criticized as reflecting "poor analytical, research, and writing skills."[12] Except for the constitutional court, the majority of judges continued in their formalist reading of the law rather than performing their assumed transitional role. Improperly supported by their education, judges often sought a way out of more difficult legal cases by disposing them based on purely formalistic grounds. In this way, the simplified version of textual positivism and the ideology of bound judicial decision-making were able to survive the process of judicial reform. Legacies of old legal culture, although without connection to the former political system, thus remain alive and continue to influence contemporary legal thought. At the same time, education in law schools very often lacks any practice orientation, and even judicial and bar examinations only test applicants' technical legal knowledge.

In an attempt to improve the quality of the judiciary, Judicial Academies specialized in initial and/or continuous education of judges have been established in all countries with the exception of Kosovo, where the Kosovo Judicial Institute was established. However, Judicial Academies are not a part of the regular educational system, but rather an integral part of the judicial system. Their main purpose is to provide professional performance of the judicial function through implementation of initial training of candidates legally integrated into the process of recruitment, and continuous professional training of judges. However, a worrisome trend observed in all case study countries is the neglect of the legislative requirement for recruitment of the Judicial Academy graduates to the judicial positions. The irregularity of the implementation of the merit based recruitment has, in Macedonia for instance, led to a gradual decrease in applicants to the initial training program offered at the Judicial Academy.

The continuous lack of human, technical and financial resources hampers the implementation of more efficient judiciary in the Western Balkans. As a rule Judicial Academies receive state funding only for their annually set priorities within initial and continuous training programs. Crucial parts of the program, such as the training on public procurement issues, the use of alternative dispute settlement procedures, etc., lack financial resources. For this reason, enhancement of the effectiveness of judges is additionally supported by a number of foreign aid donors and domestic expert NGOs, for example the Council of Europe, Foundation Open Society Institute, Soros—Representative Office Montenegro, and American Bar Association/Central and East-European Legal Initiative (ABA/Ceeli), Association of Judges, Centres for Human Rights, etc. On the other hand, it is striking, particularly bearing in mind the common legal tradition of the WB countries, both the lack of regional law journals and the nonexistence of a regional community of lawyers to exchange ideas and experiences and discuss problems common to all of their countries.

The way forward for the improvement of judiciary in the WB

Despite the evident progress achieved in the reform of the judiciary in the WB countries over the past decade, the reform momentum needs to be additionally strengthened in particular to ensure implementation of the undertaken reforms. This is also mentioned in the latest European Commission Enlargement Strategy document that reads that the rule of law reform in accession countries must move "beyond declarations to tangible results."[13] In a nutshell, countries need to ensure full independence of state judicial councils, provide more sound procedures for the appointment of judges, and to additionally improve quality and efficiency of justice. Bearing this in mind, this book offers a list of open questions/recommendations on the improvement of the judiciary reform in the WB countries (see Table 8.2).

Table 8.2 Recommendations for judiciary improvement

	Recommendations			
Country/Benchmark	*Independence*	*Efficiency*	*Accountability*	*Effectiveness*
Bosnia-Herzegovina	1 Consider establishment of clear rules for financing the work of judiciary at the state level. 2 HJPC should be provided with an explicit constitutional basis. 3 Provide greater budgetary competences to the HJPC.	1 Reduce the backlog of cases. 2 Move "utilities" cases from the courts. 3 Transfer non-judicial parts of enforcements to private or public enforcement agencies. 4 Increase number of judges. 5 Modernize case management software. 6 Link the Case Management System with the Police database. 7 Provide the court staff with sets of practical skills, such as decision writing, administrative management, etc.	1 Increase the role of NGO "watchdogs" and society in control of accountability of judges. 2 Fight the corruption of the judiciary. 3 Establish clear mechanisms to ensure the accountability of judges, i.e. disciplinary procedure.	1 Establish single judicial training left at the state level. 2 Set professional qualifications as the standard for appointment of judges rather than "equal rights and representation of constituent people and others." 3 Introduce courses on harmonization of the legislation with the *Acquis* at the Judicial and Prosecutorial Training left. 4 Modernize curricula at law faculties.

	Recommendations			
Country/Benchmark	*Independence*	*Efficiency*	*Accountability*	*Effectiveness*
Kosovo	1 Include the Kosovo Judicial Council in the drafting of judiciary-related legislation. 2 Establish transparent process for the adoption of the judicial budget. 3 Respect the principle of equal ethnic representation in judiciary. 4 Limit the veto rights of the President of Kosovo in the process of appointment of judges. 5 Increase financial independence of the judicial branch. 6 Limit political interference in judiciary.	1 Establish the Case Management Information System in all courts. 2 Improve court infrastructure and modernize equipment. 3 Reduce the case backlog. 4 Modernization of judicial administration. 5 Improve the professional skills of mediators licensed by the Ministry of Justice and public notaries. 6 Implement the Brussels Agreement on Normalization of Relations between Serbia and Kosovo in relation to court structure.	1 Increase the role of NGO "watchdogs" and society in control of accountability of judges. 2 Fight the perceived corruption of the judiciary. 3 Increase the public trust in judiciary.	1 Modernize the curriculum at the law faculties. 2 Improve the quality of writing of judicial decisions. 3 Introduce mandatory continuous training for sitting judges. 4 Secure access to judicial training particularly for members of minority communities.

Table 8.2 (continued)

	Recommendations			
Country/Benchmark	*Independence*	*Efficiency*	*Accountability*	*Effectiveness*
Macedonia	1 Increase the number of Council members coming from the ranks of judges. 2 Strengthen judicial independence in order to eliminate "soft pressure" from other branches of government. 3 Provide budgetary independence of courts.	1 Improve court infrastructure. 2 Decrease the backlog of pending cases at the Administrative and Supreme Court. 3 Improve procedural rules in order to resolve lengthy court proceedings and case backlog. 4 Improve the administrative capacity of courts. 5 Promote alternative dispute resolution.	1 Fight the perceived corruption of judiciary. 2 Increase the role of NGO "watchdogs" and society in control of accountability of judges. 3 Set clear criteria for qualitative evaluation of the work of judges. 4 Set legal provisions distinguishing between disciplinary and dismissal proceedings against judges. 5 Improve predictability and precision of the current legislation governing the dismissal of judges. 6 Improve the proportionality of the application of the disciplinary proceedings by the Judicial Council.	1 Establish a clear set of educational requirements for the election of judges, bearing in mind mandatory recruitment of judges and prosecutors from the Academy for Training of Judges and Prosecutors graduates. 2 Introduce mandatory continuous training for judges. 3 Improve curricula at law faculties.

	Recommendations			
Country/Benchmark	*Independence*	*Efficiency*	*Accountability*	*Effectiveness*
Montenegro	1 Implement constitutional amendments on independence of the judiciary. 2 Fully implement new recruitment system. 3 Strengthen the capacity of Judicial Council.	1 Decrease the case backlog of unenforced court decisions. 2 Develop judicial information system. 3 Provide incentives for alternative dispute settling procedures.	1 Fight the perceived corruption of judiciary. 2 Implement the disciplinary proceedings rules. 3 Introduce system of individual and periodical evaluation of judges. 4 Strengthen the principle of proportionality in regards to disciplinary sanctions.	1 Strengthening and better streamlining of the judicial training. 2 Strengthen the training on public procurement and the use of mediation. 3 Improve curricula at law faculties.
Serbia	1 Introduction of transparency in the work of the High Judicial Council. 2 Set new criteria for appointing the Supreme Court president and court presidents. 3 Revoke the extensive power of the court presidents to reassign cases.	1 Foster alternative ways of dispute settlement. 2 Secure enforcement of court judgments. 3 Modernization of judicial administration 4 Enforcement of existing legal framework in an effort to reduce excessive delays in court proceedings. 5 Increase the budget intended to improve courts' infrastructure. 6 Provide incentives for alternative dispute settling procedures.	1 Set clear criteria for qualitative evaluation of the work of judges. 2 Increase the role of NGO "watchdogs" and society in control of accountability of judges. 3 Secure the accountability of judges by more systematic application of the disciplinary rules. 4 Combat the perceived corruption of judiciary.	1 Modernize the curriculum at the law faculties. 2 Provide incentives for judges to participate at the voluntary continuous training. 3 Legally define the place of the Judicial Academy within the judicial system.

Notes

1 F. Fukuyama. 1992. *The End of History and the Last Man* (New York: Avon Books).
2 B. Z. Tamanaha. 2004. *On the Rule of Law: History, Politics and Theory* (Cambridge: Cambridge University Press).
3 Ibid. 1.
4 See for example T. Carothers (ed.). 2006. *Promoting the Rule of Law Abroad: The Problem of Knowledge* (Washington, D.C.: Carnegie Endowment for International Peace); F. Fukuyama and M. McFaul. 2007. "Should Democracy be Promoted or Demoted? Bridging the foreign policy divide." Stanley Foundation. Available online at http://www.stanleyfoundation.org/publications/other/fukuymcfaul07.pdf; J. M. Trebilcock and J. R. Daniels. 2008. *Rule of Law Reform and Development: Charting the Fragile Path of Progress* (Northampton: Edward Elgar); A. Magen and L. Morlino. 2008. *International Actors, Democratization and the Rule of Law* (London and New York: Routledge); A. Magen, T. Risse and M. McFaul. 2009. *Promoting Democracy and the Rule of Law* (New York: Palgrave Macmillan); L. Morlino and G. Palombella (eds.). 2010. *The Rule of Law and Democracy: Internal and External Issues* (Leiden: Brill Publishing).
5 T. Carothers (ed.), *Promoting the Rule of Law Abroad*, cit.: 3–15.
6 See A. Magen. 2007. "Transformative Engagement through Law. The *Acquis Communautaire* as Instrument of EU External Influence," *European Journal of Law Reform* 9(3): 361–393.
7 F. Schimmelfenning. 2000. "International Socialization in the New Europe: Action in a Rational Institutional Environment," *European Journal of International Relations* 6(1): 109–139.
8 A. Mungiu-Pippidi. 2008. "The EU as a Transformation Agent. Lessons Learned from Governance Reforms in East Central Europe," *Hertie School of Governance – Working Papers* 33: 7.
9 Detailed explanation of the logic of functional interdependance is available in works of J. Marko. 2008. "The Law and Politics of Diversity Management: A Neo-Institutional Approach," *European Yearbook of Minority Issues* 6 (2006/07: Brill): 252–279; and J. Marko and M. Handstanger. 2009. "The Interdependence of Law and Political Science: About the 'Essence and Value' of a 'Juristenpolitologie'-approach: Wolfgang Mantl for his 70th Birthday," *Vienna Online Journal on International Constitutional Law* 3(2).
10 According to Dietrich's typology, two types of Judicial Councils predominate: the Southern European model, currently in use in France, Italy, Spain, and Portugal, characterized by the role of the council being largely limited to the appointment, promotion, and disciplining of Judges; and the Northern European model, found in Sweden, Ireland, and Denmark, where the primary role of the councils is to oversee the management of the courts, administer the budget for the judiciary, and conduct judicial training. A third model exists in countries that do not have judicial councils at all, i.e. Austria and Germany. In these countries, appointment, advancement, and disciplining of judges, as well as the management of the courts, falls within the competence of the Ministry of Justice. See M. K. Dietrich. 2008. "A Comparative Review of Judicial Councils in the Former Yugoslavia," East West Management Institute. Occasional Papers Series. Available at http://ewmi.org/Pubs/EWMIOPSJudicialCouncils.pdf.
11 L. J. Cohen and J. R. Lampe. 2011. *Embracing Democracy in the Western Balkans: From Post-conflict Struggles toward European Integration* (Washington D.C.: Woodrow Wilson Center Press): 335.

12 American Bar Association. *2010. Judicial Reform Index for Kosovo*, Volume IV: 79. Available online at http://apps.americanbar.org/rol/publications/kosovo_jri_vol_iv_12_2010_en.pdf.

13 European Commission, Enlargement Strategy and Main Challenges 2014–15, (Brussels: 2015). Available at http://ec.europa.eu/enlargement/pdf/key_documents/2014/20141008-strategy-paper_en.pdf.

9 Scope, depth and limits of EU rule of law promotion in the Western Balkans

Does the EU rule of law promotion in candidate countries work?

Over the past 15 years EU policy makers have placed a growing emphasis on the rule of law, particularly the reform of the judiciary, in the transition countries of the Western Balkans. In spite of the EU's efforts and the publicly announced commitment to implement the far-reaching reform of the judiciary declared by the leading politicians in the Western Balkans, the reform process still suffers from instability and incoherence.

In order to measure the EU's influence this study has established a differentiation of four phases within the "rule adoption spiral" which consist of rule transfer, rule adoption, rule implementation and norm socialization. Through utilizing the spiral theory of rule of law adoption, it can be concluded that the main problem observed in all case study countries is the incomplete and/or selective implementation of the adopted norms. Rewriting laws and constitutions and the far-reaching institutional reform comprised of court system reconstruction, improvement of court infrastructure and retraining judges, is only the first and 'easiest' step that potential EU membership candidates need to undertake. The following step in the spiral which is the implementation of law, a formal operation of introducing legal texts into the domestic system of law, is still only partially completed. Finally, the EU rule of law promotion has yet to bring the Western Balkan accession countries to norm socialization which is the last phase of the proposed rule of law adoption spiral. Reaching this phase will signal the achievement of legal norms having become rooted in the domestic culture via the evolutionary process, through which social interaction with the EU has led the Western Balkan accession countries to adopt and endorse a prescribed "way of thinking, feeling and acting."[1]

The comparative research conducted in this book has confirmed that the EU's strategy of promoting the rule of law in the Western Balkans relies on the demand to comply with certain political criteria in combination with the supply of institutional ties, technical and economic assistance on one hand, and socialization of national elites on the other. This points to a distinctive characteristic of the EU rule of law promotion strategy which is based on the dichotomy of "rationalist" and "constructivist" institutionalism.

However, the obstacles and false assumptions preventing the full implementation of the judicial reform in the Western Balkans are neither few nor minor, and the following sections will address them in detail.

Mediating factors and constraints

Two sets of obstructing factors explain the gap between the adoption and internalization of norms related to the rule of law in the Western Balkans. On the supply side, i.e. on the side of the EU processes and strategies, these are the lack of *clarity* and *credibility* of EU conditionality while on the demand side, concerning the domestic drive for reforms, these relate to the obstructionist potential of *gatekeeper elites* and *legacies* of the past.

Obstructing factors on the supply side

Firstly, on the supply side, bearing in mind the current EU approach to enlargement, this study has noticed the lack of a clearly elaborated set of EU standards in the sphere of the judiciary, according to which accession countries would be able to align themselves should they choose to do so. As described in Chapter 1 of this book, in addition to the issue of vagueness of the rule of law criterion *per se*, even judicial organizations and judicial and legal systems throughout EU differ from one another. Despite the non-legally binding recommendations developed recently by the Council of Europe, the European Network of Councils for Judiciary (ENCJ), the Consultative Council of European Judges, The European Judicial Training Network, the European Judicial Network, and particularly the European Commission via the EU Justice Scoreboard, the idea of common European judicial standards still remains in its infancy. The establishment of an unambiguous and coherent EU policy for the quality of justice, which addresses not only aspiring members but also existing member states, would significantly enhance the effectiveness of rule of law implementation during the EU accession process. In other words, for the process of the pre-accession reforms to become smoother, accession countries should know when and how they are considered to be progressing. Therefore, the EU should abandon the 'moving target' strategy in the field of the rule of law conditionality, and should instead distil the particular criteria and indicators on the basis of which countries will be graded.

Moreover, the clarity of conditionality is closely linked with the ability of the EU to efficiently monitor the fulfillment of its requirements. Consequently, the EU has invested significant efforts in developing its monitoring mechanism. Progress on the path towards accession is measured in Progress Reports on the basis of "legislation actually adopted, [...] and measures actually implemented."[2] This snapshot of a candidate's development during the 12 months following the previous monitoring period provides the European Commission with the necessary information for concluding an objective assessment of the candidate country in terms of its preparation for accession.

Since 2015, Progress Reports provide clearer guidance for what a country is expected to do in the following year in order to fully meet EU conditions. However, more precise mid and long-term guidance is still missing. Although the transparency of the overall monitoring process has increased with the adoption of recalibrated progress reports, additional efforts should nevertheless be made with regard to providing open public access to the European Commission's opinion on key legislation in accession countries, as well as on the reports of the EU's peer review missions used in preparation of the progress reports.

Finally, this study has confirmed that the lack of credible reward obstructs the desired compliance of a rational target state. The credibility of EU conditionality has two sides, meaning that the candidate countries must be certain of receiving the promised rewards after meeting the EU's conditions, but only after they fully meet all of the demands. The premature accession of Bulgaria and Romania in 2007 could have undermined the credibility of the rule of law conditionality in the subsequent accession negotiations. However, this risk was averted with the merit-based application of the rule of law conditionality in the 2013 accession of Croatia, and subsequently introduced safeguard clause which is now part of Montenegro's membership negotiating process. This clause allows the Commission and/or Member States to put the overall negotiation process on hold if the progress in chapters 23 and 24 is lagging too far behind. However, the other part of credibility is particularly problematic because the goal of membership remains distant and elusive for the current accession countries. The meticulous approach that the EU has undertaken in its enlargement to the WB means that the member states favor a more hands-on approach than in previous rounds and as a result some countries, such as France, have announced a referendum on any further enlargement of the Union. While the intervention of member states in EU integration is not an entirely new feature, a persisting impression is that the frequency of instances in which member states block or delay decisions on enlargement has increased—even in relation to early milestones on the EU path. Although this trend is mostly motivated by domestic politics in the member states at a time of crisis, its real danger lays in the possible multiplication of bilateral conditionality in the region. In addition to the existing outstanding bilateral issues between Greece/Bulgaria-Macedonia, and Romania-Serbia, following the accession of Croatia into the EU, Croatian authorities have signaled on several occasions that they will take advantage of the accession negotiations of Serbia as a means of pressure in order to achieve a regulated border between the two countries and to address various other legacies of the recent conflict.[3] The more active role of member states in the EU integration process creates an additional obstacle on the accession path for the WB countries. Additionally, the new bilateral conditionality risks duplicating the Macedonian scenario whereby the Greek veto provided a cover for the current government to delay reforms, which ultimately resulted in a backslide of the rule of law benchmarks.

Obstructing factors on the demand side

On the demand side, which concerns the drive for reforming the rule of law coming from the accession countries, this study has observed problems relating to the obstructive role of domestic ruling elites and legacies from the past.

The main domestic obstacles to judiciary reform in the Western Balkans are not technical or financial, but rather political. The legal transformations promoted by the EU indirectly aim at extending the accountability of individuals to the legislation of the state. This endeavor threatens the rent-seeking interests of established political elites by increasing the prospects of them losing their position in power, and possibly even resulting in them facing criminal indictment and imprisonment. The recent conviction of the Croatian former Prime Minister Ivo Sanader for corruption[4] serves as the most striking example of the 'harmful' effects that judicial reform can present for established elites.

According to the rational-strategic logic, the elites calculate the costs incurred at the national level before they accept or block rule of law implementation. Despite the publicly declared support for the rule of law reforms, the actions of local veto players are dominantly focused on the refusal to cede traditional impunity and vested interest. Hence, domestic elites follow up with regularized patterns of delaying key reforms that would lead to a substantive improvement of the judiciary, particularly in the sphere of its independence. In other words, if the price for the ruling elites is too high in comparison to the benefits, integration will not be pursued. On the other hand, if the expected costs are deemed to be insignificant, EU integration will be considered a free lunch.

Alternatively, the interactional dimension that would reach deeper beyond the institutional (state) structure in order to socialize, empower and provide the wider public with the skills necessary to hold the elites accountable is missing.[5] This research identified a number of 'champions of change' in the WB, which act as a countervailing force against anti-reform elements. These include expert NGOs, various civil society organizations, independent investigative journalists, Ombudsperson, Commission for Protection of Competition, Securities Commission, Commissioner for Information of Public Importance and Personal Data Protection, Commissioner for Protection of Equality, Judicial Academy, etc., as well as constructive grassroots initiatives i.e. Ne da(vi)mo Beograd,[6] Mjehur na mreži,[7] Student Plenums,[8] Open University,[9] and others. However, their voice is largely marginalized and dependent on the willingness of government incumbents to hear it.

Over the last couple of years, the EU has demonstrated a growing understanding of the role that civil society plays in extracting cooperation from state institutions.[10] Since 2012 the Commission holds permanent consultations between the EU and civil society organizations in Bosnia-Herzegovina and Kosovo within the framework of the Structured Dialogue on Justice with Bosnia-Herzegovina and the Structured Dialogue on the Rule of Law with Kosovo. These consultations are intended to guarantee that the voice of civil society reaches EU decision-makers, but their underlying agenda is still to "acculturate"[11] the WB national elites into the "European" discourse. Without advocating a civil society paradigm that glorifies NGOs as universally altruistic and honest, it is crucial that credible and responsible civil society organizations complement the work of state institutions. Bearing in mind the potential impact and value of NGO contribution to the rule of law promotion, the support for this sector should continue to be the exclusive focus of a part of the EU rule of law assistance programs, and should also be introduced as a component in most others. In the future, NGO empowerment should include the strengthening of expertise, capacities and technical organization, in addition to providing international networking possibilities and opportunities. In a nutshell, the EU should maintain its support for the inclusion of responsible NGOs, grassroots movements and individual experts in an effort to create pressure on the government to do its job better.

The second obstacle at the domestic level that mediates EU influence over the rule of law implementation relates to the role of legacies as deep conditions preventing judicial reforms in the WB. The empirical research performed within this book has established a persistence of obstructing legacies from the communist and post-communist periods. A common feature for both phases is the neglect of constitutional and legal guarantees for the independence of the judiciary and its instrumentalization as a tool for political oppression. Over decades, holders of judicial functions were subjected to a complex and subtle interplay of professional, bureaucratic and political influence that prevented them from attaining acceptable political non-conformism in performing their judicial service. Furthermore, covert political influence was also exercised from within the judiciary through the role of the court's administration, which manipulated the assignments of politically sensitive cases and influenced the court budgets. Paradoxically, the institutions which were supposed to be under control of the courts, the executive and legislative bodies, were electing the judges that controlled them.[12] The erosion of professionalism in the judiciary peaked under conditions of continuous political pressure in post-communist turmoil in the Balkans, this particularly significant in Serbia and Montenegro as a consequence of the authoritarian rule of Slobodan Milošević, and in Kosovo and Bosnia and Herzegovina due to the armed conflicts that ravaged their societies.

During 60 years of onerous judicial practice, WB societies have developed certain cultural predispositions that impede the reform of the judiciary today. Well-developed lawyers' tactics of excessive delays of court procedures—i.e. symptomatic failures to appear, to produce evidence, or to meet court deadlines—are simply some of the manifestations of the cultural predispositions created over the past decades. The displayed cultural predispositions and deep legacies still matter in the WB judiciaries because they impact the administrative and technical capacities of courts, pedagogy at the law schools, budgetary constraints, court proceedings, enforcement of judgments, independence of the judiciary, and other various institutions and actors on a daily basis. Without a doubt, the pre-existing judicial systems in the WB candidate countries create disabling conditions for the EU-led internalization of the reform of judiciary. Presupposing that legacies have not permanently altered the judicial culture of future Member States, the question remains to what degree such legacies and cultural predispositions operate as structural constraints, and more importantly, if and how they could be successfully influenced via the EU's conditionality policy.

Wrong assumptions

Besides the evident obstructions, this study has identified five false assumptions that impede the process of rule of law promotion in the WB. Namely, the EU's rule of law promotion focuses mostly on judiciary reform under the hypothesis that the improvement in performance of judiciary is the most direct way to improve the legal certainty in the target country. While the role of formal public institutions is important for the respect of the law, this approach fails to deal with the problem of local cultural predispositions, to address the issue of informal institutions and centers of power and to include the wider society in the reform process. Therefore, matters such as the fairness and legitimacy of laws and court procedures, the effectiveness and accountability of the judiciary, and the role of civil society remain marginalized. Bearing this in mind, this book outlines a list of false assumptions on which the EU rule promotion is conducted in the WB before proceeding with a way forward for Europeanization by rule of law implementation in Bosnia-Herzegovina, Kosovo, Macedonia, Montenegro and Serbia.

An institutional approach is the answer

Despite the promise made by the former European Commissioner for Enlargement, Štefan Füle, that the accession negotiations would not simply involve ticking boxes about legislative approximation (see Chapter 1), the EU's rule of law promotion policy to candidate countries still translates rule of law into an institutional checklist, with a primary emphasis on the judiciary.[13] Moreover, the terms judicial reform and rule of law are frequently applied interchangeably by the rule of law promotion actors. Although the EU practitioners define the rule of law as their ultimate goal, they implicitly identify its institutional attributes as the most conveniently measurable ends. Namely, the extension of law in the rule of law often dissuades non-lawyers from engaging in criticism of the institutional approach, and when lawyers think about what seems to be the core of the rule of law, "they think about the core institutions of law enforcement."[14]

First of all, the institutional approach to the rule of law promotion in the accession countries does not work beyond the norm-adoption, as convincingly demonstrated above. Secondly, the focus on institutional aspects of the rule of law neglects the need for an honest democratic reform. By choosing to strengthen institutions in unconsolidated democracies, the institutional approach does not fulfil its primary purpose—to create a system in which citizens trust the law and state institutions. Instead, an institutional approach to the rule of law promotion further stabilizes semi-authoritarian rulers by providing them with additional tools to exercise their authority.

Governments are the key to achieving legal reform

The EU accession negotiations are conducted with national governments, whose role in the implementation of legal and political reforms is without a doubt essential for the success of the whole process. However, it seems that EU practitioners have overemphasized the extent of the governments' role in the rule of law reform process. That is to say, WB governments are not always able or even willing to implement the reform process. Some of the obstacles addressed earlier within this book include: established informal practices within/beyond the institutional sphere, the high level of corruption prevalent among government officials, lack of expertise, lack of technical capacities, and lack of cooperation between highly fragmented levels of government. Furthermore, WB governments, even in countries furthest along in the accession process, fall short of providing a satisfactory level of political transparency in their work and accountability towards their citizens. Hence, the inclusion of civil society is essential for overcoming the potential problems which accompany a governmental approach.

New laws are the answer

No matter how good the legislative solutions adopted by national parliaments are, they are not able to compensate for the lack of quality of the judicial authorities. In other words, even the best laws make little sense if law enforcement bodies are incompetent. The application of law is conducted by judges and lawyers, and it is by their competence that we recognize them to have sound judgment, professional erudition, and skill to prosecute or render judgments effectively in accordance with the law. In order to achieve this goal, the judiciary is reliant on law schools, judicial academies, paralegal training, learning through experience by soliciting advice from NGO personnel, and expert exchange programs. As learned throughout the implementation of this study, the education in WB law schools is lacking in skills training while the judicial and bar examinations only test the technical legal knowledge of applicants. Clearly, the lack of judicial capacity to implement adopted legislation efficiently and effectively cripples compliance with the EU rule of law conditionality in the pre- and post- accession periods alike.

For these reasons, capacity-building of the judicial sector and strengthening the effectiveness of its administrative mechanisms deserve more attention during the EU accession process. Particular focus should be placed on the capacity building of the newly established Judicial Academies. Judicial

Academies are the central institutions aiming to eradicate the features of Socialist legal education, which was marked by rigid, authoritarian and formalistic training, state maintained control over the curriculum, and an almost complete absence of analytical study of case law. The role of non-state actors, such as local and international NGOs, should also not be neglected during this process. The effects of capacity building would be significantly increased through the inclusion of non-state actors in the process which would employ the mechanism of socialization to complement the efforts invested in the conditionality.

Governments know what they are expected to comply with

Clarity of EU conditionality presupposes that the target governments know precisely what they are expected to do, should they decide to comply with the EU conditions. Nevertheless, as established in this study, accession country governments experience a high level of uncertainty in regards to the rule of law conditions set upon them by the EU. Problems surrounding the clarity of EU demands may be found in the ever-growing body of EU law and the absence of a single European model of judiciary. Additionally, the benchmarks related to the negotiations on the Judiciary and fundamental rights and Justice, freedom and security Chapters, unlike those for any other chapter, place more importance on the political principles and constitutional values rather than on the "hard" *Acquis Communautaire*. Moreover, the European Commission sometimes includes additional benchmarks even during the negotiation process. Since 2015, recalibrated Progress Reports provide clearer guidance for what the country is expected to do in the year to come in order to fully meet EU conditions, however, more precise mid and long-term guidance is still missing. All of these factors add to the lack of clarity regarding the EU's rule of law demands, and consequently affect the effectiveness of the rule transfer.

There is no ready-made solution that can be appropriately used in any given candidate country regarding the rule of law accession criteria. Instead, a package solution based on a complex preparatory operationalization that consists of three interconnected parts needs to be applied. First, the EU needs to have a better understanding of the situation of the judiciary in the candidate country prior to the start of the accession process, and not just before the opening of negotiations, particularly bearing in mind legacies of the past that influence the independence of judiciary. Historical legacies need to be taken seriously, not only because of their inherent significance in post-communist democratization but also due to their ability to shape the relationship between the candidate countries and the EU. Secondly, the use of benchmarks on independence, accountability, efficiency, and effectiveness of the judiciary in the accession negotiations serves as an important catalyst for the rule of law reform. Nevertheless, it is not clear what the exact expectations are under each of these benchmarks. This is why it is important that the Commission elaborates on each of these benchmarks in more detail. The benchmarks should be clear and predictable to the domestic actors in the candidate country prior to the start of the accession process. Otherwise the reforms are driven by a country strategy that is prepared on an *ad hoc* basis which then faces the potential risk of diminishing the effects of already achieved progress with every change of the ruling elite in the target country. An example of this can be witnessed in Serbia, where after the 2012 elections the newly elected government made its priority to re-assess judicial reform which has resulted in delaying the end result of an already slow transformation.

Membership incentive is sufficient

There is no doubt that conditionality is at the heart of EU relations with the WB countries. In most of these countries, EU conditions have triggered the rule of law reforms. Surely the "credible" prospect of full membership has been the "golden carrot" convincing target governments to implement tasks agreed within their respective SAAs. Additionally, rewards attached to the EU conditionality sometimes even provided "an excuse"[15] for national governments to proceed with unpopular policies.

However, a sustainable reform process requires certain domestic conditions to prevail. First and foremost, reforms proved to be impossible without the civic pro-reform political parties and a broad consensus among the political, economic and social elites as well as the citizens as to the necessity of EU-guided reforms. Despite academic and popular mythology, the distant prospect of membership has proven to be incapable of mobilizing the civic politics proposed by the EU and regional NGO activists for the past two decades. This democratic deficit keeps the gatekeeper elites incumbent in the WB, effectively blocking the rule of law reform. The lack of commitment on the EU side, which is reflected in the deficit of actual membership perspective for the WB countries and the non-existence of interim rewards tied to a gradual prospect of rule of law implementation, is part of the problem instead of the solution in the WB. Without any intention to advocate for "short-cut conditionality," this book recalls that the promise of EU integration actually holds the WB together, while alternatively, postponing the accession to the indefinite future undermines hard-won peace and stability in the region.

Clearly, the distant promise of EU membership is not enough of an incentive for the non-consolidated WB countries. In order to create a momentum for reforms the EU should set up an intermediary system of tangible rewards to be gained upon the achieved interim goals. The recent visa liberalization in the region serves as a good example for the mechanics of "soft" EU pressure. There are three lessons to be learned from the visa liberalization process: (1) the EU should motivate state institutions and civil sector to take part in the reform process, (2) the EU has to set out an explicit and detailed conditions map, and (3) the EU has to create a comprehensive implementation strategy with a measurable interim system of goals and rewards so that the domestic actors have a clear and immediate rationalist-based motivation to adhere to the rule of law conditionality.

Notes

1 A. I. Johnston. 2001. "Treating International Institutions as Social Environments," *International Studies Quarterly* 45: 487–515, at 487.

2 A. F. Tatham. 2009. *Enlargement of the European Union*, (Kluwer Law International: Alphen aan den Rijn): 248.

3 See "Croatia Demanding More War Crimes Indictments if EU Entry Talks With Serbia are to Advance." *Croatia Week*. (13 November 2014). Available at http://www.croatiaweek.com/croatia-demanding-more-war-crimes-indictments-if-eu-entry-talks-with-serbia-are-to-advance/.

4 "Former Croatia PM Ivo Sanader convicted of corruption," *BBC* (11 March 2014). Available at http://www.bbc.com/news/world-europe-26533990.

5 See J. Ker-Lindsay. 2013. "Conclusion," in V. Bojicic-Dzelilovic, J. Ker-Lindsay, and D. Kostovicova, (eds.) *Civil Society and Transitions in the Western Balkans*. (Basingstoke: Palgrave Macmillan): 257–264.

6 Ne da(vi)mo Beograd is a grass roots initiative gathering organizations and individuals interested in sustainable urban development and equitable use of shared resources contesting the controversial and non-transparent Belgrade Waterfront project. See https://nedavimobeograd.wordpress.com/o-inicijativi/.

7 The Mjehur na mreži initiative promotes the idea of independent internet radio broadcasting in the region amidst ongoing media freedom deterioration. See https://www.mixcloud.com/MjehurNaMre%C5%BEi/.

8 Students in Skopje rallied around an informal movement called the Student's Plenum in early 2015, demanding the immediate suspension of a controversial law on higher education.

9 Open University is a platform for public discussion of social, political and artistic alternatives and non-formal education in Bosnia and Herzegovina.

10 T. Beichelt, I. Hahn-Fuhr, F. Schimmelfennig, S. Worschech (eds.). 2014. *Civil Society and Democracy Promotion* (Basingstoke: Palgrave).

11 G. Sasse, J. Hughes and C. Gordon. 2006. "Sub-National Governance in Central and Eastern Europe: Between Transition and Europeanization," in W. Sadurski, A. Czarnota and M. Krygier (eds), *Spreading Democracy and the Rule of Law: The Impact of EU Enlargement on the Rule of Law, Democracy and Constitutionalism in Post-Communist Legal Orders* (Netherlands: Springer): 121–147, at 138.

12 See Chapter 5.

13 "Institutional definitions of the rule of law are not new. Their heritage stretches back to Ancient Greek discussions of the need for standing laws, impartial courts, and enforcement mechanisms (although the latter were often religious, political, or cultural structures, not modern-day law-enforcement bodies)." R. Kleinfeld, "Competing Definitions of the Rule of Law," in T. Carothers, *Promotion of the Rule of Law Abroad*, cit.: 47.

14 Ibid. 20.

15 O. Anastasakis and D. Bechev. April 2003. *EU Conditionality in South East Europe: Bringing Commitment to the Process* (South East European Studies Programme: European Studies Centre St Antony's College: University of Oxford).

10 Conclusions

Theoretical conclusions

While the EU accession of the WB countries continues to depend mostly on the rigorous application of conditionality, poor rule implementation and extremely weak rule internalization of the judiciary reform in the Western Balkans are caused by the presence of veto players armed with rationalist calculations of social costs of deviation, and by inadequate institutional and administrative capacities in the target countries which are caused by legacies of the past. In order for EU rule of law conditionality to be functional, domestic adaptation costs must not be higher than the reward; otherwise the ruling elites of a rational target state will not comply. Moreover, despite the proper precautions such as later accession dates, the use of safeguard clauses and post-accession monitoring, the EU does not have a functional mechanism under which EU conditionality can be genuinely effective against the observed "legacies as deep conditions."[1] Finally, the EU's established rule of law conditionality proved to be particularly incapable to answer the country-specific challenges of (1) high political fragmentation which hampers Bosnia-Herzegovina, (2) ethnic cleavages that seriously impact processes in Bosnia-Herzegovina, Kosovo and Macedonia, and (3) the lack of fully affected state-building.

On the other hand, constructivist institutionalism suggests the processes of socialization and persuasion to be the central mechanisms of the EU's domestic impact, through which national elites become convinced of the need to internalize the EU's rules. A particular problem regarding this approach lies in the fact that the EU demands unilateral adjustments while the candidate countries did not participate in the setting of the rules that they need to adopt. In order to impact the public and domestic elites to positively identify with the EU demands and be more open to persuasion, the EU employs "transnational networks"[2] as a facilitating factor for its influence. However, the success of EU socialization and persuasion strategies is highly dependent on both the de-politicization of projects and the expertise of individuals involved. By focusing exclusively on institutional socialization the EU has thus far failed to influence the wider community, particularly the expert public, in order to empower it to become part of the cognitive convergence pressure group and thus exercise bottom-up pressure on the political elites in the target country.

In practical terms, this implies that *rationalist* and *constructivist* strategies for the promotion of the rule of law in Bosnia and Herzegovina, Kosovo, Macedonia, Montenegro and Serbia must not be considered as mutually exclusive, but rather as *complementary* approaches for the enhancement of the EU's influence. The rule of law reform is a lengthy, potentially life-long process, during which the social and cultural continuity of the transferred norms is eventually attained, particularly by providing every responsible member of society with the skills and habits necessary for their implementation. Therefore, in order to achieve the goal of Europeanization by rule of law implementation, i.e. the goal of internalizing adopted norms in everyday life, it is necessary to include wider social strata into the rule of law transformation process.

Basically, it is *essential* to achieve the transformation of traditional top-down power structures in which governments are at liberty to influence both legislative and judiciary branch through clientelistic networks and/or methods of more or less open pressure into a horizontally structured civil society based on the rule of law. This exercise is not simply a superficial creation of healthier and less dependent relations between the state and civil society. It has much more serious consequences, particularly within the process of EU integration. As presented in Figure 3.1, the creation of civic networks composed of Judicial Associations, expert NGOs, various civil society organizations, independent investigative journalists, Ombudsperson, Commission for Protection of Competition, Securities Commission, Commissioner for Information of Public Importance and Personal Data Protection, Commissioner for

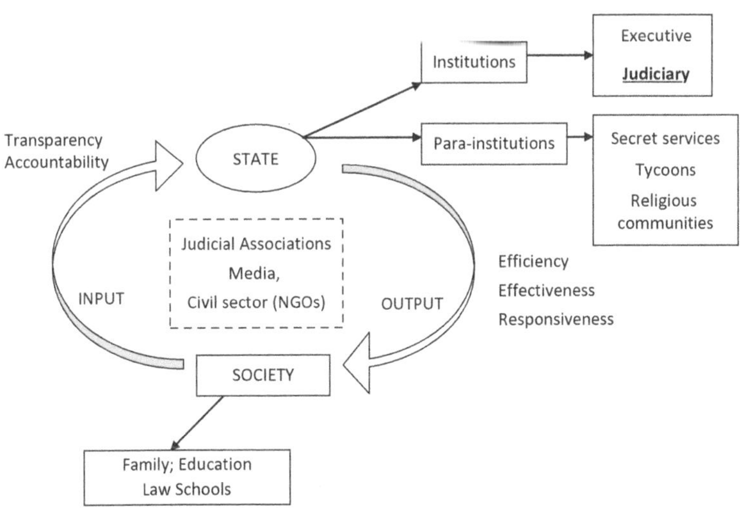

Figure 10.1 Good Governance Scheme

Protection of Equality, Judicial Academy, and so forth is crucial for ensuring the transparency and accountability of the state by providing control over its efficiency, effectiveness and responsiveness. Furthermore, this horizontal power structure is central to the prevention of the pervasive veto power of gatekeeper elites embodied in government representatives, and other para-institutional actors such as secret services, tycoon networks, influential religious leaders, and so forth.

Still, the proposed scheme would not yield sustainable results without the credible promise of full EU membership. As Montenegro currently displays, a credible membership perspective is an effective mechanism in persuading national governments to adopt rules, create institutions, and establish relations with the civil society, they would otherwise resist. On the other hand, where the credibility of the EU promise is either weak or distant, such as can be observed in Kosovo, Bosnia-Herzegovina, and Macedonia, the achievement of formal compliance with the EU rule of law conditionality has proven to be less complete.

This in turn opens a legitimate concern about how to influence the reform processes in the current laggards of EU integrations; namely Kosovo and Bosnia and Herzegovina, but also Macedonia, whose accession has effectively been blocked for almost a decade now due to the Greek veto.

The theory of "leverage and linkage"[3] between the EU and the accession countries suggests that the success of the EU's influence in democracy and rule of law export is conditioned by high leverage, as manifested in an asymmetrical power relationship between the EU and the target state, and dense linkages through density of ties between the negotiating parties. The more an accession country becomes "entangled" in linkages with the EU, the more "vested interests will consolidate on both sides,"[4] which ultimately leads to the natural desire of the holders of vested interests to preserve such ties. In other words, opening the gates wider would produce a path-dependency that in the long run constrains the maneuverability of gatekeeper elites. At the moment, newly established mechanisms of the European Commission, Structured Dialogue on Justice with Bosnia-Herzegovina, Structured Dialogue on the Rule of Law with Kosovo, and the High Level Accession Dialogue with Macedonia aim to advance structured relations on the implementation of the rule of law with aspiring member countries prior to the SAAs entering into force. However, while socializing the elites, Structured Dialogues still do not provide credibility in regards to the membership perspective. Hence, the question of the way forward towards the sustainable and long-lasting EU rule of law promotion to candidate countries remains open.

The way forward: policy recommendations

The top-down institutional approach employed by the EU, empowered by the golden carrot of full membership, has generated unique, broad-based and long-term support for rule of law reform and progress towards EU membership in the Western Balkans. However, while EU conditionality has an important role in prompting reforms, a sustainable rule of law reform process also requires certain domestic conditions to prevail—most notably the reduction of the number of veto players and the elimination of institutional obstructions exhibited in clientelistic relationships among the domestic ruling elites and institutions prone to corruption, and administrative obstacles caused by the legacies of the communist past. Additionally, this approach has limited reach in non-consolidated democracies due to the fact that it runs counter to democratization by favoring ruling elites and depoliticizing civil society.

On the other hand, bottom-up soft socialization mechanisms are not used equitably enough in order to strengthen the capacity of civic society organizations, and to create a consensus among the ruling and oppositional elites on the necessity of socialization of the adopted norms. Furthermore, on the EU side, the actual lack of European standards in judiciary has raised important questions as to whether it is fair to ask aspiring members to incorporate changes from which the EU member states are exempted. Finally, the technocratic, vague and short-term nature of the EU rule of law conditionality coupled with the increasing lack of credibility of the overall enlargement process at best leads to redistributive, capacity-related and short-term outcomes rather than sustainable and transformative change. Hence, it comes as no surprise hearing about the EU's guerilla tactics in the sphere of the rule of law promotion, whereby it only pretends to reform while aspiring member states pretend to be reformed in order to advance in the accession process.[5]

So what can be done in order to strengthen the rule of law promotion in accession countries? This book provides suggestions and answers on how the EU can improve its rule of law conditionality toolbox in order to guide domestic reforms beyond the phase of norm adoption. Below is a list of ready-made policy recommendations that need to be taken into account by relevant actors.

Create clear criteria and indicators for the rule of law conditionality

The apparent thinness of the *Acquis Communautaire* in the field of the judiciary contrasts with the centrality of this issue in the accession negotiations process. The lack of codified institutional rules influences the use of soft conditions and individually tailored guidelines. For a smoother process of the pre-accession reforms candidate countries should know when and how they are considered to be progressing. In this regard, the EU has to distil particular criteria and indicators on the basis of which the progress of the candidate countries will be graded. Furthermore, rule of law specialists, including EU practitioners, should continue their efforts to reach a definitional consensus on the concepts of "Rule of Law" and "Judiciary Reforms."

Produce interim benchmarks

Europeanization through rule of law implementation works under certain conditions but only for the adoption of norms that are not necessarily followed through with rule internalization. Continuous efforts are needed to ensure sustainability of reforms by norm-socialization of adopted rules. Bearing in mind problems of implementing the rule of law in non-consolidated democracies, the EU should elaborate the overall and interim objectives with regard to good governance and rule of law.

Redefine progress reports

Annual progress reports are and should remain the EU's key tool in assessing the progress towards membership of the aspiring candidates. In November 2015, the European Commission published its "recalibrated" progress reports. Within its remodeled reports, the Commission has increased strategic focus on the "fundamentals first" approach as strengthened reporting is now visible in areas which are closely related to the fundamentals—rule of law, public administration reform, economic development and competitiveness, as well as the three *Acquis* chapters (public procurement, statistics, financial control). In addition to reporting on progress in these areas, the Commission has dedicated more scrutiny to the actual state of play and preparedness for taking on the obligations of membership of the accession countries. However, the EU progress reports still focus more on the bureaucratic measures of opening and closing chapters, rather than on substance related to the rule of law reforms. Furthermore, the progress reports are still written in a technocratic language which is often difficult to understand for the broader public. It is important that the EU clearly and accurately scrutinize target country's annual approximation towards the set objectives and publicizes its findings in direct communication with citizens. While the transparency of the overall monitoring process has increased with the adoption of recalibrated progress reports, additional efforts should nevertheless be made with regard to providing open public access to the European Commission's opinion on key legislation in accession countries, as well as on the reports of the EU's peer review missions used in preparation of the progress reports. Finally, as already indicated above, more precise mid and long-term guidance for what the country is expected to do in order to fully meet EU conditions is still missing.

Include civil society in the EU integration process

Under the "rule-of-law orthodoxy," civil society is at best adjunct to the institution building process. This book argues for the need of a more inclusive bottom-up approach to the EU rule of law promotion, in which civil society actors will be empowered to play a rights-holder's role vis-à-vis public authority in order to push for compliance of key laws, monitor their implementation and influence norm socialization, both during or before negotiations. The broad inclusion of civil society in the accession process can help to build broader constituency in favor of EU accession in the Western Balkans, and help to keep the reforms on track.

Open Chapters 23 and 24

The new EU strategy on rule of law conditionality envisages that both Chapter 23 on Judiciary and fundamental rights and Chapter 24 on Justice, freedom and security should be tackled early in the negotiations in order to allow maximum time to establish the necessary legislation, institutions, and solid track records of implementation before the negotiations are closed. Moreover, the EU has established the Structured Dialogue; this is is a new mechanism for countries that are still not negotiating their EU membership that will assist them in moving further along their path towards the EU. The focus of the Structured Dialogues falls precisely on the rule of law. However, thus far, it has had very limited success. Hence, the EU should enter into a screening process and open Chapters 23 and 24 with all of the Western Balkans countries on the basis of the earlier described new approach as soon as possible. The benefits of this proposal are threefold. First of all, it replicates the success of the visa liberalization process by opening simultaneous negotiations with all the countries of the region, which will develop a competitive dynamic in which no country wants to be left behind. It is hoped that this will encourage faster reforms among laggards and will help them to avoid falling further behind. Secondly, this proposal will increase the density of ties and linkages between the EU and domestic elites in the Western Balkans, which will effectively consolidate the natural desire of the holders of vested interests to preserve such ties, ultimately weakening the veto potential of gatekeeper elites. Finally, this proposal would give the biggest possible leverage to the EU to influence the establishment of an effective rule of law system in its immediate neighborhood.

Monitor the state of democracy

The extent to which the rule of law exists in a particular regime reflects the entire democratic quality of that regime. Conversely, as this research has proven, internalization of the judicial reforms is crucially dependent on the political and legal stability in countries of concern. In this regard democracy and the rule of law remain mutually interconnected. However, as Chapter 1 describes in detail, the two concepts are not identical. Regardless of the obvious prominence of the rule of law in the process of EU accession, the current, institution-based method of the EU rule of law promotion fails to address non-judiciary related factors that in turn crucially impact judicial performance in accession states. However, democracy cannot be engineered through smart design of formal institutions. Therefore, it is essential that the EU pays greater attention to the whole forest and not just the trees when it comes to the rule of law promotion in membership candidate countries. In a nutshell, the EU should focus on gearing the aspiring members towards stable and prosperous democracies governed by the rule of law.

The problems observed in this book are not entirely novel insights. For instance, similar critiques were made of the international efforts for the judiciary reforms in Latin America of the 1960s by Wade Channel.[6] World Bank rule of law specialist Richard Messick, accounted for comparable shortcomings in his study on Africa, Latin America and Southeast Asia 20 years ago.[7] Indeed, due to an apparent lack of applicable incentive structures within the legal reform industry, lesson learning is a gradual process among the current generation of EU rule of law specialists. This is why this book has shown that only through accepting *rationalist* (conditionality) and *constructivist* (socialization) institutionalism strategies for the promotion of the rule of law as *complementary* approaches; it would be possible to address the regional peculiarity of the Western Balkans in a way that safeguards the long-term sustainability of judiciary reform process.

Notes

1 A. M. Cirtautas and F. Schimmelfennig. 2010. "Europeanization Before and After Accession: Conditionality, Legacies and Compliance," cit.: 431.
2 Ibidem.
3 The theory was developed in S. Levitsky and L. Way. 2005. "International Linkage and Democratization," *Journal of Democracy* 16(3): 20–34, and further elaborated in S. Levitsky and L. A. Way. 2006. "Linkage versus Leverage: Rethinking the International Dimension of Regime Change," *Comparative Politics* 38(4).
4 J. Tolstrup. "When can External Actors Influence Democratization? Leverage, Linkages, and Gatekeeper Elites," cit.: 22.
5 See M. Mendelski. 2013. "Does the EU Make a Difference? Judicial Reforms in South-Eastern Europe," in A. Elbasani (ed.), *EU Enlargement and Europeanization in the Western Balkans* (London: Routledge).
6 See W. Channell. May 2005. *Lessons not Learned about Legal Reform, in Carothers, Promoting the Rule of Law Abroad* (Washington, D.C.: Carnegie Endowment for International Peace): 137–159.
7 R. E. Messick. 1999. "Judicial Reform and Economic Development: A Survey of the Issues," *World Bank Research Observer* 14(1).

Bibliography

Academy for Judges and Public Prosecutors. 2014 *Report on the Work of the Academy for Judges and Public Prosecutors for 2013* (Skopje).

Anastasakis, O. and D. Bechev. April 2003. *EU Conditionality in South East Europe: Bringing Commitment to the Process* (Oxford: European Studies Centre St Antony's College, University of Oxford).

Anderson, R.D., M.S. Fish, S.E. Hanson, and G.R. Philip (eds.). 2001. *Postcommunism and the Theory of Democracy* (Princeton: Princeton University Press).

Arestis, P. and M. Sawyer (eds.). 2012. *The Euro Crisis* (New York: Palgrave Macmillan).

Assembly of the Republic of Kosovo. 2010. *Law on Courts. No.03/L-199*, Article 3 (Pristina).

Assembly of the Republic of Kosovo. 2008. *Constitution of Republic of Kosovo.* Article 102. Official Gazette of Republic of Kosovo no.25 (Pristina).

Assembly of the Republic of Kosovo. 2010. *Law on Kosovo Judicial Council* 03/L-233. Article 3. (Pristina).

Assembly of the Republic of Kosovo. 2010. *Law on the Special Prosecution Office of the Republic of Kosovo* 03/L-052 (Pristina).

Assembly of the Republic of Kosovo. 2006. *Law on Arbitration* 02/L-75 (Pristina).

Assembly of the Republic of Kosovo. 2008. *Law on Notary* 04/L 002 (Pristina)

Assembly of the Republic of Kosovo. 2008. *Law on Establishing the Kosovo Judicial Institute*, Official Gazette No. 02/L-25 O (Pristina).

Bailer, S., R. Hertz and D. Leuffen 2009. "Oligarchization, Formalization, Adaptation? Linking Sociological Theory and EU Enlargement Research," *Journal of European Public Policy* 16(*1*): 162–174.

Baland, T. and K.N. Wood. 2010. *Report on the Work of Kosovo's Independent Judicial and Prosecutorial Commission* (Pristina: Independent Judicial and Prosecutorial Commission).

Balfour, R. and C. Stratulat. 2013. "Between Engagement and Cold Feet: Ten Years of the EU in the Western Balkans," in E. Prifti (ed.), *The European Future of the Western Balkans: Thessaloniki @10 (2003–2013)* (European Union Institute for Security Studies): 19–25.

Balfour, R. and Stratulat C. (2012) *The Enlargement of the European Union*, EPC Discussion Paper (Brussels: European Policy Centre).

Balkans in Europe Policy Advisory Group. 2015. *Unraveling the Political Crisis in Macedonia: Toward Resolution or Calm Before the Storm?* Available at http://www.suedosteuropa.uni-graz.at/biepag/node/158.

Balkans Investigative Network. 21 Oct 2013. "*Macedonia Jails Journalist Tomislav Kezarovski*," Skopje.

Baltić, N. and T. Milej. 2007. "Human Rights under the Yugoslav System, Processes of Ethnic Mobilization and EU Crisis Management," *MIRICO Working Papers*, Bolzano.

Barnett, M.N. and M. Finnemore. 1999. "The Politics, Power, and Pathologies of International Organizations," *International Organization* 53(*4*): 699–732.

Beichelt, T., I. Hahn-Fuhr, F. Schimmelfennig and S. Worschech (eds.). 2014. *Civil Society and Democracy Promotion* (Basingstoke: Palgrave).

Berger, P.L. and T. Luckmann. 1966. *Die gesellschaftliche Konstruktion der Wirklichkeit* (Frankfurt am Main: Fischer).

Bertelsmann Stiftung. 2014. *BTI 2014 – Serbia Country Report* (Gütersloh: Bertelsmann Stiftung).

Bibežić, A. and M. Kmezić. 2014. "Approximation of Membership as an Impetus for Rule of Law," in M. Kmezić (ed.), *Europeanization by Rule of Law Implementation in the Western Balkans* (Skopje: Institute for Democracy): 159–182.

Bieber, F. 2010. "Bosnia and Herzegovina since 1990," in S. P. Ramet (ed.), *Central and Southeast European Politics since 1989* (Cambridge: Cambridge University Press): 311–328.

Bieber, F. 2012. "The Western Balkans are Dead – Long Live the Balkans! Democratization and the Limits of the EU," in V. Džihić and D. Hamilton (eds.), *Unfinished Business: The Western Balkans and the International Community* (Washington D.C.: Brookings Institution Press): 3–10.

Bieber, F. 2013. "Building Impossible States? State-Building Strategies and EU Membership in the Western Balkans," *Europe-Asia Studies* 63(*10*): 1783–1802.

Bieber, F. 2014. "Greater Serbia and Greater Albania Do Not Exist: The Myth of Bad Serb-Albanian Relations," *Balkans in Europe Policy Blog*.

Bieber, F. and I. Ristić. 2012. "Constrained Democracy: The Consolidation of Democracy in Yugoslav Successor States," *Southeastern Europe* 36(*3*): 373–397.

Bobić, M. and R. Božić. 2012. "Civil Society in the Process of European Integration – From Constructive Dialogue to Successful Negotiations," *European Movement in Serbia*, Belgrade.

Börzel, T. 2011. When Europe Hits Limited Statehood. Europeanization and Domestic Change in the Western Balkans," *KFG Working Papers* No. 30.

Börzel, T.A. and T. Risse. 2012. "From Europeanisation to Diffusion. Introduction," *West European Politics* 35(*1*): 1–19.

Börzel, T.A. and T. Risse. 2000. "When Europe Hits Home: Europeanization and Domestic Change," *European Integration Online Papers (EIoP) 4*(*15*).

Bosnia and Herzegovina Ministry of Justice. June 2008. *Bosnia and Herzogovina Justice Sector Reform Strategy 2008–2012* (Sarajevo).

Bosnia-Herzegovina–EU: Deep Disappointment on Sejdić-Finci Implementation. 18 February 2014. European Commission MEMO (Sarajevo). Available at http://europa.eu/rapid/press-release_MEMO-14–117_en.htm?locale=en.

Bovens, M. 2007. "Analysing and Assessing Accountability A Conceptual Framework," *European Law Journal* 13(*4*): 447–468.

Brčko District Assembly. 2007. *Law on Judicial Commission of Brčko District of BiH*, Official Gazette of the Brčko District of BiH, No. 7.19 (Brčko).

Bunce, V. 1999. *Subversive Institutions: The Design and Destruction of Socialism and the State* (Cambridge: Cambridge University Press).

Carothers, T. (ed.). 2006. *Promoting the Rule of Law Abroad* (Washington, D.C.: Carnegie Endowment for International Peace).

Case 294/83 Les Verts v. Parliament. 1986. European Court of Justice 1339: para. 23.

Čavoški, K. 1991. *Tito-Tehnologija vlasti* (Belgrade: Dosije).

Channell, W. 2006. "Lessons Not Learned About Legal Reform," in T. Carothers (ed.), *Promoting the Rule of Law Abroad* (Washington, D.C.: Carnegie Endowment for International Peace).

Checkel, J.T. 2005. "International Institutions and Socialization in Europe: Introduction and Framework," *International Organization* 59(*4*): 801–826.

Cierco, T. 2014. "Albania's Difficult Path towards Democracy," *Canadian-American Slavic Studies* 48(*4*): 468–491.

Cirtautas, A.M. and F. Schimmelfennig. 2010. "Europeanisation Before and After Accession: Conditionality, Legacies and Compliance," *Europe-Asia Studies* 62(*3*): 421–441.

Cohen, L.J. 1989. *The Socialist Pyramid: Elites and Power in Yugoslavia* (Oakville: Mosaic Press).

Cohen, L. 1985. "Judicial Elites in Yugoslavia: The Professionalization of Political Justice," *Review of Socialist Law* 11(*1*): 313–344.

Cohen, L. and J.R. Lampe (eds.). 2011. *Embracing Democracy in the Western Balkans: From Post-conflict Struggles toward European Integration* (Washington, D.C.: Woodrow Wilson Center Press).

Cohler, A.M., B.C. Miller and H.S. Stone (eds.). 1989. *The Spirit of the Laws by Charles de Secondat baron de Montesquieu* (Cambridge: Cambridge University Press).

Constitutional Assembly of the Federal People's Republic of Yugoslavia. 1946. Constitution of the Federal People's Republic of Yugoslavia, *The Official Gazette of the Federal People's Republic of Yugoslavia*, Year II, No. 10 (Belgrade).

Commission of the European Communities. 9 November 2005. *Communication from the Commission – Commission Opinion on the Application from the Former Yugoslav Republic of Macedonia for Membership of the European Union* {SEC(2005) 1425} {SEC(2005) 1429} /* COM/2005/0562 final (Brussels).

Communication from the Commission to the European Parliament, the Council, the European Central Bank, the European Economic and Social Committee and the Committee of the Regions. 2014. *2014 EU Justice Scoreboard*, COM(2014) 155 final (Brussels).

Cortell, A., P. Davis Jr. and W. James. 2000. "Understanding the Domestic Impact of International Norms: A Research Agenda," *International Studies Review* 2(*1*): 65–87.

Council of Europe. 1950. *European Convention for the Protection of Human Rights and Fundamental Freedoms* (Strasbourg).

Council of Europe. 1950. *Convention for the Protection of Human Rights and Fundamental Freedoms* (*European Convention on Human Rights*, as amended by the provisions of Protocol No. 14 (CETS no. 194) from its entry into force on 1 June 2010) (Rome).

Council of the European Union. 26 March 2001. *Stabilisation and Association Agreement between the European Communities and their Member States, of the one part, and the former Yugoslav Republic of Macedonia, of the other part* (6726/01) (Brussels).

Council of the European Union. 2007. *Stabilisation and Association Agreement between the European Communities and their Member States of the one part, and the Republic of Montenegro, of the other part*. 11566/07 COWEB 117.

Council of the European Union. 2011. *Council Conclusions on Enlargement and Stabilization and Association Process* (Brussels).

Council of the European Union. 29 March 2012. Ministerial Meeting Opening the Intergovernmental Conference on the Accession of Montenegro to the European Union – Negotiating Framework. 8339/12 Limite ELARG31. Available at http://ec.europa.eu/enlargement/pdf/st20002_05_mn_framedoc_en.pdf.

Council of the European Union. 2014. *First Accession Conference with Serbia.* 5486/14 (OR. en) PRESSE 15.

"Croatia Demanding More War Crimes Indictments if EU Entry Talks With Serbia are to Advance." 13 November 2014. *Croatia Week.* Available at http://www.croatiaweek.com/croatia-demanding-more-war-crimes-indictments-if-eu-entry-talks-with-serbia-are-to-advance/.

Czarnota, A. 2006. "Barbarians ante portas or the Post-Communist Rule of Law in Post-Democratic European Union," in W. Sadurski, A. Czarnota, M. Krygier (eds.), *Spreading Democracy and the Rule of Law?* (Netherlands: Springer): 283–297.

Dallara, C. 2014. *Democracy and Judicial Reforms in South-East Europe* (Bern: Springer).

Delegation of European Union to Bosnia and Herzegovina. 2011. First Set of Preliminary Recommendations from the European Commission, Inaugural meeting of the "SAA Structured Dialogue on Justice between the European Union and Bosnia and Herzegovina" (Banja Luka: 6–7 June 2011). Available at http://www.delbih.ec.europa.eu/Download.aspx?id=734&lang=EN.

Delegation of the European Union to Bosnia and Herzegovina and European Union Special Representative in Bosnia and Herzegovina. 2011. "10 Facts To Know About the EU-BiH Structured Dialogue On Justice" (Sarajavo: June 2011). Available at http://europa.ba/Download.aspx?id=736&lang=EN.

Dietrich, M.K. 2008. "A Comparative Review of Judicial Councils in the Former Yugoslavia," East West Management Institute. Occasional Papers Series. Available at http://ewmi.org/Pubs/EWMIOPSJudicialCouncils.pdf.

Dimitrova, A. and D. Toshkov. 2009. "Post-accession Compliance between Administrative Co-ordination and Political Bargaining," *European Integration Online Papers.* Special Issue: 2–13.

Dimitrova, A.L. 2010. "The New Member States of the EU in the Aftermath of Enlargement: Do New European Rules Remain Empty Shells?" *Journal of European Public Policy* 17(*1*): 137–148.

Dimitrova, A. 2015. *The Effectiveness and Limitations of Political Integration in Central and Eastern European Member States: Lessons from Bulgaria and Romania,* MAXCAP Working Papers No. 10.

Dimovski, S. and S.J. Marušić. 27 July 2011. "*Macedonia's A1 TV Bankrupt, Facing Closure*" (Skopje: Balkansinsight).

Dolenec, D. 2013. *Democratic Institutions and Authoritarian Rule in Southeast Europe* (Essex: ECPR Press).

Đilas, M. 1985. *Rise and Fall* (New York: Harcourt Brace Jovanovich).

Đokić, I. and M. Sumpor 2013. *The Role of Croatian Civil Society Organisations in the European Union Accession Process* (Zagreb: TACSO).

Đordjević, J. 1982. *Ustavno pravo* (Belgrade: Savremena Administracija).

Đuričić, M. 1978. *Ustav Socijalisticke Federativne Republike Jugoslavije: Strucno objasnjenje* (Belgrade: Institute for Political Studies of the Faculty of Political Sciences).

Džihić, V. and D. Segert. 2009. "Das jugoslawische Rätsel: Enklavendemokratie, Staatsschwäche und Probleme externer Demokratieförderung," *Südosteuropa Mitteilungen 03–04*/2009: 51–63.

East-West Management Institute. 2014. Separation of Powers Program – Best Practices Guide for Backlog Reduction and Prevention, *Newsletter July 2014* (Belgrade).

Economides, S. and J. Ker-Lindsay. 2015. "'Pre-Accession Europeanization': The Case of Serbia and Kosovo," *JCMS: Journal of Common Market Studies* 53(5): 1027–1044.

Ekiert, G. and S.E. Hanson (eds.). 2003. *Capitalism and Democracy in Central and Eastern Europe: Assessing the Legacy of Communist Rule* (Cambridge: Cambridge University Press).

Elbasani, A. (ed.) 2013. *European Integration and Transformation in the Western Balkans: Europeanization or Business as Usual?* (New York: Routledge).

Elbasani, A. 2014. "EU Conditionality Curve and State Capacities in the Balkans," *Balkans in Europe Policy Blog*.

Elgstrom, O. and M. Smith (eds.). 2006. *The European Union's Role in International Politics: Concepts and Analysis* (London: Routledge): 118–135.

Engstad, N.A., Lærdal Frøseth, A. and Tønder. B. 2014. *The Independence of Judges* (Den Haag: Eleven Publishing House).

European Commission. March 2000. *EU Roadmap. Steps to be Taken by Bosnia and Herzegovina to Prepare for a Launch of a Feasibility Study.*

European Commission. July 2004. "Re-enforcement of the Rule of Law. Division of Competences and Interrelations between Courts, Prosecutors, the Police, Executive and the Legislative Powers in the Western Balkans Countries," *Strategic Studies in CARDS 2003*. Final Report.

European Commission. 20 April 2005. *Communication from the Commission – A European Future for Kosovo* (COM/2005/0156 final) (Brussels).

European Commission. 16 July 2007. *Agenda 2000: For a Stronger and Wider Union* [COM(97) 2000]. Brussels.

European Commission. October 2008. *2008 Progress Report of Bosnia and Herzegovina accompanying the Communication from the Commission to the European Parliament and the Council, Enlargement Strategy and Main Challenges 2008–2009*, COM(2008) 674 (Brussels).

European Commission. 14 October 2009. *Communication of the European Communities. Communication from the Commission to the European Parliament and the Council. Kosovo*-Fulfilling its European Perspective* (Brussels).

European Commission. 9 October 2010. *Commission Opinion on Montenegro's Application for Membership of the European Union*. SEC (2010) 1334 (Brussels).

European Commission. July 2011. *Technical Information Requested by the European Commission*. European Union-Bosnia and Herzegovina SAP Structured Dialogue on Justice (Brussels).

European Commission. 12 October 2011. *Enlargement Strategy and Main Challenges 2011–2012, Communication from the Commission to the European Parliament and the Council*, COM(2011) 666 final (Brussels).

European Commission. 15 March 2012. *Start of the High Level Accession Dialogue with the Government of the Former Yugoslav Republic of Macedonia, European Commission* – MEMO/12/187 (Skopje).

European Commission. 30 May 2012. *Structured Dialogue on the Rule of Law with Kosovo, Conclusions* (Brussels).

European Commission. 10 October 2012. *Communication from the Commission to the European Parliament and the Council on a Feasibility Study for a Stabilization and Association* (Brussels).
European Commission. 12 November 2012 *Screening Report Montenegro, Chapter 23 – Judiciary and Fundamental Rights*, MD 281/12 (Brussels).
European Commission. 16 April 2013. *EU Commission HLAD Spring Report* (Strasbourg).
European Commission. 22 April 2013. *Recommendation for a Council Decision Authorising the Opening of Negotiations on a Stabilisation and Association Agreement between the European Union and Kosovo**, COM(2013) 200 (Brussels).
European Commission. 1 August 2013. *Statement on the Adoption of Constitutional Amendments in Montenegro.* MEMO/13/735 (Brussels).
European Commission. 16 October 2013. *The Former Yugoslav Republic of Macedonia 2013 Progress Report*, SWD(2013) 413 final (Brussels).
European Commission. 16 October 2013. *Serbia 2013 Progress Report*, SWD(2013) 412 final (Brussels).
European Commission. 16 October 2013. *Bosnia and Herzegovina 2013 Progress Report 2013*, SWD(2013) 415 final (Brussels).
European Commission. 16 October 2013. *Kosovo* 2013 Progress Report*, SWD(2013) 416 final (Brussels).
European Commission. 16 October 2013. *Montenegro 2013 Progress Report*, SWD (2013) 411 final (Brussels).
European Commission. 12 November 2015. *The Former Yugoslav Republic of Macedonia 2015 Progress Report*, SWD(2015) 211 final (Brussels).
European Commission. 10 November 2015. *Enlargement Strategy and Main Challenges* 2015. *Communication from the Commission to the European Parliament and the Council* (COM [2015] 611) (Brussels).
European Commission for the Efficiency of Justice. 2012. *European Judicial Systems. Edition 2012 (2010 data), Efficiency and Quality of Justice* (Strasbourg).
European Commission for Democracy through Law (Venice Commission). 6 July 2012. *Draft Amendments to the Constitutional Provisions Relating to the Judiciary of Montenegro.* Opinion No. 677/2012 Strasbourg.
European Commission for Democracy through Law (Venice Commission). 2012. *Opinion on Legal Certainty and Independence of Judiciary in Bosnia and Herzegovina*, Opinion No. 648/2011.
European Commission for Democracy through Law (Venice Commission). 4 April 2011. *Report on the Rule of Law Adopted by the Venice Commission at its 86th plenary session* (Strasbourg).
European Council. 16 June 2003. *The Thessaloniki Agenda for the Western Balkans – Moving towards European Integration. Conclusions of the General Affairs and External Affairs Council* (Thessaloniki).
European Council. 2012. *Conclusions – 1/2 March 2012*. EUCO 4/3/12 REV 3.
European Council. 22 March 2004. *Council Regulation of on the Establishment of European Partnerships in the Framework of the Stabilisation and Association Process* (EC) No 533/2004.
European Council. 19 and 20 June 2003. *Thessaloniki Presidency Conclusions*, 11638/ 03 (Thessaloniki).
European Council. 21–22 June 1993. *Copenhagen Presidency Conclusions*, SN 180/93. (Copenhagen).

European External Action Service. 2013. *First Agreement of Principles Governing the Normalisation of Relations.*

European Parliament. 23 October 2008. *European Parliament Legislative Resolution of* 23 October 2008 on the Proposal for a Council and Commission Decision on the Conclusion of the Stabilisation and Association Agreement between the European Communities and their Member States, of the one part, and Bosnia and Herzegovina, *of the other part*, 8225/2008 – COM(2008)0182 – C6–0255/2008–2008/0073(AVC).

European Parliament. 2000. *Charter of Fundamental Rights of the European Union*, Article 47, *Official Journal of the European Communities* C364/1 (Brussels).

European Union Council. 2006. *EU Council Conclusions on Montenegro*, 2737 External Relations Council meeting, CL06–123EN.

Fagan, A. 2009. *Europe's Balkan Dilemma. Paths to Civil Society or State-Building?* (London: I. B. Tauris).

Fagan, A. 2015. "Democracy Promotion in Kosovo: Mapping the Substance of Donor Assistance and a Comparative Analysis of Strategies," *Cambridge Review of International Affairs* 28(*1*): 115–135.

Falkner, G. 2003. "Comparing Europeanisation Effects: From Metaphor to Operationalisation," *European Integration Online Papers 7*(*13*).

Falkner, G. and M. Hartlapp. 2009 "Problems of Operationalization and Data in EU Compliance Research," *European Union Politics* 10(*2*): 281–304.

Federal Assembly of the Federal People's Republic of Yugoslavia. 1954. Law on Courts, *Official Gazette of the Federal People's Republic of Yugoslavia* 30/54 (Belgrade).

Federal Assembly of the Federal People's Republic of Yugoslavia. 1974. Constitution of the Socialist Federal Republic of Yugoslavia, *Official Gazette* 9/74 (Belgrade).

Federal Assembly of the Federal People's Republic of Yugoslavia. 1954. Law on Financial Courts, *Official Gazette of the Federal People's Republic of Yugoslavia* 31/54 (Belgrade).

Federal Assembly of the Federal People's Republic of Yugoslavia. 1954. Law on Public Prosecutors, *Official Gazette of the Federal People's Republic of Yugoslavia*, 51/54 (Belgrade).

Federal Assembly of the Federal People's Republic of Yugoslavia. 1963. Constitution of the Socialist Federal Republic of Yugoslavia, *Official Gazette* 14/63 (Belgrade).

Fira, A. 1980. "Transformation of Executive and Judicial Functions in Yugoslavia," *Yugoslav Law, II* (Belgrade).

Fish, S. 2005. *Democracy Derailed in Russia: The Failure of Open Politics* (Cambridge: Cambridge University Press).

Fisher, S. 2006. *Political Changes in Post-Communist Slovakia and Croatia. From Nationalist to Europeanist* (London: Palgrave).

Fleiner, T., L.R. Basta Fleiner. 2009. *Constitutional Democracy in a Multicultural and Globalized World* (Berlin, Heidelberg: Springer).

"Former Croatia PM Ivo Sanader Convicted of Corruption." 11 March 2014. *BBC*. Available at http://www.bbc.com/news/world-europe-26533990.

Freyburg, T. and S. Richter. 2008. *National Identity Matters: The Limited Impact of EU Political Conditionality in the Western Balkans.* National Centre of Competence in Research (NCCR). Challenges to Democracy in the 21st Century. Working Paper 19.

Freyburg, T. and S. Richter. 2010. "National Identity Matters: The Limited Impact of EU Political Conditionality in the Western Balkans," *Journal of European Public Policy* 17(*2*): 262–280.

Frydman, B. 2007. "The Evolution of Criteria and Methods for Monitoring the Quality of Judicial Decisions," Working Papers. Perelman Center for Philosophy of Law 2007/4.
Füle, Š. 9 November 2010. *European Commissioner for Enlargement and Neighbourhood Policy. Presentation of Enlargement Package. European Parliament – Foreign Affairs Committee* (AFET) (Brussels).
Fukuyama, F. 1992. *The End of History and the Last Man* (New York: Avon Books).
Fukuyama, F. and M. McFaul. 2007. "Should Democracy be Promoted or Demoted? Bridging the Foreign Policy Divide." Stanley Foundation. Available online at http://www.stanleyfoundation.org/publications/other/fukuymcfaul07.pdf.
Goetz K.H. and J-H. Meyer-Sahling. 2008. "The Europeanisation of National Political Systems: Parliaments and Executives," Living Reviews in *European Governance* 3(*2*).
Gordon, C. 2009. "The Stabilisation and Association Process in the Western Balkans: An Effective Instrument of Post-conflict Management?" *Ethnopolitics* 8(*3*): 325–340.
Gordon, C., M. Kmezić and J. Opardija (eds.). 2013. *Stagnation and Drift in the Western Balkans: The Challenges of Political, Economic and Social Change* (Bern: Peter Lang AG).
Grabbe, H. 2006. *The EU's Transformative Power: Europeanization through Conditionality in Central and Eastern Europe* (London: Palgrave Macmillan).
Grabbe, H., Knaus G. and Korski, D. 2010. "Beyond Wait-and-See: The Way Forward for EU Balkan Policy," *European Council on Foreign Relations.*
Grabbe, H. 2014. "Six Lessons of Enlargement Ten Years On: The EU's Transformative Power in Retrospect and Prospect," *Journal of Common Market Studies 52*, Issue Supplement S1: 40–56.
Gray, A. 2014. "The Criminal Consequences of Kosovo's Post-War Disorder," *Birn.*
Grimm, S. and O.L. Mathis. 2015. "Stability First, Development Second, Democracy Third: The European Union's Policy towards the Post-Conflict Western Balkans, 1991–2010," *Europe-Asia Studies* 67(*6*): 916–947.
Gunsteren, H.R. v. 1986. "The Ethical Context of Bureaucracy and Performance Analysis," in F.-X. Kaufmann, G. Majone, V. Ostrom and W. Wirth (eds.), *Guidance, Control, and Evaluation in the Public Sector: The Bielefeld Interdisciplinary Project* (Berlin: De Gruyter).
High Judicial and Prosecutorial Council of Bosnia and Herzegovina. 2011. *Mid-Term Strategic Plan for 2012–2015, Initial and Continuous Judicial and Prosecutorial Training* (Sarajevo).
High Judicial and Prosecutorial Council of Bosnia and Herzegovina. 2012. *Rules on Measures for the Performance of Judges, Legal Associates and Other Employees in the Courts in Bosnia and Herzegovina, Official Gazette of Bosnia and Herzegovina* 43/12 (Sarajevo).
High Judicial and Prosecutorial Council of Bosnia and Herzegovina. 2006. *Code of Judicial Ethics and the Code of Prosecutorial Ethics, Official Gazette of Bosnia and Herzegovina* 13/06 (Sarajevo).
High Judicial and Prosecutorial Council of Bosnia and Herzegovina: 2004. *Rules of Procedure of the High Judicial and Prosecutorial Council of Bosnia and Herzegovina, Official Gazette of Bosnia and Herzegovina* 59/04 (Sarajevo).
Hillion, C. (2010) *The Creeping Nationalisation of the EU Enlargement Policy* (Stockholm: SIEPS, Swedish Institute for European Policy Studies).
Hobsbawm, E. and T. Ranger (eds.). 1983. *The Invention of Tradition* (Cambridge: Cambridge University Press).

Human Rights Watch. 2015. *Difficult Profession: Media Freedom Under attack in the Western Balkans.*

Höcker-Weyand, C. 1978. *Verfassungsgerichtsbarkeit in Jugoslawien* (Cologne: Bundesinstitut für Ostwissenschaftliche und Internationale Studien).

Inter-American Specialized Conference on Human Rights. 1969. *American Convention on Human Rights*, Articles 8–10. OAS Treaty Series No. 36 (San Jose).

International Court of Justice. 26 February 2007. Judgment. *Bosnia and Herzegovina v. Serbia and Montenegro*, Case 91.

International Monetary Fund. 2015. *The Western Balkans: 15 Years of Economic Transition*. Regional Economic Issues, Special Report.

Jacoby, W. 2004. *The Enlargement of the European Union and NATO: Ordering from the Menu in Central Europe* (Cambridge: Cambridge University Press).

Jano, D. 2010. *The Europeanization of Western Balkans: A Fuzzy Set of Qualitative Comparative Analysis of the New Potential EU Member States* (Saarbrücken: VDM Verlag).

Jelinčić, J. and Đurović, S. 2011. *Europeanization of Serbia: Civil Society.* (Belgrade: Fund for an Open Society Serbia).

Johnston, A.I. 2001. "Treating International Institutions as Social Environments," *International Studies Quarterly 45*: 487–515.

Judicial Reform in Europe. 2012. European Network of Judicial Councils (Dublin).

Judicial Training Centre. 2013. *Annual Activity Report Judicial Training Centre of Montenegro for the Year 2012* (Podgorica).

Judicial Council of Montenegro. 2007. Rules of Procedure of the Judicial Council, *Official Gazette* 11/2007 (Podgorica).

Judicial Council of Montenegro. 2014. *Operation Analysis 2008–2013* (Podgorica).

Kadribašić, A. 2014. "Democratic Transition, Rule of Law and Europeanization: Limited Progress in Bosnia and Herzegovina," in M. Kmezić (ed.), *Europeanization by Rule of Law Implementation in the Western Balkans* (Skopje: Institute for Democracy): 63–90.

Keil, S. 2013. "Europeanization, State-building and Democratization in the Western Balkans," *Nationalities Papers* 41(*3*): 343–353.

Keil, S. and Z. Arkan. (eds.). 2015. *The EU and Member State Building: European Foreign Policy in the Western Balkans* (New York: Routledge)

Ker-Lindsay, J. 2013. "Conclusion," in V. Bojicic-Dzelilovic, J. Ker-Lindsay and D. Kostovicova (eds.) *Civil Society and Transitions in the Western Balkans* (Basingstoke: Palgrave Macmillan): 257–264.

Kitschelt, H.P. 2003. "Accounting for Postcommunist Regime Diversity: What Counts as a Good Cause?" in E. Grzegorsz and H. Stephen, *Legacies of Communism* (Cambridge: Cambridge University Press): 49–86.

Kleinfeld, R. 2006. "Competing Definitions of the Rule of Law," in T. Carothers (ed.), *Promoting the Rule of Law Abroad* (Washington, D.C.: Carnegie Endowment for International Peace): 31–73.

Kmezić, M. 2014. *Europeanization by Rule of Law Implementation in the Western Balkans* (Skopje: Institute for Democracy).

Kmezić, M. 2014. "Lack of Clarity and Credibility in the EU Rule of Law Promotion," *Balkans in Europe Policy Blog.*

Kmezić, M. 2014. "Overcoming the Crisis od EU Enlargement," *Contemporary Southeastern Europe 1*(*1*).

Kmezić, M. 2015. "The Judicial Academy as conditio sine qua non for the Effectiveness and Efficiency of the Serbian Judiciary," *European Public Law 21*(*3*): 509–525.

Kmezić, M. 2015. *The Western Balkans and EU Enlargement: Lessons Learned, Ways Forward and Prospects Ahead*, European Parliament, Directorate-General for External Policies.

Kochenov, D. 2005. "EU Enlargement: Flexible Compliance with the Commission's Pre-Accession Demands and Schnittke's Ideas on Music," CSEP Working Paper (Centre for the Study of European Politics and Society, Ben-Gurion University of the Negev): 1–16.

Kochenov, D. 2007. *The Failure of Conditionality: Pre-accession Conditionality in the Fields of Democracy and the Rule of Law: A Legal Appraisal of EU Enlargement* (Rijksuniversiteit Groningen).

Kochenov, D. 2008. *EU Enlargement and the Failure of Conditionality: Pre-accession Conditionality in the Fields of Democracy and the Rule of Law* (The Hague: Kluwer Law International).

Koppell, J.G.S. 2005. "Pathologies of Accountability: ICANN and the Challenge of 'Multiple Accountabilities Disorder'," *Public Administration Review* 65(*1*): 94–108.

Kosovo Judicial Council. 2012. *Kosovo Judicial Council Annual Report 2011* (Pristina).

Kosovo Judicial Council. 2014. *Kosovo Judicial Council 2013 Statistical Report* (Pristina).

Kosovo Judicial Council. 14 July 2014. *Annual Report of Kosovo Judicial Council* (Pristina).

Kosovo Judicial Council. 2 April 2012. *Regulation on the Evaluation of Performance of Judges*, decision no: KJC 50/1–2012, dated April 2, 2012, and KJC no.85/2013, dated September 6, 2013. Adopted on 24.02.2012, amended on 2 May 2013 and 10 June 2013.

Kosovo Judicial Institute. 2014. *Annual Report 2013* (Pristina).

Kostovicova, D. and V. Bojičić-Dželilović (eds.). 2008. *Transnationalism in the Balkans* (New York: Routledge).

Kratochwil, F. 2009. "Has the 'Rule of Law' become a 'Rule of Lawyers'? An Inquiry into the Use and Abuse of an Ancient Topos in Contemporary Debates," in G. Palombella and N. Walker, *Relocating the Rule of Law* (Oxford: Hart): 171–196.

Krygier M. 2009. "The Rule of Law: Legality, Teleology, Sociology," in G. Palombella and N. Walker, *Relocating the Rule of Law* (Oxford: Hart): 51–79.

Kuhn, Z. 2011. *The Judiciary in Central and Eastern Europe* (Leiden: Martin Nijhoff Publishers).

Kujundžić, L. 2000. "Naručene sudije," *NIN*, No. 2586 (20 July).

Ladrech, R. 1994. "Europeanization of Domestic Politics and Institutions: The Case of France," *Journal of Common Market Studies* 32(*1*): 69–88.

Ladrech, R. 2009. "Europeanization and Political Parties," Living Reviews in *European Governance* 4(*1*).

Landes, W.M. and R.A. Posner. 1975. "The Independent Judiciary in an Interest-Group Perspective," *Journal of Law and Economics 18*: 875–901.

Larkins, M.C. 1996. "Judicial Independence and Democratization: A Theoretical and Conceptual Analysis," *American Journal of Comparative Law 44*: 605–626.

Lavanex, S. and D. Lehmkuhl (eds.). 2009. "Switzerland's Flexible Integration in the EU: A Conceptual Framework," *Swiss Political Science Review* (Special Issue) *15(4)*.

Lavenex, S. 2004. "EU External Governance in 'Wider Europe'," *Journal of European Public Policy* 11(*4*): 680–700.

Levitsky, S. and L.A. Way. 2002. "The Rise of Competitive Authoritarianism," *Journal of Democracy 13*: 51–65.

Levitsky, S. and L.A. Way. 2005. "International Linkage and Democratization," *Journal of Democracy* 16(*3*): 20–34.
Levitsky, S. and L.A. Way. 2006. "Linkage versus Leverage: Rethinking the International Dimension of Regime Change," *Comparative Politics* 38(*4*).
Linz, J. and A. Stepan. 1996. *Problems of Democratic Transition and Consolidation: Southern Europe, South America, and Post-Communist Europe* (Baltimore: The John Hopkins University Press).
Magen, A. 2007. "Transformative Engagement through Law. The *Acquis Communautaire* as Instrument of EU External Influence," *European Journal of Law Reform* 9(*3*): 361–393.
Magen, A. and L. Morlino. 2008. *International Actors, Democratization and the Rule of Law* (London and New York: Routledge).
Magen, A., T. Risse and M. McFaul. 2009. *Promoting Democracy and the Rule of Law* (New York: Palgrave Macmillan).
Mandelski, M. 2013. "They Have Failed Again! Donor-driven Promoting of the Rule of Law in Serbia," *Südosteuropa 61*: 79–113.
Mansfield, E.D. and J. Snyder. 1995. "Democratization and the Danger of War," *International Security* 20(*1*): 5–38.
March, J.G. and J.P. Olsen. 2004. "The Logic of Appropriateness," *Arena Working Papers 04/09* (Oslo).
Marčić, S. 2015. "Informal Institutions in the Western Balkans: An Obstacle to Democratic Consolidation," *Journal of Balkan and Near Eastern Studies* 17(*1*): 1–15.
Marko, J. 2008. "The New Kosovo Constitution in a Regional Comparative Perspective," *Review of Central and East European Law 33*: 437–450.
Marko, J. 2008. "The Law and Politics of Diversity Management: A Neo-Institutional Approach," *European Yearbook of Minority Issues 6* (2006/07: Brill): 252–279.
Marko, J. 2009. "A Response to the Interview with Michael Leigh, Director-General of the European Commission," *Journal of Southeastern Europe 33*(*1*).
Marko, J. and M. Handstanger. 2009. "The Interdependence of Law and Political Science: About the 'Essence and Value' of a 'Juristenpolitologie' Approach: Wolfgang Mantl for his 70th birthday," *Vienna Online Journal on International Constitutional Law* 3(*2*).
Marko, J., Palermo F. and Woelk, J. July 2004. "Re-enforcement of the Rule of Law. Division of Competences and Interrelations between Courts, Prosecutors, the Police, Executive and the Legislative Powers in the Western Balkans Countries," *Strategic Studies in CARDS 2003*. Final Report.
Mcfaul, M. 2002. "Transitions from Postcommunism," *Journal of Democracy* 16(*3*): 5–19.
Mendelski, M. 2013. "Does the EU Make a Difference? Judicial Reforms in South-Eastern Europe," in A. Elbasani (ed.), *EU Enlargement and Europeanization in the Western Balkans* (London: Routledge).
Mendelski, M. 2013. "They Have Failed Again! Donor-driven Promotion of the Rule of Law in Serbia," *Südosteuropa 61*(*1*): 79–113.
Messick, R.E. 1999. "Judicial Reform and Economic Development: A Survey of the Issues," *World Bank Research Observer* 14(*1*).
Micklitz, H.W. and De Witte, B. 2012. *The European Court of Justice and the Autonomy of the Member States* (Cambridge: Intersentia).
Ministerial Meeting Opening the Intergovernmental Conference on the Accession of Montenegro to the European Union, European Commission. 27 June 2012 (Brussels).

Modić, H. 1957. "Pravo v prehodnem razdobju," *Ekonomski Zbornik II*.
Morlino, L. and A. Magen. 4–5 October 2004. "EU Rule of Law Promotion in Romania, Turkey and Serbia-Montenegro: Domestic Elites and Responsiveness to Differentiated External Influence," Paper for CDDRL (Stanford: SIIS).
Morlino, L. and G. Palombella (eds.). 2010. *The Rule of Law and Democracy: Internal and External Issues* (Leiden: Brill Publishing).
Muharremi, R. 2008. "Kosovo's Declaration of Independence: Self-Determination and Sovereignty Revisited," *Review of Central and East European Law 33*: 401–435.
Mungiu-Pippidi, A. 2008. "The EU as a Transformation Agent. Lessons Learned from governance reforms in East Central Europe," Hertie School of Governance – Working Papers. No. 33.
Mungiu-Pippidi, A. 2014. "The Transformative Power of Europe Revisited," *Journal of Democracy*, 25(1): 20–32.
National Assembly of the Republic of Macedonia. 1991. The Constitution of the Republic of Macedonia Article 98 para.2, *Official Gazette of Republic of Macedonia* No. 52/91, 31/98, 91/01 (Skopje).
National Assembly of the Republic of Macedonia. 2006. Law on Courts, Article 11 para 2, Official Gazette of the Republic of Macedonia No.58/2006 (Skopje).
National Assembly of the Republic of Macedonia. 2006. The Law on the Judicial Council, Official Gazette of the Republic of Macedonia No.60/2006 (Skopje).
National Assembly of the Republic of Macedonia. 2003. Law on Court Budget, Official Gazette of the Republic of Macedonia" no. 60/03, 37/06, 103/08, 145/2010 (Skopje).
National Assembly of the Republic of Macedonia. 2006. Law on the Academy for the Training of Judges and Prosecutors, *Official Gazette of the Republic of Macedonia* 13/2006, 88/2010, 166/2012 and 26/2013 (Skopje).
National Assembly of the Republic of Macedonia. 2007. Law on Judges' Salaries, *Official Gazette of the Republic of Macedonia* No.110/2007 (Skopje).
National Assembly of the Republic of Serbia. 2006. Constitution of the Republic of Serbia, *Official Gazette of the Republic of Serbia* 83/2006 (Belgrade).
National Assembly of the Republic of Serbia. 2009. Decision on the Number of Judges in Courts, *Official Gazette of the Republic of Serbia* 43/2009, 91/2009 and 35/2010 (Belgrade).
National Assembly of the Republic of Serbia. 2009. Decision on the Establishment of Criteria and Standards for Evaluation of Qualification, Competence and Worthiness for Election of Judges and Presidents of Courts, High Judicial Council, *Official Gazette of the Republic of Serbia* 49/09 (Belgrade).
National Assembly of the Republic of Serbia. 2006. Constitution of the Republic of Serbia, *Official Gazette of the Republic of Serbia* 83/2006 (Belgrade).
National Assembly of the Republic of Serbia. 26 May 2006. National Judicial Reform Strategy, *Official Gazette of the Republic of Serbia* 44/2006 (Belgrade).
National Assembly of the Republic of Serbia. 2014. Decision on Number of Judges, *Official Gazette of the Republic of Serbia* 106/13,115/13 and 5/14. (Belgrade).
National Assembly of the Republic of Serbia. 1 July 2013. National Judicial Reform Strategy for the Period 2013–2018, *Official Gazette of the Republic of Serbia* 57/2013 (Belgrade).
National Assembly of the Republic of Serbia. 1 July 2003. Law on the Organization and Competencies of Government Authorities in Prosecuting Perpetrators of War Crimes, *Official Gazette of the Republic of Serbia* 67/03 (Belgrade) as amended,

Official Gazette of the Republic of Serbia 135/04 (Belgrade); *Official Gazette of the Republic of Serbia* 61/05.

National Assembly of the Republic of Serbia. 2009. Law on Organisation and Jurisdiction of Government Authorities in Suppression of High Technological Crime. *Official Gazette of the Republic of Serbia* 61/2005 and 104/2009 (Belgrade).

National Assembly of the Republic of Serbia. 2009. The Law on Judicial Academy, *Official Gazette of the Republic of Serbia* 104/2009 (Belgrade).

National Assembly of the Republika Srpska. 2002. The Law on the Judicial and Prosecutorial Training Centre in Republika Srpska, *Official Gazette of* Republika *Srpska* 49/02 and 77/02 (Banja Luka).

Nations in Transit. 2015. Freedom House. Available at https://freedomhouse.org/sites/default/files/FH_NIT2015_06.06.15_FINAL.pdf.

Negriz, N. 2015. "The Role of the Mass Media on Shaping the Public Opinion about the Enlargement of the European Union," in N.O. Taskiran and R. Yilmaz. *Handbook of Research on Effective Advertising Strategies in the Social Media Age* (Hershey: IGI).

Noutcheva, G. 2009. "Fake, Partial and Imposed Compliance: The Limits of the EU's Normative Power in the Western Balkans," *Journal of European Public Policy*: 1065–1084.

Noutcheva, G. 2012. *European Foreign Policy and the Challenges of Balkan Accession: Conditionality, Legitimacy and Compliance* (London: Routledge).

Organization of African Unity. 1981. *African Charter on Human and Peoples' Rights*, Article 7, OAU Doc. CAB/LEG/67/3 rev. 5, 21 I.L.M. 58, entered into force 21 October 1986 (Banjul).

Organization for Security and Co-operation in Europe. December 2009. *Legal Analysis. Independence of the Judiciary.* Spillover Mission in Skopje (Skopje).

Ott, K. 28 June 2013. *Croatia and the EU: The Catch-Up Issue* (CEPS Commentary). Available online at www.ceps.eu/ceps/dld/8210/pdf.

Päivi, L. 2002. "Rights, Rules and Democracy in the EU Enlargement Process: Between Universalism and Identity," *Austrian Review of International and European Law 7*: 53–80.

Panagiotou, R. 2013. "The Greek Crisis as a Crisis of EU Enlargement: How Will the Western Balkans Be Affected?" *Southeast European and Black Sea Studies* 13(*1*): 89–104.

Parliamentary Assembly of Bosnia and Herzegovina. 2005. Law on High Judicial and Prosecutorial Council of Bosnia and Herzegovina, Article 17. *Official Gazette of Bosnia and Herzegovina* 25/04 and 93/05 (Sarajevo).

Parliamentary Assembly of Bosnia and Herzegovina. 1994. Constitution of the Federation of Bosnia and Herzegovina, *Official Gazette of the Federation of Bosnia and Herzegovina*, 1/94, 13/97, 16/02, 22/02, 52/02, 60/02, 18/03, 63/03; and National Assembly of the Republic of Srpska. Pale: 1992. Constitution of the Republic of Srpska, *Official Gazette of the Republic of Srpska* 3/92, 6/92, 8/92, 15/92 and 19/92, and Amendments I-CXXII (Sarajevo).

Parliamentary Assembly of Bosnia and Herzegovina. 2002. The Law on the Judicial and Prosecutorial Training Centre in Federation of BiH, *Official Gazette of Federation of BiH* 24/02, 40/02, 52/02 and 21/03 (Sarajevo).

Parliament of the Republic of Montenegro. 2008. Law on Notaries, *Official Gazette of the Republic of Montenegro* 68/05 and 49/08 (Podgorica).

Parliament of the Republic of Montenegro. 2011. Law on Public Enforcement Officers, *Official Gazette of the Republic of Montenegro* 61/2011 (Podgorica).

Parliament of the Republic of Montenegro. 2006. The Law on Judiciary Training, *Official Gazette of the Republic of Montenegro* 27/2006 (Podgorica).
Parliament of the Republic of Montenegro. 2006. Constitution of the Republic of Montenegro, *Official Gazette* 1/2007 (Podgorica).
Parliament of the Republic of Montenegro. 2002. Law on Courts. *Official Gazette of the Republic of Montenegro* 5/2002, 49/2004; *Official Gazette of the Republic of Montenegro*. No. 22/2008 and 39/2011 (Podgorica).
Parliament of the Republic of Montenegro. 2008. Law on the Judicial Council. *Official Gazette of the Republic of Montenegro* 13/2008 and 39/2011 (Podgorica).
Parliament of the Republic of Montenegro. 2003. Law on State Prosecutor's Office. *Official Gazette of the Republic of Montenegro* 69/2003; *Official Gazette of the Republic of Montenegro* 40/2008 and 38/11 (Podgorica).
Parliament of the Republic of Montenegro. 2006. Law on Education in Judicial Bodies. *Official Gazette of the Republic of Montenegro* 27/2006 (Podgorica).
Pavlović, A. and S. Ćirić. 2014. "Opportunity On-Hold: Edi Rama's Visit to Belgrade in the Light of 'the Drone Incident'," *Balkans in Europe Policy Blog*.
Peci, E. 2013. "Kosovo Parliament Rejects Family 'Revenge' Murders Probe," *Birn*.
Pech, L. 2009. "The Rule of Law as a Constitutional Principle of the European Union," *Jean Monnet Working Paper* 04/09.
Peerenboom, R. 2002. "Let One Hundred Flowers Bloom, One Hundred Schools Contend: Debating the Rule-of-Law in China," *Michigan Journal of International Law* 23(*3*): 471–544.
Piana, D. 2010. "Beyond Judicial Independence: Rule of Law and Judicial Accountabilities in Assessing Democratic Quality," in L. Morlino and G. Palombella (eds.), *Rule of Law and Democracy: Inquiries Into Internal and External Issues* (Leiden: Koniklijke Brill): 65–93.
Piana, D. 2010. *Judicial Accountabilities in New Europe* (London: Ashgate).
Piana, D. 2011. "In Search of A New Judicial Professionalism: Intertwining Legal and Extra-Legal Values in Post-Authoritarian Training Programs," *Web Journal of Current Legal Issues*.
Pippan, C. 2004. "The Rocky Road to Europe: The EU's Stabilisation and Association Process for the Western Balkans and the Principle of Conditionality," *European Foreign Affairs Review* 9(*2*): 219–245.
Pop-Eleches, G. 2007. "Between Historical Legacies and the Promise of Western Integration: Democratic Conditionality after Communism," *East European Politics and Societies* 21(*4*): 142–161.
Popović, S. 16 November 1990 "Ideja suvereniteta je luda," *Stav* 66: 26–29.
Pound, R. 1908. "Mechanical Jurisprudence," *Columbia Law Review 8*: 605–623.
Putnam, R. 1988. "Diplomacy and Domestic Politics: the Logic of Two Level Games," *International Organization*.
Radaelli, C. 2003. "The Europeanization of Public Policy," in K. Featherstone and C. Radaelli (eds.), *The Politics of Europeanization* (Oxford: Oxford University Press): 27–56.
Radić, S. (ed.). 2004. *Dva veka prvog suda u Srbiji* (Belgrade: Judges Association of Serbia).
Radeljić, B. 2013. "Democratising and Europeanising the Western Balkans: Contexts, Challenges and Prospects," *East European Politics* 29(*2*): 245–251.
Radulović, V., B. Gorjanc Prelević and T.A. Šoć. 2013. *Judicial Council of Montenegro: Operation Analysis 2008–2013* (Podgorica: Golbiprint).

Rakić-Vodinelić, V. 14 February 2014. "Corrupt Obsolescence 'Reformed' Judiciary," *Peščanik*.

Ramet, S.P. (ed.). 2010. *Central and Southeast European Politics since 1989* (Cambridge: Cambridge University Press).

Ramet, S. and V. Pavlaković (eds.). 2005. *Serbia since 1989: Politics and Society Under Milosevic and After* (Seattle: University of Washington Press).

Ramseyer, J. 1998. "Judicial Independence," in P. Newman, *The New Palgrave Dictionary of Economics and the Law* (New York: Stockton Press): 383–387.

Ramseyer, J. 1994. "The Puzzling (In)dependence of Courts: A Comparative Approach," *Journal of Legal Studies* 23(2): 721–747.

Ranković, A. 1951. 4 June 1951. "Za dalje jačanje pravosuđa i zakonitosti," *Četvrti plenum centralnog Komiteta Komunističke partije Jugoslavije*.

Regional Cooperation Council. 2015. *Balkan Barometer 2015 Public Opinion Survey* (Sarajevo).

Republika Srpska Government, Federation of Bosnia and Herzegovina Government and the Council of Ministers of Bosnia and Herzegovina. 11 March 2004. *Agreement on the Transfer of Certain Entity Responsibilities through the Establishment of the High Judicial and Prosecutorial Council of Bosnia and Herzegovina* (Sarajevo).

Ribičič, C. (ed.). 1986. *Ustavno pravo SFR Jugoslavije* (Ljubljana: Časopisni Zavod Uradni List SR Slovenije).

Risse, T., S. Ropp and K. Sikkink. 1999. *The Power of Human Rights* (Cambridge: Cambridge University Press).

Rupnik, J. 1999. "The Postcommunist Divide," *Journal of Democracy* 10(*1*): 57–62.

Sadurski, W., A. Czarnota and M. Krygier (eds.). 2006. *Spreading Democracy and the Rule of Law: The Impact of EU Enlargement on the Rule of Law, Democracy and Constitutionalism in Post-Communist Legal Orders* (Netherlands: Springer).

Sasse, G., Hughes, J. and C. Gordon. 2006. "Sub-National Governance in Central and Eastern Europe: Between Transition and Europeanization," in W. Sadurski, A. Czarnota and M. Krygier (eds.), *Spreading Democracy and the Rule of Law: The Impact of EU Enlargement on the Rule of Law, Democracy and Constitutionalism in Post-Communist Legal Orders* (Netherlands: Springer): 121–147.

Schapiro, M. 1981. *Courts: A Comparative and Political Analysis* (Chicago: University of Chicago Press).

Schimmelfennig, F. 2000. "International Socialization in the New Europe: Action in a Rational Institutional Environment," *European Journal of International Relations* 6(*1*): 109–139.

Schimmelfennig, F. 2008. "EU Political Accession Conditionality after the 2004 Enlargement: Consistency and Effectiveness," *Journal of European Public Policy*: 918–937.

Schimmelfennig, F. 2010. "Europeanisation Beyond the Member States," *Zeitschrift für Staats- und Europawissenschaften* 8(*3*): 319–339.

Schimmelfennig, F. 2010. "The Normative Origins of Democracy in the European Union: Towards a Transformationalist Theory of Democratization," *European Political Science Review* 2(*2*): 211–233.

Schimmelfennig, F. 2012. "Europeanization beyond Europe," Living Reviews in *European Governance* 7(*1*).

Schimmelfennig, F. 2015. "EU Enlargement," in J. Richardson and S. Mazey (eds.), *European Union: Power and Policy-Making* (London: Routledge): 261–282.

Schimmelfennig, F. and U. Sedelmeier. 2004. "Governance by Conditionality: EU Rule Transfer to the Candidate Countries of Central and Eastern Europe," *Journal of European Public Policy* 11(*4*): 661–679.

Schimmelfennig, F. and U. Sedelmeier. (eds.). 2005. *The Europeanisation of Central and Eastern Europe* (Ithaca: Cornell University Press).

Schimmelfennig, F. and U. Sedelmeier. (eds.). 2005. *The Politics of European Union Enlargement: Theoretical Approaches Routledge Advances in European Politics* (New York: Routledge).

Schimmelfennig, F. and H. Scholtz. 2010. "Legacies and Leverage: EU Political Conditionality and Democracy Promotion in Historical Perspective," *Europe-Asia Studies* 62(*3*): 443–460.

Schimmelfennig, F. and A.M. Cirtautas. 2010. "Europeanisation Before and After Accession: Conditionality, Legacies, and Compliance," *Europe-Asia Studies* 62(*3*): 421–441.

Sciarini, P., A. Fischer and S. Nicolet. 2004, "How Europe Hits Home: Evidence from the Swiss Case," *Journal of European Public Policy* 11(*3*): 353–378.

Sedelmeier, U. 2006. "Europeanization in New Member and Candidate States," Living Reviews in *European Governance* 1(*3*).

Sedelmeier, U. 2006. "The EU's Role as a Promoter of Human Rights and Democracy: Enlargement Policy Practice and Role Formation," in O. Elgstrom and M. Smith (eds.), *The European Union's Role in International Politics: Concepts and Analysis* (London: Routledge): 118–135.

Sedelmeier, U. 2010. "The EU and Democratization in Central and Southeastern Europe since 1989," in S.P. Ramet (ed.), *Central and Southeast European Politics since 1989* (Cambridge: Cambridge University Press): 519–536.

Sedelmeier, U. 2011. "Europeanization in New Member and Candidate States," *Living Reviews in European Governance* 6(*1*).

Sedelmeier, U. 2014. "Anchoring Democracy from Above? The European Union and Democratic Backsliding in Hungary and Romania after Accession," *Journal of Common Market Studies* 52(*1*): 105–121.

Sedelmeier, U. 2015. "Enlargement: Constituent Policy and Tool for External Governance," in H. Wallace, M. Pollack and A. Young (eds.), *Policy-Making in the European Union* (Oxford: Oxford University Press): 407–435.

Shetreet, S. 1985. "Judicial Independence: New Conceptual Dimensions and Contemporary Challenges," in S. Shetreet and J. Deschenes (eds.) *Judicial Independence: The Contemporary Debate* (Dordrecht: Martinus Nijhoff): 590–681.

Shklar, J. 1987. "Political Theory and the Rule of Law," in A.C. Hutchinson and P. Monahan (eds.) *The Rule of Law: Ideal or Ideology?* (Toronto: Carswell Legal Publications).

Smilov, D. 2006. "EU Enlargement and the Constitutional Principle of Judicial Independence," in W. Sadurski, A. Czarnota and M. Krygier (eds.) *Spreading Democracy and the Rule of Law?: The Impact of EU Enlargement for the Rule of Law, Democracy and Constitutionalism in Post-Communist Legal Orders* (Dordrecht: Springer).

Spaić, T. 2014. "Judiciary Reform or How to Make the Serbian Judiciary Worthy?" *The New Century 07*.

Spaić, T., V. Cvijić, M. Ilić and N. Latković. 2014. "Crimes in Serbia Barred by the Authorities," *Blic* (23 March).

State Statistical Office of the Republic of Macedonia: 2014 "Average Monthly Net Wage Paid per Employee" (Skopje).

Standard Eurobarometer. 2013. "Tables of Results: Public Opinion in the European Union," No. 79, Spring 2013, T84.

Statistical Bulletin No 3. 2011. (Zagreb: Centre for Public Employment Services of South East European Countries).

Strobl, M., I. Kristan and C. Ribičić (eds.). 1986. *Ustavno pravo SFR Jugoslavije* (Ljubljana: Časopisni Zavod Uradni List SR Slovenije).

Structured Dialogue on Justice. 10–11 November 2011. *Recommendation from the Second Meeting of the Structured Dialogue on Justice* (Sarajevo).

Supreme Court of Montenegro. 2012. *Annual Report on Work of the Judicial Training Center for 2011* (Podgorica: Centre for Judicial Training).

Tamanaha, B.Z. 2004. *On the Rule of Law: History, Politics and Theory* (Cambridge: Cambridge University Press).

Tansey, O. 2010. *Regime-Building: Democratization and International Administration* (Oxford: Oxford University Press).

Tatham, F.A. 2009. *Enlargement of the European Union* (Alphen aan den Rijn: Kluwer Law International).

The Balkans in Europe's Future. 2005. Report of the International Commission on the Balkans (Sofia: Centre for Liberal Strategies).

The General Framework Agreement for Peace in Bosnia and Herzegovina. 1995. Initialled Dayton, Ohio: 21 November 1995, signed Paris: 14 December 1995, agreed to by Bosnia and Herzegovina, Croatia and Federal Republic of Yugoslavia, 35 (1996) ILM 75.

Trajković, J. 1987. "Pravosuđe u sistemu organizacije vlasti i samoupravljanja u društveno-političkim zajednicama" in *Društveno-političke zajednice i njihova organizacije vlasti* (Belgrade: Prosveta): 229–294.

Trajković, J.1984. *The Judicial System of Yugoslavia* (Belgrade: Jugoslovenski Pregled).

Tolstrup, J. 2010. "When can External Actors Influence Democratization? Leverage, Linkages, and Gatekeeper Elites," *CDDRL Working Papers 118*: 1–31.

Toshkov, D. 2008. "Embracing European Law: Compliance with EU Directives in Central and Eastern Europe," *European Union Politics* 9(*3*): 379–402.

Transparency International. 2014. *Montenegro: Overview of Political Corruption*. Available at http://www.transparency.org/files/content/corruptionqas/Montenegro_Overview_of_Political_Corruption_2014.pdf.

Trauner, F. 2009. "From Membership Conditionality to Policy Conditionality: EU External Governance in South Eastern Europe," *Journal of European Public Policy*: 774–790.

Trauner, F. 2011. *The Europeanisation of the Western Balkans: EU Justice and Home Affairs in Croatia and Macedonia* (Manchester: Manchester University Press).

Trebilcock, J.M. and J.R. Daniels. 2008. *Rule of Law Reform and Development: Charting the Fragile Path of Progress* (Northampton: Edward Elgar).

Treib, O. 2008. "Implementing and Complying with EU Governance Outputs," Living Reviews in *European Governance* 3(*5*).

Treib, O., H. Bähr and G. Falkner. 2007. "Modes of Governance: Towards a Conceptual Clarification," *Journal of European Policy* 14(*1*): 1–20.

Trivunović, M., V. Devine and H. Mathisen. 2007. *Corruption in Montenegro 2007: Overview over Main Problems and Status of Reforms* (Bergen: Chr. Michelsen Institute).

Tsebelis, G. 1990. *Nested Games: Rational Choice in Comparative Politics* (Berkeley: Berkeley University Press).

Turkalj, K. 29–30 April 2010. "Negotiations for the Accession of the Republic of Croatia to the European Union in the Area of Justice ('State of Play for Chapters 23 and 24')," Paper presented at the Conference 'Croatia on the Eve of EU Accession: The Path of Reform' (Zagreb, Croatia).

Towfigh, E.V. 2009. "Complexity and Normative Clarity – Or: Legal Statutes are Made for Lawyers," *Der Staat 48(1)*: 29–74.

United Nations. 1948. *Universal Declaration of Human Rights*, Article 10. United Nations General Assembly Resolution 217A (III), ratified 16 December 1949 (New York).

United Nations. 1985. *United Nations Basic Principles on the Independence of the Judiciary*, United Nations General Assembly resolutions 40/32 of 29 November 1985 and 40/146 of 13 December 1985 (New York).

Vachudova, M.A. 2009. "Democratization in Post-Communist Europe: Illiberal Regimes and the Leverage of the European Union," in V. Bunce, M. McFaul and K. Stoner-Weiss (eds.), *Democracy and Authoritarianism in the Post-Communist World* (Cambridge: Cambridge University Press): 82–106.

Vachudova, M. 24 February 2014. "The Thieves of Bosnia: The Complicated Legacy of the Dayton Peace Accords," *Foreign Affairs*.

Vachudova, M. 2014. "EU Leverage and National Interests in the Balkans: The Puzzles of Enlargement Ten Years On," *Journal of Common Market Studies* 52(*1*): 1–17.

Vasilijević, V. 20 August 1990. "Ko sudi sudijama?" *NIN*, No. 2016: 25–26.

Vasilić, J. 2014. "*The Judiciary Is Not Independent Due to Government*," *NIN* 3336 (4 December).

Voigt, S. 2005. "The Economic Effects of Judicial Accountability: Some Preliminary Insights," International Centre for Economic Research Working Paper No. 19.

Wade, J. 1999. "Priest and Patient: The European Union as a Force in the Domestic Politics of Eastern Europe," *East European Constitutional Review 8*(*1–2*): 62–67.

Weller, M. 2009. *Contested Statehood: Kosovo's Struggle for Independence* (Oxford: Oxford University Press).

Winland, D. 2008. "Ten Years Later: The Changing Nature of Transnational Ties in Post-independence Croatia," in D. Kostovicova and V. Bojicic-Dzelilovic. *Transnationalism in the Balkans* (New York: Routledge): 79–93.

Wood S. 2009. "The European Union: A Normative or Normal Power?" *European Foreign Affairs Review 14*: 113–128.

Yein Ng, G., M. Velicogna, and C. Dallara. 2007. *Monitoring and Evaluation of Court System: A Comparative Study* (European Commission for Efficiency of Justice).

Zielonka, J. 2006. *Europe as Empire. The Nature of the Enlarged European Union* (Oxford: Oxford University Press).

Zirk-Sadowski, M. 2006 "*Transformation and Integration of Legal Cultures and Discourses – Poland*," in W. Sadurski, A. Czarnota, M. Krygier (eds.), *Spreading Democracy and the Rule of Law?* (Netherlands: Springer): 299–311.

Zubek, R. and K.H. Goetz. 2010. "Performing to Type? How State Institutions Matter in East Central Europe," *Journal of Public Policy* 30(*1*): 1–20.

Internet sources

<http://www.encj.eu>.

<http://www.coe.int/t/DGHL/cooperation/ccje/default_en.asp>.

<http://www.ejn-crimjust.europa.eu/ejn/EJN_StaticPage.aspx?Bread=2>.
<http://www.encj.eu/images/stories/pdf/GA/Vilnius/encj_vilnius_declaration.pdf>.
<http://ec.europa.eu/justice/effective-justice/files/justice_scoreboard_communication_en.pdf>.
<http://europa.eu/rapid/press-release_MEMO-12–187_en.htm?locale=en>.

Index